PRISON STATE

Since the late 1970s, the prison population in America has shot upward to reach a staggering 1.5 million by the end of 2005. This book takes a broad, critical look at incarceration, the huge social experiment of American society. The authors investigate the causes and consequences of the prison buildup, often challenging previously held notions from scholarly and public discourse. By examining such themes as social discontent, safety and security within prisons, and the impact on crime and on the labor market, Bert Useem and Anne Morrison Piehl use evidence to address the inevitable larger questions: where should incarceration go next for American society, and where is it likely to go?

Bert Useem is a professor of sociology at Purdue University. He previously taught sociology at the University of New Mexico, where he was Director of the Institute for Social Research. He is the author of *Resolution of Prison Riots: Strategy and Policies* (with Camille Camp and George Camp, 1996) and *States of Siege: U.S. Prison Riots, 1971–1986* (with Peter A. Kimball, 1989).

Anne Morrison Piehl is an associate professor in the Department of Economics at Rutgers University and a research associate at the National Bureau of Economic Research. She previously taught public policy at the John F. Kennedy School of Government at Harvard University. She has been published widely in journals in economics, law, criminology, sociology, and public policy.

CAMBRIDGE STUDIES IN CRIMINOLOGY

Other books in the series:

Life in the Gang: Family, Friends, and Violence, by Scott H. Decker and Barrik van Winkle

Delinquency and Crime: Current Theories, edited by J. David Hawkins

Recriminalizing Delinquency: Violent Juvenile Crime and Juvenile Justice Reform, by Simon I. Singer

Mean Streets: Youth Crime and Homelessness, by John Hagan and Bill McCarthy

The Framework of Judicial Sentencing: A Study in Legal Decision Making, by Austin Lovegrove

The Criminal Recidivism Process, by Edward Zamble and Vernon L. Quinsey

Violence and Childhood in the Inner City, by Joan McCord

Judicial Policy Making and the Modern State: How the Courts Reformed America's Prisons, by Malcolm M. Feeley and Edward L. Rubin

Schools and Delinquency, by Denise C. Gottfredson

Delinquent-Prone Communities, by Don Weatherburn and Bronwyn Lind

White Collar Crime and Criminal Careers, by David Weisburd, Elin Waring, and Ellen F. Chayet

Sex Differences in Antisocial Behavior: Conduct Disorder, Delinquency, and Violence in the Dunedin Longitudinal Study, by Terrie Moffitt, Avshalom Caspi, Michael Rutter, and Phil A. Silva

Delinquent Networks: Youth Co-Offending in Stockholm, by Jerzy Sarnecki

Criminality and Violence among the Mentally Disordered, by Sheilagh Hodgins and Cari-Gunnar Janson

Corporate Crime, Law, and Social Control, by Sally S. Simpson

Companions in Crime: The Social Aspects of Criminal Conduct, by Mark Warr

Series list continues following the index.

Prison State

The Challenge of Mass Incarceration

Bert Useem

Purdue University

Anne Morrison Piehl

Rutgers University

CAMBRIDGE
UNIVERSITY PRESS

CAMBRIDGE UNIVERSITY PRESS
Cambridge, New York, Melbourne, Madrid, Cape Town,
Singapore, São Paulo, Delhi, Tokyo, Mexico City

Cambridge University Press
32 Avenue of the Americas, New York, NY 10013-2473, USA

www.cambridge.org
Information on this title: www.cambridge.org/9780521713399

First published 2008
Reprinted 2011

A catalog record for this publication is available from the British Library.

Library of Congress Cataloging in Publication Data

Useem, Bert.
Prison state : the challenge of mass incarceration / Bert Useem, Anne Morrison Piehl.
p. cm. – (Cambridge studies in criminology)
ISBN 978-0-521-88585-0 (hardback) – ISBN 978-0-521-71339-9 (pbk.)
1. Prisons – United States. 2. Prison administration – United States. 3. Prisons – Overcrowding – United States. 4. Corrections – United States. I. Piehl, Anne Morrison, 1964– II. Title.
HV9469.U83 2008
365′.973–dc22 2007031644

ISBN 978-0-521-88585-0 Hardback
ISBN 978-0-521-71339-9 Paperback

Contents

Acknowledgments

We are grateful to the National Science Foundation, the National Institute of Justice, and the Harry Frank Guggenheim Foundation for grants to support this work. Purdue University and Rutgers University provided funds that helped us complete the work.

We have several intellectual debts, as our approach to the ground covered in this book was developed during work with several collaborators. Professor Raymond Liedka, Oakland University, worked with us to develop much of the statistical analysis underlying several themes in the book, especially calculating the effects of prison on crime. Professor John DiIulio, with whom we collaborated on the inmate surveys, always understood that opinion about criminal justice had to be informed by the impacts within the justice sector and on families and neighborhoods. And Stefan LoBuglio, a practitioner and a scholar, always provided feedback tempered with the wisdom of both fields of endeavor. We are very grateful to them all.

We also appreciate the helpful comments on drafts of chapters from Howard Waitzkin, Patricia Useem, David Rubinstein, Daniel Maier-Katkin, Anthony Oberschall, Harry Holzer, Phyllis Bursh, Arthur Stinchcombe, and Jack Bloom. Melissa Stacer provided outstanding research assistance. Our editor at Cambridge University Press, Ed Parsons, helped us in numerous ways. Riley Bursh, Lauren Useem, and Hanna Useem provided welcome distraction, a support in its own way. Of course, we alone are responsible for the views expressed in this book.

CHAPTER ONE

The Buildup to Mass Incarceration

The era of big government is over.[1]

Every culture, every class, every century, constructs its distinctive alibis for aggression.[2]

It's too soon to tell.[3]

The change began with little official notice or fanfare. There were no presidential speeches to Congress, such as the ones pledging to land a person on the moon within a decade or declaring war on poverty. No catastrophic event, such as the attack on Pearl Harbor or 9/11, mobilized the United States. No high-profile commission issued a wake-up call, as the Kerner Commission did in warning the nation that it was moving toward two separate and unequal societies and, decades later, as the 9/11 Commission did in exposing the country's vulnerabilities to terrorism. Indeed, to see the change of interest – the massive buildup of the U.S. prison population that began in the 1970s – one has to look to the statistical record. There was little bark (at least at first), but a great deal of bite.

Beginning with modern record keeping in 1925 and continuing through 1975, prisoners represented a tiny segment of the U.S. population. In 1925, there were 92,000 inmates in state and federal prisons. By 1975, the number behind bars had grown to 241,000, but this increase merely kept pace with the growth of the general population. The *rate* of imprisonment remained stable, at about 110 inmates per 100,000 residents.[4] Indeed, during the early 1970s, two well-known criminologists argued that society kept this ratio (inmates over population) at a near constant to meet its need for social integration.[5] As the crime rate went up or down, like a thermostat, society would adjust its imprisonment decisions to ensure that the rate of imprisonment would remain close to 110. Then, in the mid-1970s, the thermostat was disconnected. The imprisonment furnace was turned on full blast.

The number of prisoners shot upward and would continue on that trajectory for 25 years. By the end of the twentieth century, there were 476 prison inmates per 100,000 U.S. residents, or more than 1.36 million people in prison.[6] And the furnace has not yet been put to rest. By year-end 2005, the number behind prison bars had risen even further, to 1.5 million.[7] In the 12-month period ending in December 2005, for example, the prison population increased by 21,500 inmates, an annual growth rate of about 1.9%.

To add some perspective, if assembled in one locality, the prison population would tie Philadelphia for the fourth largest U.S. city. If "prisoner" could be thought of as an occupation, one in fifty male workers would have this "job"; there would be more people in this line of "work" than the combined number of doctors, lawyers, and clergy. For certain demographic groups, the proportion serving time in prison has become extraordinarily high. By year-end 2004, 8.1% of black males between the ages of 25 and 29 were in prison.[8] About one-third of all African American males are predicted, during their lifetime, to serve time in a state or federal prison.[9] In 1975, 241,000 inmates in state and federal prisons were serving 8.4 million inmate-days. By the end of 2005, 1.5 million inmates were serving more than a half-*billion* inmate-days per year and consuming 1.6 trillion meals.

Our topic is the prison population buildup. Why did the United States embark on this course? What were the consequences for society? This transformation did not occur spontaneously, and it has had consequences. There are a profusion of claims about this choice. Proponents of the buildup tend to see only virtue and necessity. We had to build more and more prisons, in this view, to stem the tide of disorder and crime on the streets. The buildup was a farsighted investment in our future, and we are now reaping the benefits. Critics tend to see only vice and human folly. The buildup has done far more harm than good. In one argument, putting more people in prison adds fuel to the fire by stigmatizing millions of low-level offenders as hard-core felons and schooling them in crime. Mass prison is not only a massive waste of public resources, but it is also socially destructive. Hard-nosed realism requires something other than more prisons.

These points of view have been expressed on the opinion/editorial pages of newspapers and television talk shows, been the subject of numerous stump speeches by politicians seeking elected office, and, from time to time, been given serious study by scholars. Still, we may be no closer now to consensus over the "prison question" than we were halfway through the buildup. With the arguments well worn, both sides now play the common-sense card: everyone *knows* that more prison causes (or does not cause) less crime and that the motives behind the buildup were noble albeit tough minded (or ill conceived). The goal of this book is to get past these self-confident assertions.

PRISON BUILDUP: CONSTRUCTIVE OR DESTRUCTIVE?

Prison is the ultimate intrusion by the state into the lives of its citizens. Prisons impose on their residents near-complete deprivation of personal liberties, barren living conditions, control centers that regulate movement within the prison, exterior fences draped with concertina wire, lines painted on hallway floors that limit where inmates may walk, little and ill-paid work, and endless tedium. The prison buildup was commonly and appropriately called the "get tough" approach to crime control.

Was the buildup generally constructive or destructive? If there is satisfaction in the buildup, from what does it spring – the harnessing of aggression to get a grip on the plague of crime, especially violent crime, or the satisfaction that comes with demolition and denigration?[10] Is the prison buildup an ennobling enterprise? Or are such lofty claims merely alibis for aggression or, worse yet, an effort at repression by some groups over other groups?

To take stock, "more prisons" is *not* merely a policy preference in the way one might prefer more bike trails, better schools, or lower taxes. More prisons means the greater exercise of coercive power by some people (mere human individuals) over other people. Mass imprisonment is an emphatic expression of aggression; that is obvious. But what kind of aggression? And with what consequences? Answering these questions is the central purpose of this book.

Much of the sociological literature on prisons and the prison buildup construes the buildup as an effort at social domination and exploitation. This argument is developed most famously by Michel Foucault, the French social critic, and, more recently, by a group of scholars that include David Garland, Loïc Wacquant, William Chambliss, Jerome Skolnick, and James Q. Whitman. The U.S. prison buildup has no rational content. Prison's formal purposes – retribution and crime control – are nothing more than alibis for aggression. Behind the mass movement demanding more prisons are excited but unaware masses, politicians taking advantage of these lower sentiments, and large doses of collective irrationality. One formulation portrays the buildup as coming out of the emotional lift stirred by treating people as inferior and placing them in harsh conditions.[11] We consider these arguments and search for evidence to support them. Unfortunately, for these authors, we do not come up with much.

An alternative position is that society has mandates that are not arbitrarily chosen tasks but are the core of what is needed for society to function. In a modern economy, schools must teach true lessons about physics today so that tomorrow's flood-control levies can be built without structural flaws. The judiciary must be independent of family, clan, and special interests; judges must be competent; and the rule of law must mean something; otherwise, the judiciary cannot serve as an instrument of economic development.[12] Likewise, prisons gain or lose their legitimacy according to whether they achieve their mission, their social ends – retribution and crime control. Prisons achieve, or are supposed to achieve, a substantive outcome. This outcome is important to society.

The position we ultimately take is much more in line with the second stance. However, it is important to emphasize that because prison growth can achieve something substantively important, it does not follow that such gains are always achieved. There may be a threshold beyond which more prisons yield minimal crime reductions, and possibly even more crime. Thus, it is an empirical question whether we currently use incarceration in a way that is effective. There is a small literature (in economics, sociology, and policy analysis) that takes such an empirical approach. We address this empirical question in Chapter 3.

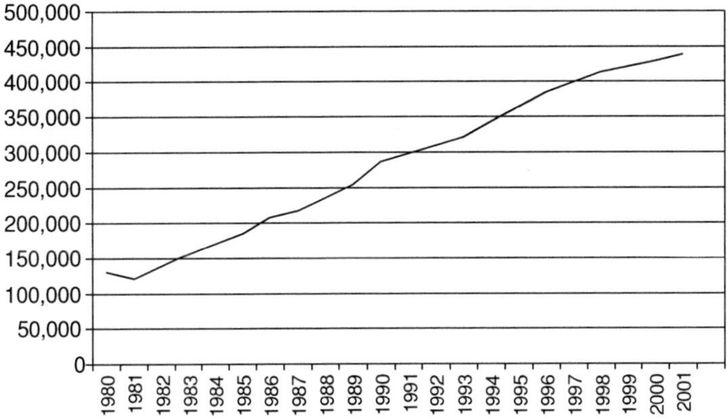

Figure 1.1. Prison employees, 1980–2001. *Source: Corrections Yearbook*, South Salem, NY, and Middletown, CT: Criminal Justice Institute, annually, 1980–2002.

BUILDUP AS BIG GOVERNMENT AND FAILED GOVERNMENT

The prison buildup is sometimes described as adding more prison beds. This is a shorthand term for more recreation yards and infirmaries, custody and treatment staff, visiting rooms and educational programs, food preparation facilities and guard towers, wardens and associate wardens, and sheets and towels – in short, the components that differentiate a fully functioning prison from a mere dormitory or housing unit. "More beds" imposes ever-greater demands on the public fisc and requires more government employees. It also raises questions of governance: can a mass of inmates be governed without an organizational collapse? Should we anticipate high rates of violence and rebellion?

Big Government

In 1979, there were 855 state and federal adult correctional prisons. By 2000, the number of prisons had almost doubled to 1,668.[13] More prisons, of course, require more public funds to build and operate them and more government employees to staff them. Figure 1.1 shows the growth in prison employees, from 121,000 in 1981 to 440,000 in 2001. The money side is shown in Table 1.1. In 1980, states spent $7.2 billion

TABLE 1.1. *Federal and State Prison Expenditures**

Year	Expenditures, state prisons in $1,000s	Expenditures, federal prisons in $1,000s	State and federal prisons' cost per resident ($)
1980	7,197,338	715,300	32
1981	8,180,148	704,500	35
1982	8,185,889	800,440	35
1983	8,978,005	883,050	38
1984	10,152,592	873,250	42
1985	11,393,521	1,024,820	52
1986	11,718,582	978,020	53
1987	12,461,390	1,365,210	57
1988	14,265,336	1,559,580	64
1989	15,681,836	2,201,650	72
1990	17,505,068	3,589,700	85
1991	19,226,855	2,258,630	85
1992	19,404,816	2,663,450	87
1993	19,723,011	2,612,370	87
1994	21,417,090	2,665,870	93
1995	23,627,083	3,015,040	101
1996	24,029,310	3,250,750	103
1997	25,059,538	3,510,890	107
1998	26,120,090	3,363,330	109
1999	27,182,280	3,505,900	113
2000	27,569,391	3,769,630	111
2001	29,491,268	4,303,500	119

* Inflation adjusted to 2001 constant dollars, using the consumer price index.

Source: State data, 1980–1985, *State Government Finances*, various years (Washington, DC: Bureau of Census); 1986–2001, James J. Stephen, *State Prison Expenditures, 2001* (Washington, DC: U.S. Department of Justice, Bureau of Justice Statistics, 2001). Federal data, U.S. Department of Justice, "Budget Trend Data 1975 through the President's 2003 Request to the Congress," Table, Federal Prison System Budget, 1975–2003, www.usdoj.gov/jmd/budgetsummary/btd/1975_2002/btd02tocpg.htm.

on prisons, and the federal government spent $715 million (in 2000 dollars). In 2001, states spent $29 billion on prisons, and the federal government spent $4.3 billion.[14] If we combine federal and state prison expenditures, prison spending for each U.S. resident increased from $32 in 1980 to $119 in 2001.

These figures point in one direction – "big government" becoming bigger. Or do they? The proper yardstick to measure the "size" of government is less obvious than it might first appear.[15] Consider the growth of the U.S. Postal Service (USPS), which employs almost one-third of the federal civilian labor force.[16] Since the early 1970s, the USPS increased from 740,000 employees to 850,000 employees – a 15% increase. Yet the volume of mail delivered more than doubled during this period. Also, the USPS began to generate a hefty profit (on the order of $400 million per year), while decreasing average delivery time. If one's agenda is to trim the size of big government, one could say that the USPS was part of the problem (an increase in the number of employees) or part of the solution (a decreasing ratio of employees to mail delivered, operating in the black, quicker service). The embarrassment of more postal employees in a period of less government is superficial. What about correctional buildup?

This question loops us back to where we started – the issue of the optimal scope of government depends at least in part on whether one accepts the legitimacy of this or that governmental effort. Only the most rigid anti–big government advocate would object to the employment of more USPS employees when asked to deliver more mail. Likewise, only the most dogmatic anti–big government advocate would object to more correctional workers, if this would cause a large decline in the crime rate. If one really believes that one will see substantial crime reduction with more prisons, then increasing size may not be hard to swallow – even for the anti–big government advocate. However, if the prison buildup is all folly, then the buildup is but another instance of the state overstepping its mandate. There is nothing illogical about wanting to trim the size of government, in the belief that doing so is vital to economic prosperity, while granting exceptions. Perhaps corrections should be an exception.

Privatization as an Antidote to Big Government?

Some researchers in the field of policy studies draw a distinction between the provision of government services and bearing the cost. From this perspective, privately provided corrections services, although paid for by state and federal governments, would not be criticized as "big government" because little government bureaucracy would be involved.[17] Despite years of interest in privatization as a means to save costs, this movement has not led to a substantial private prison sector. There has been a dramatic increase in private provision of particular services such as health care, education, and food services, much as in other parts of the economy.[18] However, the direct provision of custodial control is largely the province of government. Currently, 6.7% of all inmates are held in privately operated facilities. Furthermore, the growth of private prisons appears to have reached a plateau and may not expand beyond its current small share of the correctional market.[19] The proportion of inmates in private facilities grew modestly between 2000 and 2005, from 6.5% to 6.7% of all inmates.[20]

To take the issue a bit further, some observers have argued that the impact of the privatization on public corrections cannot be measured by size alone because private prisons force public corrections to achieve greater efficiency. Correctional employees and managers, it is argued, respond to the challenge of private prisons, "whether from fear of being privatized themselves, or pride in showing that they can compete, or from being compared by higher authority."[21] There may be something to this. A recent study examined the possibility that states adopting private facilities will experience a reduction in the costs of their *public* facilities.[22] The data were collected for the period 1999–2001. At least for this period, states with private prisons (thirty states) experienced lower rates of growth in expenditures per inmate for their public prisoners than states without private prisons (nineteen states, one state with missing data). Privatization then may be a counterforce to big governmental bureaucracy and inefficiency. It remains an open question whether the existence of private prisons will have this effect in the future. The shock toward greater efficiency may be one time only, occurring just in the period studied or thereabouts. Our main point is that privatization does not solve the big government issue, although it may help at the margins.[23]

Failed Government?

Much of the debate of modern politics concerns the scope of government. Conservatives favor smaller government, lower taxes, and less government regulation and intervention into daily lives, in the belief that restraining public entitlements and subsidies is crucial to economic prosperity. Liberals advocate larger government, higher taxes, greater regulation, and a more generous safety net, in the belief that society must help those who struggle in the open marketplace. Recently, a number of scholars, including Frances Fukuyama and Peter Evans, have argued that our preoccupation with the scope of government has given short shrift to a second dimension of state power, its strength.[24] *Scope* refers to the range of governmental activities undertaken and the resources applied to them. *Strength* refers to the ability of a state to execute policies effectively and without massive resistance. Fukuyama states that, based on the evidence, "strength of state institutions is more important in a broad sense than scope of state function."[25] Large or small is less crucial than how, and how well, state institutions are led and managed.

Critics of the buildup argue that prisons on a mass scale are unworkable. They will become tense, dangerous, and too weak to prevent high rates of individual and collective violence. Prisons, under mass incarceration, will resemble "failed states." Yet the critics have not given this worrisome forecast the simplest empirical test. We are far enough down the buildup road to test their prediction. We do this in Chapter 4.

THE SORTING MACHINE

Metaphorically speaking, the justice system operates like a giant sorting machine that distributes offenders into four main forms of correctional supervision.[26] Both *probation* and *parole* are community-based sanctions, in the sense that offenders reside in the community rather than in a correctional facility.[27] *Probation* is a court-ordered sanction, which serves as the main alternative to incarceration. Typically, probationers are required to comply with specific rules of conduct. If the offender violates those rules, or if she or he commits a new offense, this may result in tighter restrictions or incarceration. *Parole* is correctional supervision for offenders after they have served some time behind bars. As with probation, if the parole term does not go well, the offender may be (in this instance) reincarcerated. *Jail* confines defendants awaiting and during trial, offenders who have been sentenced to a term of 1 year or less, and offenders waiting transfer to state or federal prison after conviction. *Prison* confines inmates to a correctional facility, normally to serve a sentence of 1 year or more.

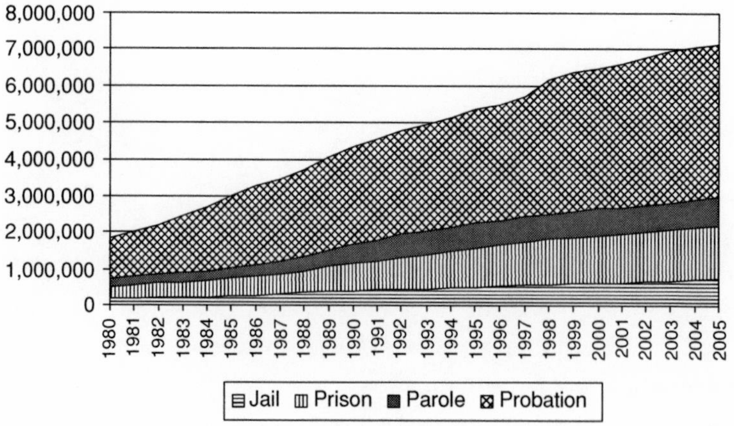

Figure 1.2. Correctional populations, 1980–2005. *Source:* "Number of Persons under Correctional Supervision" (Washington, DC: Bureau of Justice Statistics), www.ojp.usdoj.gov/bjs/glance/tables/corr2tab.htm.

How much sorting goes on? Consider the following. In 2004, there were 13.9 million arrests for crimes.[28] Of these, 2.2 million were charged with a serious violent crime (murder, forcible rape, robbery, and aggravated assault) or a serious property crime (burglary, larceny-theft, motor vehicle theft, and arson). For those charged with a felony, 68% were convicted, 25% were not convicted, and the remaining 9% received another disposition (e.g., diversion).[29] Some (unknown) portion of those convicted was innocent – the sorting was harmfully defective. Of those convicted of a felony, 32% were sentenced to prison, 40% were sentenced to jail, 25% were sentenced to probation, and the remaining 3% were sentenced to other sanctions (e.g., fine, community service, restitution, treatment).[30]

Figure 1.2 shows the end product of the sorting, as measured by the number of persons assigned to each of the big four. Several facts about correctional supervision in the United States become apparent. The first is overall growth. At year-end 1980, there were 1.8 million offenders serving sentences under one form or another of correctional supervision. By year-end 2005, there were more than 7 million offenders under correctional supervision. In 1980, 0.8% of the U.S. population was under some form of correctional supervision. In 2005, 2.4% of the U.S. population was under correctional supervision. Second, community corrections is the punishment of choice. In 2004, 70% of those under correctional supervision were either on probation or on parole. Probation, in particular, dominates. Of the nearly 7 million offenders under correctional supervision, 60% are on probation. Third, the raw numbers themselves tell us little about how good a job the sorting system does. In Chapter 3, we address this issue, asking "who" goes to prison and how this has changed during the prison buildup.

Finally, if one thinks of probation as the dispositional alternative to prison, then the sheer number of probationers suggests that even modest changes in the boundary between the two alternatives could have large consequences. If it becomes even slightly easier to assign offenders to prison rather than probation, one can expect significant changes in the number of individuals behind bars. Furthermore, these changes would certainly increase the percentage of Americans who come under the control of state correctional agencies at some time in their lives. A recent study from the Bureau of Justice Statistics estimates that, based on 2001 incarceration rates, the lifetime chance of going to prison is about 32% for blacks males, 17% for Hispanic males, and 6% for white males.[31] (Males comprise the majority of prisoners, so the corresponding estimates for females are about six times lower.) As with most projections, these calculations are extrapolations of current conditions and must be interpreted cautiously.[32]

Nonetheless, one might want to consider that increases in the use of imprisonment are likely to increase Americans' (already high) lifetime incidence of incarceration. Any additional increases that failed to promote public safety in a cost-effective way would be difficult, if not impossible, to justify.

ORGANIZATION OF THE BOOK

Our charge is to assess the buildup, both its causes and its consequences. Starting with causes, Chapter 2 examines the social forces that brought about the buildup. A lot has been said on this topic, especially by sociologists who attempt to connect the buildup to broad changes in American society. We assess these arguments, as well as the idea that the prison buildup was an instrumental effort to push down the crime rate.

As is brought out in this first chapter, the crime rate soared in the late 1960s, yet the initial response was to decrease the rate of imprisonment. This was followed by a massive, unrelenting increase in the number of citizens behind bars. A central question to ask about this policy change is whether it decreased the crime rate. Chapter 3 approaches this question from two angles. One approach is to examine changes in the composition of "who" goes to prison. If the buildup was achieved by imprisoning increasingly less serious offenders, this would suggest that its crime reduction capacity diminished over time. A second approach takes advantage of the fact that some states imprison at higher rates than others. This allows us to determine whether variation in the rate of imprisonment among states can be linked statistically to variation in the crime rate among states. Does more prison, holding constant other factors, mean less crime? Also, using this sort of regression approach, we can consider the possibility that past a certain threshold, more prison may actually generate more crime.

During the 1970s and 1980s, prison riots and high rates of violence wreaked havoc on U.S. prisons. Many saw this experience as a bad trend that would only become worse under the buildup. The prognosis was an unavoidable organizational collapse. Chapter 4 assesses this worrisome possibility, using several indicators to track the pattern of individual and collective violence during the buildup period. All indicators point in the same, although not in the expected, direction. This chapter relates the observed patterns to broader theories of prison order.

Chapter 5 addresses prisoner reentry into society. Given that almost all prisoners are eventually released (only about 5% of the current population will not be released), the prison buildup could be expected to eventually lead to an explosive growth in the numbers of ex-offenders released to the streets. In fact, about two-thirds of those released are rearrested within 3 years of release, and half are returned to prison either for a new crime or for violating the terms of their release. Recognizing the dimensions of this problem, policy makers have begun to devote a great deal of attention to how to make this transition more successful. Researchers have tried to find out what works and what might work better. This chapter discusses these efforts.

Chapter 6 considers the impact of the prison buildup on the labor market. Motivating this chapter is the concern that mass imprisonment has two pernicious effects. It conceals the true rate of unemployment in American society. Mass imprisonment generates unemployment, by damaging the employment prospects of those released from prison. For critics of the buildup, these are two more reasons that it is a misguided policy.

We conclude that many of the worries about the buildup did not come to pass. In fact, prison conditions have improved during the same period that the incarcerated population multiplied. We also conclude that there were gains in terms of crime reduction that resulted from this expansion of incarceration. In addition, we conclude that the negative impacts of incarceration on labor markets are modest.

However, our overall assessment of the buildup is not as sanguine as these observations first suggest. Although earlier expansions of prison capacity may have yielded solid crime reductions, the scale of imprisonment is now so great that the gains from further expansions are rapidly declining. Society is still struggling with how to change policy and practice to accommodate the large numbers of inmates that leave secure confinement each year. Mass incarceration also requires substantial fiscal resources, primarily at the state level. The human costs are not evenly spread across the population because poor and minority demographic groups are vastly overrepresented among the incarcerated. Together, these observations inform the judgment in Chapter 7 that, at this time, both justice and pragmatism challenge the policies that have led to mass incarceration.

Causes of the Prison Buildup

> Few people in the mid-1970s could have predicted the massive growth in prison and jail populations that was about to occur.[1]

However one calculates the numbers, the late twentieth century saw a massive increase in the extent of incarceration in the United States. From 1973 to 2005, the number incarcerated per 100,000 U.S. residents increased five-fold, from 96 to 491. To understand the buildup in its various aspects, we address the social forces that summoned it forth, the impact of the buildup on order behind bars, and the impact of the buildup on the broader society, including the crime rate and the labor market. That is, we should consider the cause of the buildup, its course, and its consequences. This chapter investigates the first of these issues – what brought about the buildup – leaving the other two for subsequent chapters. We begin by examining the scholarly work on this issue. Much of this literature relates the prison buildup to the large-scale social changes that occurred over the past several decades, even, in some formulations, to grand historical themes.

The literature can be divided into two blocks. In the first block, researchers agree that a broad-based social movement supported the buildup, but then disagree over whether the movement is best characterized as the by-product of social discontents associated with rapid social change or as an instance of purposeful people seeking solutions to a problem. In the second block, the buildup is seen as having nothing to do with popular demands or social movements. Instead, the powers-that-be weave a system of controls that, by means of detailed monitoring and subtle coercion, creates a docile and obedient citizenry. The buildup is an element of this insidious project. This perspective merits consideration, too, and we take it up following our assessment of social movement explanations for the buildup.

It should be pointed out that the victims' rights movement emerged in this period, but with a somewhat different agenda than the broader prison buildup movement. The advocates of victims' rights sought to enhance the services provided to crime victims, especially those suffering domestic violence and sexual assault. Financial restitution programs would compensate victims for the crimes they suffered. In addition, the victims' movement sought to change criminal procedure to allow victims (or their families in murder cases) to testify in the sentencing phase of trial concerning the impact of the crime. They demanded, and in many jurisdictions were given, a "voice" in the legal proceedings. Concerns over the rights of victims are related to the broader effort to increase punishment, but are not conterminous with them.[2]

A SOCIAL MOVEMENT FROM BELOW – TWO VIEWS

Some scholars see the prison buildup as growing out of the discontents and social problems of modern society. For example, in *The Culture of Control*, David Garland develops a broad account of the role of imprisonment in modern society. Although the argument is complex and draws on an impressive array of sources, the core point can be straightforwardly stated: the prison buildup was the product of a reactionary social movement driven by the strains of modern society and disruptive social change. Garland argues,

> The risky, insecure character of today's social and economic relations is the social surface that gives rise to our newly emphatic, overreaching concern with control. . . . It is the source of the deep-seated anxieties that find expression in today's crime control culture, in the commodification of security, and in a built environment designed to *manage space and to separate people.*[3]

The linchpin of the effort to "manage space and separate people" is the prison buildup, as achieved in the United States and (to a lesser extent) Great Britain. Garland does not identify the relevant comparison period as to when social relations were less risky and insecure, although the immediate post–World War II period suggests itself. (As a side note, Garland does not consider whether that earlier period of security was achieved through otherwise undesirable social arrangements, such as racial domination, patriarchy, or stifling conformity.)

Along the same lines as Garland, Thomas Blomberg and Karol Lucken argue that the prison buildup is the culmination of a downward spiral:

> When progressivism's promise of a science and government cure to the crime problem failed to materialize, society was stripped of all hope and expectations. As a result, frustration, rather than reason, determined crime control policy. Tucked away in current formulations [of crime control policy] is evidence of the resignation and confusion that presumably typifies modern society.[4]

William Lyons and Stuart Scheingold state that "the anxieties associated with unwelcome social, economic, and cultural transformations generate anger, and punishment becomes a vehicle for expressing that anger."[5] Katherine Beckett maintains that the pro-prison movement served as a channel to express the diffuse anxieties associated with the breakdown of gender and racial hierarchies: "Economic pressures, anxiety about social change, and a pervasive sense of insecurity clearly engender a great deal of frustration, and the scapegoating of the underclass has been a relatively successful way of tapping and channeling these sentiments."[6] This scapegoating took the form of irrational demands for more severe sentencing.

The most fully elaborated argument is by Michael Tonry, who sought to explain the "public hysteria [that] leads to adoption of cruel and intemperate policies."[7] Tonry observes that the United States has undergone "wrenching social change" since the early 1970s.[8] The shocks to the system include the overthrow of Jim Crow laws, the civil rights and feminist movements, mass entry of women into the workforce, transformation of gender roles, mass migration of foreign citizens into the United States, and the "fundamental restructuring" of the economy. These changes have little to do with crime, but have "raised enormous anxieties." Playing on these anxieties for short-term electoral gains, politicians stoke public fears about crime and seek votes by promising more severe punishments for criminal offenders. "In the 1970s and 1980s," Tonry argues, "crime issues acted both as a code word for racial animosity and as an appeal to voters who were anxious about many changes in their lives."[9]

Recently, several researchers have sought to moderate this strong emphasis on social problems as the cause of the prison buildup movement, allowing for crime and crime control to play a significant role.[10] The emphasis in this "governance through crime" approach is that governmental elites take advantage of the crime problem – recognized to be real – to shore up their power. Theodore Caplow and Jonathan Simon, for example, argue that although "a great surge of violent crime did take place in the United States between 1967 and 1975,"[11] this cannot fully account for the buildup. Rather, governmental elites used the crime surge to help pull themselves out of difficult circumstances. "In the face of losses in its perceived competence, purposes, and boundaries, the state finds the intensification of crime control attractive.... Crime control has come to be a rare source of agreement in a factionalized public."[12]

Along the same lines, Anthony Bottoms[13] identifies the "disembedding process of modernity" as the underlying force that has given rise to the prison buildup. Disembedding is the conjuncture of several broad developments, including the erosion of class, the decline of intermediate-level social groups, and the subjective experience of living in a highly technological world. Disembedding causes both widespread insecurities among the public and higher crime rates. Bottoms dismisses as implausible the rationale that higher rates of imprisonment reduce the crime rate. Instead, politicians seeking public approval "tap into the electorate's insecurities by promising tough action."[14] Crime and tougher punishments are correlated, but only because they arise from a common cause: dissolution of the social web that binds people into a social unity.

In the following, we undertake a direct analysis of what caused the buildup in incarceration in the United States at the end of the twentieth century. To do this, we first connect the previous discussion to broader debates over the causes of social movements. We then describe the pattern of prison growth in the United States, followed by a review of relevant scholarly literature. We present fresh evidence. Specifically, we use data to test the plausibility of theories that a social movement was responsible for the buildup and to distinguish among hypotheses about its form. We particularly highlight theories emphasizing social disconnection and those emphasizing instrumental concerns regarding crime. Finally, we consider an alternative position, that the prison buildup is a by-product of the system's need to maintain domination over its population.

SOCIAL MOVEMENT THEORIES AND THE BUILDUP

Scholars from a number of disciplines (sociology, political science, economics, and law) have studied the conditions that give rise to social movements. No single theory has gained dominance, perhaps because social movements are too diverse to permit theoretical unity. The starting point of most theories is that people join social movements because of "bad" conditions. Yet, this insight does not get us very far. Bad conditions can be found almost everywhere, as long as "bad" can be defined broadly enough. However, social movements are not pervasive. Most of the time, people do not invest the time and resources it takes to change some aspect of society through social movement participation. Social movements take something more than routine participation. They require a burst of high energy to get people mobilized (committed to a new cause) and active (doing something). To be pushed over the edge toward social movement participation, people need to believe that something important *must* change. What conditions produce these bursts of high energy? Although current thinking has developed along a number of lines, the approaches most relevant to our current task are a "crisis mobilization" approach and a "system disturbance" approach.

The crisis mobilization position is that social movements emerge, and are more likely to be successful, in periods of broad social and economic crisis.[15] Outside crisis situations, society's institutions are able to regulate day-to-day activities with little disruption. Institutional leaders are paid to make competent, informed, and effective decisions. They ensure that the roads are paved, that children are educated, and that the rule of law prevails against unbridled assertions of self-interest and intense community conflict. Economic prosperity is generated. However, when routine institutional solutions seem ineffective, when leaders' commitments are the wrong ones or are poorly executed, when uncertainty about the future is high, then people can be expected to demand new solutions. Social movements are important to society because they are a source of new ideas and change in response to troubled situations. They are the seedbeds for new institutions, or major changes within them.

Social movements, in this theory, tend to emerge from "below" and may leap ahead of elites. The image is evoked well by law professor Bruce Ackerman: "The scene is dominated by mass movements mobilizing on behalf of grand ideals, and elites struggling for authority to speak in the name of their mobilized fellow citizens."[16] The people force a "switch in time." Political scientist Walter Dean Burnham, working in this tradition, suggests one marker for a switch in time: the forces of change win two or more elections in a row based on the appeal of their reform agenda.[17] Business school professor John Kotter argues that movements for change within organizations require a sense of urgency. Visible crises capture people's attention, allowing the change process to begin, or leaders may help foster a sense of crisis to achieve the same.[18] The forces for change swing into action only "when about 75% of a company's management is honestly convinced that business-as-usual is totally unacceptable."[19]

Theorists working in the system disturbance tradition assert that social movement participants tend to be confused, hapless, and unreasoning victims of large-scale social change.[20] When society undergoes a major change, such as urbanization or the modernization of gender roles, some people lose out, and many others become confused and disoriented. Unable to understand the larger forces that are swirling around them, and without reasonable solutions to their problems, people turn to social movements and other forms of collective behavior. As a consequence, social movements demand changes undisciplined by any sense of proportion or realism; they tend to be coarse, hostile, and aggressive. The "success" of a movement cannot be measured against its formal goals because they are secondary to the underlying purpose – to aggressively attack the social order, where aggression itself is the goal, or to scapegoat. Rather, the yardstick is the extent to which participants desist from their irrational behavior and are reintegrated into society.

To summarize, according to the crisis mobilization model, the fundamental process giving rise to social movements is the breakdown of existing arrangements. The future looks unpredictable and undesirable, and people take action. Elites may then need to catch up to the masses. The masses are rational in their action. In contrast, in the system disturbance model, people losing out in social change join social movements to compensate for strain and hardship. Participants are suggestible, intolerant, extreme in action, and display only the coarser emotions, such as revenge.

Social Movement and Institutions

Before we turn to the empirical evidence, two additional points will help specify the issues at hand. First, John McCarthy and Mayer Zald distinguish a "social movement" from a "social movement organization."[21] The former refers to a "set of opinions and beliefs in a population which represents preferences for changing some element of the social structure." The latter is a "formal organization which identifies its goals with the preferences of a social movement." A complete analysis of the buildup movement would give attention to both the buildup social movement and the buildup social movement organizations. We focus on the former alone because it allows us to test directly arguments connecting broad social change and the prison buildup outcome. It is this connection that has generated the greatest scholarly attention. Second, scholars' views of the social movement bringing about the buildup are strongly correlated with their views of the purposes of incarceration. Those who view the social movement supporting the buildup as having arisen from disturbed social relations tend to minimize the importance of prison's formal goals. Those goals are mainly excuses for acting aggressively, undisciplined by any consideration as to what is fair, valuable, or effective. Scholars who see the social movement as an effort to effect problem-solving institutional change view prison as an important instrument of social control. That is, the public demanded more prisons, and was willing to pay for them, to

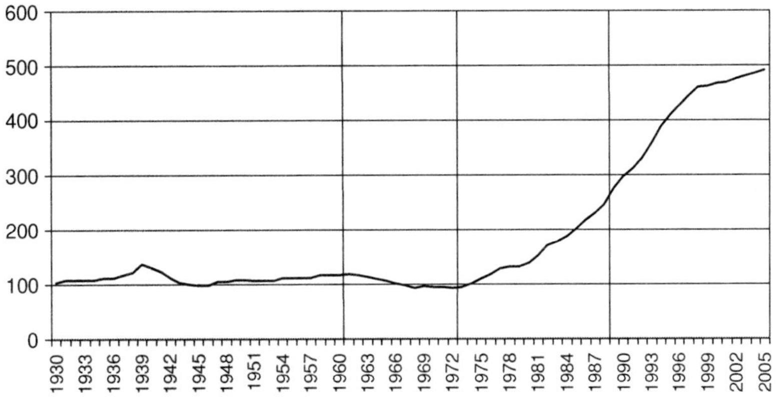

Figure 2.1. Prisoners per 100,000 population, 1930–2005. *Source: Sourcebook of Criminal Justice Statistics*, www.albany.edu/sourcebook/pdf/t6282005.pdf.

achieve gains in public safety and retribution. The old solutions were not working, and they wanted to try something new.

Our staring point is the prison buildup itself and its relationship to the crime rate.

EMPIRICS OF PRISON BUILDUP

Figure 2.1 graphs the number of prisoners in U.S. state and federal prisons per 100,000 residents from 1930 to 2005. Figure 2.2 graphs the prison population using two other denominators, the number of violent crimes and property crimes.[22] The first data point in Figure 2.2 is 1960 because crime data collected before 1960 are poorly suited for looking at trends over time.[23] The rationale behind the second figure is that a judgment about whether a society uses prisons abundantly or sparingly depends on the crime level. That is, whether a given level of imprisonment is excessive depends not only on how many people are ultimately "available" for imprisonment (one cannot directly compare the size of the prison populations of Luxembourg and China) but also on how much crime has occurred.

Four time periods suggest themselves: 1930 to 1960, 1961 to 1972, 1973 to 1988, and 1989 to 2005.[24] These are discussed in the following sections.

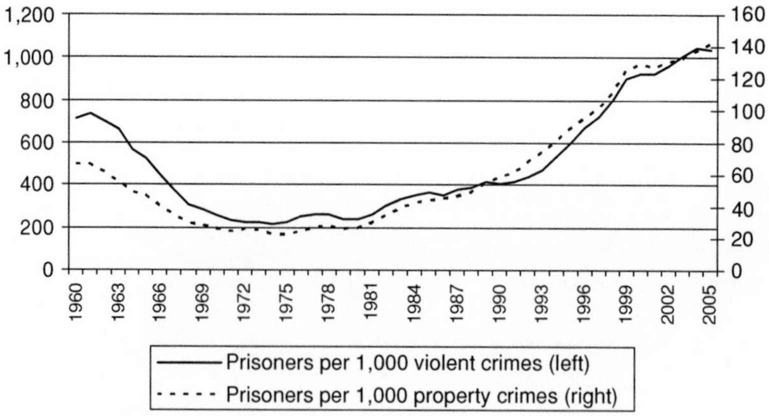

Figure 2.2. Prisoners per 1,000 violent and 1,000 property crimes. *Source: Sourcebook of Criminal Justice Statistics,* www.albany.edu/sourcebook/pdf/t31062005.pdf and www.albany.edu/sourcebook/pdf/t6282005.pdf.

Period 1, 1930 to 1960: Trendless Trend

From 1930 to 1960, the number of inmates hovered around 115 inmates per 100,000 population (Figure 2.1). There were discernible short-run trends. For example, there was a minor peak in 1939 (137 inmates/100,000 residents) and a valley in 1945 (98 inmates/100,000 residents). Still, there was no sustained drift away from the mean of 115. In 1931, there were 110 inmates per 100,000 population; in 1960, there were 117.

Period 2, 1961 to 1972: Modest to Large Decline

Starting about 1961, the United States began to turn away from imprisonment. The magnitude of this turn depends on the denominator used. Figure 2.1 shows the trend to be relatively modest. In 1961, there were 119 inmates per 100,000 population; by 1972, there were 93. The decline is much steeper if the ratio is calculated using crime as the denominator (Figure 2.2). In 1961, there were 66 inmates per 1,000 property crimes, and 733 inmates per 1,000 violent crimes. By 1972, the ratios had declined to 26 inmates per 1,000 property crimes and 227 inmates per 1,000 violent crimes.

To summarize, if population is used as a denominator, the rate of imprisonment declined by 22% between 1961 and 1972. If property crimes and violent crimes are the denominators, then the declines were 61% and 69%, respectively – a large drop in just over a decade.

Period 3, 1973 to 1988: Buildup Begins

Sometime during the mid-1970s, American society began a major, long-term buildup in its prison population. The start date depends on the denominator used. As measured by inmates per 100,000 population, the first buildup years were 1973 and 1974. In 1972, there were 93 inmates per 100,000 residents, and by 1974, 102 inmates. However, what started out slowly quickly picked up steam. By 1988, there were 247 inmates per 100,000 residents.

When property and violent crimes are used to denominate prisoners, the buildup began a bit later. The ratio of inmates to both property and violent crimes continued to decline in 1973 and 1974. The first substantial increase in both ratios did not occur until 1976 – but then increases came with a rush. Between 1976 and 1988, the number of prisoners per 1,000 property crimes nearly doubled from 25 to 49. For the same years, the number of prisoners per 1,000 violent crimes rose from 252 to 383, a 52% increase.

Period 4, 1989 to 2005: Accelerated Growth

The buildup that took hold in the 1980s accelerated in the 1990s, and continued to grow more modestly through 2005 In 1989, there were 276 inmates per 100,000 population; by 2005, this ratio stood at 491 inmates. In 1989, there were 54 and 415 inmates per 1,000 property and violent crimes, respectively. By 2005, these ratios had jumped to 142 (property) and 1,040 (violent). In the last few years, the growth has moderated substantially. It may be that in a few years, we will consider the period after 2000 as a new regime.

EMPIRICAL RESEARCH FINDINGS

Before turning to our own evidence on the prison buildup, we review efforts to validate the competing arguments on the causes of the buildup movement. Rigorous studies are few in number.

Family Values and Concern with Crime

In a study that would gain considerable attention in criminal justice circles, Tom Tyler and Robert Boeckmann interviewed a sample of 166 adults living in a community in northern California to explore the sources of support for harsh punishments.[25] Their core question was the relative importance of two sorts of factors. One set, labeled "instrumental" and "crime control" in nature, taps whether the respondents believed the world is "dangerous." Dangerousness is seen as composed of fear of crime (e.g., "I worry about being robbed or assaulted in my neighborhood at night") and perceptions of the effectiveness of courts (e.g., "The courts have been effective in dealing with the crime problem," "Most judges are honest"). The second set of variables, labeled "relational" and "noninstrumental," taps the "moral cohesion" experienced by the respondents. Moral cohesion has several dimensions, and the one that ultimately proves to have the strongest impact on punitiveness is "judgments about the family."

Tyler and Boeckmann calculated the independent effects of these two sets of variables (instrumental/crime control vs. relational/noninstrumental) on support for get-tough crime measures. These measures included support for California's three strikes initiative, support for general punitive policies, willingness to abandon procedural protections for criminal defendants, support for the death penalty, and agreement with statements such as "It is alright for a citizen to shoot someone who has just raped them to keep the criminal from running away," and "It is better to let ten people go free than to convict one innocent person by mistake."

Tyler and Boeckmann found that the instrumental/crime control variables had little or no impact on the several get-tough measures. In contrast, the relational/noninstrumental variables did far better. The authors conclude, "the primary factor driving reactions to criminals are judgments about the family." Because the instrumental/crime control variables were not important in understanding policy preferences, but noninstrumental variables were, these findings would seem to undercut the crisis mobilization position and lend strong support to the system disturbance position. This inference is drawn by Stuart Scheingold, who argues that the Tyler and Boeckmann findings show that "the principal forces driving crime control policy are not the fear of crime but rather the malaise and marginalization associated with a crisis of political authority in postliberal states."[26] We are less persuaded.

The questions that supposedly measure family cohesion seemed to be infused with strong concerns with crime. Respondents were asked to agree or disagree with these items:

1. "The risk of being robbed or assaulted by teenage gangs has increased in recent years."
2. "Teenagers in gangs will assault a person like you without feeling any guilt or remorse."
3. "Because families are failing to control teenagers, laws must be made stronger."
4. "The breakdown of family has led many children to grow up without knowing what is right or wrong."
5. "Society has become more violent and dangerous as traditional moral values have decayed."

These items not only measure concerns with crime, but also appear to do so more effectively than the questions in Tyler and Boeckmann's formal crime control scale. The first two items, in particular, would seem to capture the emotional elements of concern over crime, for example, being preyed on by teenage gangs. In contrast, some of the items that Tyler and Boeckmann used in their crime control scale seem mechanical and far less likely to evoke the emotional component of fear of crime. They include "The crime problem in my community is serious" and "The problem of becoming a crime victim in California is serious these days."

Examination of the third, fourth, and fifth items in the previous list raises another confounding issue. They seem to be asking the respondents whether they agree with an argument advanced by criminologists James Q. Wilson and John DiIulio that, if society is to maintain its equilibrium, a decline in moral constraints must be made up by more law and vice versa.[27] This "equilibrium" position could not be stated more clearly than the third item, and it is implied by the fourth and fifth. Thus, rather than tapping diffuse anxieties behind family decline, these three items seem to be getting at a logical argument behind the need for greater imprisonment, if one believes there has been a decline in morality.[28] Some scholars believe that such a decline occurred.[29]

Hate Crimes and Economic Dislocation

A number of studies have examined the causes of hate crimes against religious, ethnic, racial, and other minority groups, often testing explanations directly analogous to the system disturbance explanation of imprisonment. The basic argument is that economic dislocation, unemployment, deprivation, and the breakdown of norms and values generates hate crimes because minority groups serve as expedient scapegoats in times of social and economic distress. One only has to substitute "punitive attitudes" for "hate crimes" to see that these two arguments are hypothesizing a similar underlying process.

The classic study along this line, by Carl Hovland and Robert Sears (1940), found that the price of cotton and national economic conditions could be used to predict lynchings for the period 1883 to 1930.[30] When conditions worsened, lynchings would rise. Recently, however, researchers have reexamined these data and concluded that the association is not robust. Donald Green and colleagues found that the association was sensitive to minor adjustments in modeling techniques and data decisions.[31] For example, when additional years of data are added, extending the time series into the Great Depression, the correlation largely disappears.

Research in a contemporary context has also turned up mainly negative evidence. In one study, Alan Krueger and Jorn-Steffen Pischke could discern no relationship between economic variables, such as unemployment rates and wages, and incidents of ethnic violence across German counties in the period January 1991 to June 1993.[32] Along the same lines, Donald Green and colleagues analyzed monthly variation in the incidence of hate crimes against Asians, Latinos, blacks, whites, gays/lesbians, or Jews over a 9-year period in New York City.[33] They found no association between the incidence of these crimes and unemployment.

This line of research does not necessarily demonstrate that economic distress and frustration have no causal impact on the incidence of hate crimes. Still, if the effect exists, it is likely to be weak and indirect.

"Most Important Problem" and Prison Buildup

Katherine Beckett conducted a direct analysis of social attitudes and the prison buildup.[34] She challenged the view that public concern over rising crime rates resulted in popular demand for harsher punishments, which, in turn, drove up the rate of incarceration.[35] If crime cannot predict concern with crime, Beckett argues, then demands for more prisons must be driven by something other than concern with crime per se. This would then rule out simple instrumentalism as an explanation for the prison buildup.

Beckett focused on the years 1964 to 1974, she states, because the war on crime was begun in this period. She measured the crime rate by dividing the number of Uniform Crime Report (UCR) violent crimes by 100,000 population. Concern with crime is measured using the "most important problem" (MIP) item from the Gallup poll. Beginning in 1946, Gallup pollsters have asked samples of Americans this question, unchanged for the duration of the series: "What do you think is the most important problem facing this country today?" Graphing these data for the 1964–1974 period, Beckett observes that "the reported rates of crime . . . shifted slowly and gradually, public concern about these problems fluctuated quickly and dramatically."[36] In other words, Beckett finds the suspected disconnect between the reality of crime and public concern with crime.

Taking the analysis one step further, Beckett regressed the MIP item on crime, providing a formal test of whether the violent crime rate predicts the percentage of Americans identifying crime as the most important problem. To give the hypothesis the best chance to be found valid, Beckett experimented with various lags between the crime rate and MIP (none, 3–5 months, 6–10 months, and 9–15 months). Whatever the lag, the results are the same: "the reported incidence of crime is not associated with the propensity of members of the public to identify crime as the most important problem."[37]

In her discussion, Beckett refers to the MIP issue as "crime." MIP, however, was coded to include not only crime but also "the breakdown of law and order" and "general unrest." This slippage in language is consequential because the period under consideration experienced high rates of collective disorders, including urban riots, civil rights demonstrations, and protests on campus. Beckett correlated changes in crime with concerns about crime *and* aspects of collective disorders.

Moreover, the salience of a problem to the public need not mirror its prevalence, or *only* its prevalence, for the public to be rational. There are other considerations that may, and indeed should, enter into a rational calculation over what is the "most important problem." They include whether the problem is new on the scene, the subjective dread of the problem, whether the problem is caused by human agency or acts of god, and whether there are perceived solutions to the problem.[38] Problems can take on salience as we see solutions available or not available.

Beckett's findings have been widely cited as strong evidence against instrumentalism in the prison buildup. But the poor choice of coding conflates crime with other concerns. Moreover, the MIP data are, by design, responsive to issues of the day, leading to short term fluctuations in the data. Thus, they may not be the ideal source for testing the hypothesis of instrumentalism.[39]

Gaubatz's "Botheration-Toleration" Gap

In her 1995 study, Kathlyn Gaubatz sought to explain the historic increase in the public's punitiveness toward criminal offenders and the factors that distinguish those who support those policies ("believers") from those who do not ("dissenters").[40] Gaubatz explains that the term "believers" is intended to connote individuals who buy into the "myth of crime and punishment"; that is, they are unable to challenge the "traditional assumption" that the increased use of punishment and the renewed use of the death penalty will lower the crime rate.[41] The term "dissenters" connotes people who "refuse to endorse" this ethos, and instead, look to "new methods and experimental programs" to deal with the crime problem. Gaubatz interviewed, in depth, thirteen believers and nine dissenters, all residents of Oakland, California. She argues that a single factor, the "botheration-toleration gap," explains both the time trend and the differences between believers and dissenters. In the past, Americans could straightforwardly condemn abortion, homosexuality, equal opportunity for women and minorities, free speech for political dissenters, and cohabitation by unmarried people. The flexible-type dissenters changed with the times. The rigid-type believers continued to be bothered by their traditional concerns, but they came to recognize that protest over these issues would be futile. This gap (between what believers *believe* and what they are forced to tolerate) creates frustration and hostility. Believers vent these feelings against the only safe target available, criminal offenders.

To support her case, Gaubatz needed to show that the reservoir of hostile feelings has increased over time and that believers can be distinguished from dissenters by their higher levels of "botheration-toleration gap." Gaubatz could not address the first issue empirically because her interview data were collected at one point in time. Nonetheless, she states that the botheration-toleration gap "is a phenomenon that we may presume has only multiplied in recent decades, as American society has come to tolerate so many previously proscribed behaviors."[42] Perhaps, but evidence would surely strengthen the case.

Gaubatz claims that her interview material supports the position that believers are more "bothered" than dissenters. She shows in her sample that "all of the believers find certain things that are disturbing to them. And nearly all of the dissenters do not."[43] The problem is making the causal connection between "botheredness" and support for the prison buildup.

What is supposed to be the case, if Gaubatz's theory is correct, is that believers support more stringent punishment of criminals because they have a reservoir of hostile feelings as a result of having to put up with groups and change that bother them. They express their hostility toward criminal offenders, a safe and convenient target. It has nothing to do with solving the crime problem because the enlightened reader "knows" that more stringent punishments do not reduce crime. However, the quoted material, and especially Gaubatz's immediate interpretation of that evidence, seems to contradict that position. Even Gaubatz's extreme believer[44] expresses a desire for greater security – not merely an outlet and a balm for hostile feelings.

In the end, Gaubatz is pessimistic because the dissenters currently "make up only a tiny fraction of the American public."[45] When we turn to our own analyses in the next section, we look at opinion data for increases in hostility over time of the sort hypothesized by Gaubatz.

To summarize, the empirical work generally cited in support of the prison buildup movement suffered from lack of precision in its

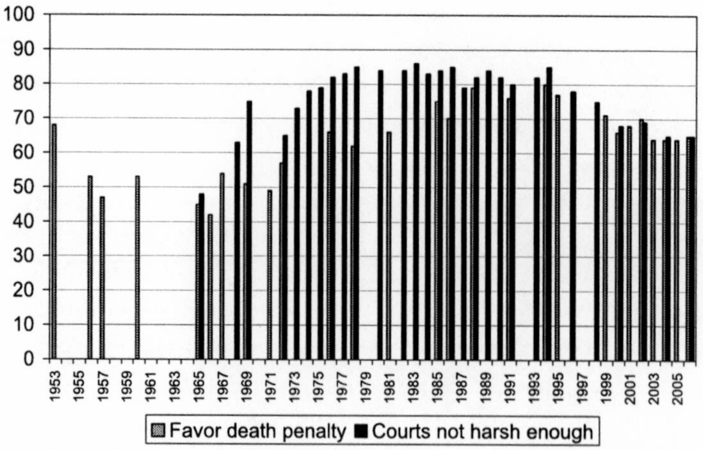

Figure 2.3. Trends in attitudes toward the death penalty and courts.
Notes: Death Penalty Question: "Are you in favor of the death penalty for a person convicted of murder?" *Source: Sourcebook of Criminal Justice Statistics,* www.albany.edu/sourcebook/pdf/t2512006.pdf, underlying data from Gallup poll.

Court Question: "In general, do you think the courts in this area deal too harshly or not harshly enough with criminals?" *Sources:* 1965–1968 data, LexisNexis Academic, underlying data from Gallup poll; 1972–2006 data, SDA: Survey Documentation and Analysis, http://sda.berkeley.edu/, underlying data from National Opinion Research Center, General Social Survey.

implementation. This provides motivation for an additional set of analyses, which we report in this chapter.

PUBLIC OPINION ON PUNISHMENT POLICY

The crisis mobilization position cannot be sustained unless there was a broad shift, from the mid-1960s through the 1980s, in public opinion toward more conservative positions on crime and punishment. The available survey data (other than the MIP) indicate a broad, slow change favoring stronger punishment. Figure 2.3 shows that support for the death penalty was fairly high in 1953 (68%), and then began to decrease, reaching a low point in 1966 (42%). After that, there was a slow rise in the proportion favoring the death penalty. By 1988, Americans overwhelmingly (79%) supported the death penalty. From 1995 through 2006, there has been a modest decrease in support for the death penalty. Similarly fluid trends appear in attitudes toward the courts. Figure 2.3 also shows that in 1965, about one-half of the respondents stated that the courts were "not harsh enough" in dealing with criminals. By 1969, there was a 25-percentage point gain in the proportion giving the "not harsh enough" response. By 1983, a large majority of Americans (86%) believed that the courts were not harsh enough on criminals. Following this peak, there was a modest decline in the percentage believing that courts are not harsh enough. In 2006, 65% stated the courts were not harsh enough.

Other data are consistent with these trends. In 1973, the General Social Survey (GSS) began to ask samples of U.S. respondents if they believed "we" were spending too much, too little, or about the right amount of money for crime control and four other problems. As reported in Table 2.1, from 1973 through 1996, about two-thirds said that they wanted more spent to halt the rising crime rate. The percentages favoring more spending on "dealing with drugs" and "improving the educational system" were about the same as on crime. In contrast, one-third or fewer favored spending more on "improving the conditions of blacks" and welfare. Respondents, then, were distinguishing among the areas they wanted their tax monies spent, and crime ranked at or near the top over a sustained period of time.

In their recent work on the three strikes law in California, Zimring and colleagues make a relevant point.[46] They argue that public anxiety may be sufficient to cause support for a symbolic, inexpensive, punitive response to crime. However, for the public to express support for expensive programs over a sustained period requires the belief that the funds expended will have an observable impact. If we accept this point, then data reported in Table 2.1 suggest that the American public was motivated by concerns specific to crime, not flashes of uncertainty or disorientation.

Support for Civil Liberties

In line with system disturbance theory, Gaubatz leads us to believe that there should be declining tolerance over time as a growing number of believers need to vent their hostility. If this argument is correct, we should see a corresponding decline in the support for the civil liberties of criminal defendants. (Crisis mobilization could imply either no trend or a similar decline in support as a means to crime control ends.)

TABLE 2.1. *Respondents Indicating Too Little Is Spent on Selected Problems in the United States*

Question: "We are faced with many problems in this country, none of which can be solved easily or inexpensively. I'm going to name some of the problems, and for each one I'd like you to tell me whether you think we're spending too much money on it, too little money, or about the right amount."

Year	Halting the rising crime rate	Dealing with drug addiction	Improving the nation's education system	Improving the conditions of blacks	Welfare
1973	68	70	51	35	21
1974	71	64	54	33	24
1975	69	59	52	29	25
1976	70	64	53	30	14
1977	71	59	50	27	13
1978	68	58	53	26	14
1980	72	65	56	27	14
1982	76	63	61	42	28
1983	69	62	62	32	22
1984	71	66	64	38	24
1985	65	65	63	32	19
1986	66	60	61	37	23
1987	73	70	66	48	28
1988	72	71	66	38	25
1989	75	73	69	37	24
1990	71	65	74	41	24
1991	68	60	71	39	24
1993	74	63	70	39	17
1994	78	63	72	34	13
1996	69	60	71	35	15
1998	64	61	71	37	16
2000	61	62	71	38	21
2002	57	55	74	33	21
2004	58	55	74	35	24
2006	61	62	74	37	25

Note: "Don't know" excluded from calculating percentages.
Source: SDA Archive, http://sda.berkeley.edu/archive.htm; underlying data from General Social Survey, National Opinion Research Center.

Several survey questions about respect for the civil liberties of criminal offenders are available for analysis. Unfortunately, they do not reach back in time as far as we would like, and the questions themselves are somewhat problematic. One set of questions asks respondents if they would approve of a police officer "striking" a citizen "in any situation you can imagine" and then in several specified conditions. Although this question appears to be designed to measure support for the civil rights of citizens against police abuse, it is far from ideal. Police, of course, are authorized by law to use force against citizens. Thus, one could be a committed civil libertarian, yet still imagine circumstances requiring a police officer to "strike" a citizen (e.g., to save a child from a murderous assault). Still, the term "striking" seems to connote something other than the lawful use of force, and civil libertarian concerns are likely to come into play in the answers to the questions. Thus, increasing levels of approval of a police officer striking a citizen may serve as an imperfect proxy for a decreasing commitment to civil liberties.

Although the trends are not even across the five questions, several of them show an increasing concern for civil liberties over the time period covered. For example, in 1973, 27% of the respondents approved of a police officer striking a citizen who had been vulgar; this decreased to 12% by 1988 (Table 2.2). Another question asks respondents if they were mainly concerned with the rights of the accused or mainly concerned with stopping crime. The percentage mainly concerned with stopping crime decreased from 1970 to 1974, but then reversed itself toward a more conservative position in 1976 and 1978. The overall change for the period was in the conservative direction, but only by about 4 percentage points (Table 2.3).

In summary, if the system disturbance argument were correct, we should anticipate Americans would have, along with their shift to the right on crime and punishment, also become less tolerant of the civil rights of accused criminals. We have seen almost no evidence that this occurred.

Victims of Change?

The crux of system disturbance theory as applied to prisons is that supporters of the prison buildup were the victims of historical change who vented their anxieties and frustrations on a vulnerable group – criminal defendants. The evidence considered thus far has been at the aggregate level, and it has not been very favorable to the theory. There are also individual-level implications. If the argument holds,

TABLE 2.2. *Respondents Indicating Whether They Approve of a Policeman Striking a Citizen*

Question 1: "Are there any situations in which you would approve of a policeman striking an adult male citizen?"

Questions 2–5: "Would you approve of a policeman striking a citizen who…"

Year	Any situation (Q.1)	…was attacking the policemen with his fists? (Q.2)	…was attempting to escape from custody? (Q.3)	…had said vulgar and obscene things to the policeman? (Q.4)	…was being questioned in a murder case? (Q.5)
1973	73	97	88	27	8
1975	76	98	89	19	7
1976	79	95	81	20	8
1978	79	94	77	18	8
1980	76	96	79	13	8
1983	81	93	79	15	9
1984	71	94	76	12	9
1986	74	95	75	14	9
1987	73	93	78	10	10
1988	75	93	80	12	9
1989	75	95	79	11	9
1990	73	94	77	12	11
1991	69	92	74	9	6
1993	77	94	76	7	7
1994	73	94	78	9	7
1996	71	93	73	7	5
1998	69	93	71	7	6
2000	67	91	70	6	6
2002	71	91	74	6	9
2004	71	89	74	8	10
2006	66	89	77	6	13

Note: "Don't know" excluded from calculating percentages.
Source: SDA Archive, http://sda.berkeley.edu/archive.htm; underlying data from General Social Survey, National Opinion Research Center.

we should anticipate that supporters of more punitive policies would disproportionately come from the ranks of the unemployed, or those who worry about unemployment in the future. They should be especially likely to be concerned about losing out at workplace advancement, especially to those groups who might otherwise be perceived as

TABLE 2.3. *Attitudes toward the Legal Rights of the Accused*

Year	Stop crime (%)
1970 (CPS)	49
1972 (CPS)	46
1974 (CPS)	42
1976 (CPS)	48
1978 (CPS)	54
1978 (WP)	48

CPS, Center for Political Studies; WP, *Washington Post.*
Note: Question (CPS): Some people are primarily concerned with doing everything possible to protect the legal rights of those accused of committing crimes. Others feel that it is more important to stop criminal activity even at the risk of reducing the rights of the accused. Where would you place yourself on this scale, or haven't you thought much about this?
Question (WP): Some people are primarily concerned with doing everything possible to protect the legal rights of those accused of committing crimes. Others feel it is more important to stop criminal activity even at the risk of reducing the rights of the accused, and others have opinions somewhere in between. Which of these views is closest to your own?
Note: "Don't know" excluded when calculating percentages.
Sources: SDA Archive, http://sda.berkeley.edu/archive.htm, underlying data from CPS; LexisNexis, underlying data from WP.

gaining, such as minorities and women. They should find themselves dissatisfied with their financial situation and the locale in which they live. These are large claims about trends among many millions of people – the American public or large segments of it. National survey data are needed to test them; fortunately, they are available.

Beginning in 1972, the University of Chicago's GSS asked representative samples of the American public about aspects of their lives and views on a range of issues. Using these data, Tables 2.4 to 2.6 report results of regression analyses designed to test whether disturbances in people's lives have led them to be more punitive toward criminal offenders. Four GSS questions are used as indicators of support for more severe punishment. They are whether the respondents (1) support the death penalty, (2) think the courts in their area deal harshly enough with criminals, (3) believe more should be spent to halt the rising crime rate, and (4) believe more should be spent on law enforcement.[47] To isolate the effects of disturbed circumstances from other circumstances that might be expected to affect punitiveness

TABLE 2.4. *Logistic Regressions of Policy Preferences on Unemployment Variables*

	Favor death penalty	Courts too lenient	Spend too little to halt crime	Spend too little on law enforcement
Intercept	2.086***	2.307***	0.521**	0.409
	(0.181)	(0.231)	(0.200)	(0.263)
Job loss likely	−0.095*	−0.052	−0.030	0.024
	(0.041)	(0.052)	(0.408)	(0.063)
Unemployed in past 10 years	−0.026	−0.197*	0.143	−0.275**
	(0.071)	(0.090)	(0.080)	(0.104)
Age	0.001	0.005	0.003	0.002
	(0.003)	(0.004)	(0.003)	(0.004)
Education: less than high school	−0.222*	−0.319	−0.060	−0.023
	(0.100)	(0.127)	(0.300)	(0.172)
Education: some college or more	−0.532***	−0.382***	−0.367***	−0.050
	(0.073)	(0.093)	(0.080)	(0.105)
Female	−0.647***	0.280***	0.261***	0.277***
	(0.065)	(0.085)	(0.072)	(0.098)
African American	−0.928***	−0.436***	0.330***	0.070
	(0.074)	(0.094)	(0.092)	(0.115)
Ns	5,465	5,515	3,806	1,762

***$p < 0.001$; **$p < 0.01$; *$p < 0.05$.

Note: High school diploma is reference group; survey years entered as dummy variables (results suppressed).

toward criminals, we include several control variables. They are race (coded white or nonwhite), education (coded less than high school, high school degree, some college, or more), gender, age, and the year that the interview was conducted.[48]

Table 2.4 presents the results of regressing the four dependent variables (dimensions of criminal punitiveness) on two aspects of unemployment, in the presence of control variables. The unemployment experiences are whether the respondents are likely to lose their jobs or be laid off in the next 12 months, and whether they have been unemployed and looking for work any time in the last 10 years. All variables are coded so that a positive coefficient indicates support for the system disturbance theory. Looking at the eight coefficients associated with the two unemployment variables, only three are statistically significant, and each is in the wrong direction to support the theory. Respondents who anticipate that they may lose their jobs in the next 12 months are less likely than other respondents to support capital punishment. Respondents who had been unemployed in the previous 10 years were less likely than other respondents to support more severe penalties for criminal defendants and additional spending on law enforcement. The theory could hardly have done worse.

Note that the control variables yield some interesting results. Women are not only more likely to oppose capital punishment, but they are also more likely to favor tougher courts and to favor more spending to halt the rising crime rate and to support law enforcement. Nonwhites are less likely than whites to believe that the courts are too lenient on offenders, less likely to favor capital punishment, and more likely than whites to favor greater spending to halt crime. Age has no effect on the four dependent variables. Education has a nonlinear relationship with the dependent variables. Both a college degree and having less education than a high school diploma are associated with favoring lenient policies toward criminal offenders; high school graduates (the reference category) are more disposed toward punitive policies.

Table 2.5 reports the results of regressing the same four dependent variables on four measures of satisfaction with current situation plus control variables. The satisfaction questions are whether the respondents are generally "not too happy," not satisfied with the city or place in which they live, not satisfied with their financial situation, and facing an increasingly worse financial situation. The results also give little comfort to supporters of the system disturbance theory. Of the sixteen coefficients on the "satisfaction" variables, five are significant – three negative and two positive. The number of cases in the first three columns (12,500–15,500) is large enough that a finding of "no effect" should be taken seriously. Thus, the results can be reasonably interpreted as finding a genuine null effect, which is consistent with the instrumental or "democracy-from-below" perspective.

TABLE 2.5. *Logistic Regressions of Policy Preferences on Satisfaction Variables*

	Favor death penalty	Courts too lenient	Spend too little to halt crime	Spend too little on law enforcement
Intercept	1.325*** (0.121)	1.526*** (0.155)	0.951*** (0.129)	0.547* (0.247)
Generally unhappy	0.081** (0.031)	0.082* (0.040)	0.032 (0.033)	−0.040 (0.066)
Not satisfied with place live in	−0.003 (0.013)	−0.012 (0.017)	−0.019 (0.014)	−0.002 (0.027)
Not satisfied with financial situation	0.010 (0.029)	−0.012 (0.037)	−0.110*** (0.013)	−0.089 (0.059)
Financial situation has gotten worse	−0.043 (0.027)	−0.085* (0.035)	−0.081** (0.029)	−0.101 (0.057)
Age	0.006*** (0.001)	0.013*** (0.002)	0.006*** (0.001)	0.003 (0.002)
Education: less than high school	−0.204*** (0.047)	−0.273*** (0.060)	−0.105* (0.050)	−0.111 (0.103)
Education: some college or more	−0.476*** (0.048)	0.383*** (0.061)	−0.238*** (0.052)	−0.178 (0.092)
Female	−0.529*** (0.038)	0.157** (0.048)	0.222*** (0.040)	0.234** (0.077)
African American	−0.934*** (0.044)	−0.386 (0.056)	0.200*** (0.052)	0.059 (0.077)
Ns	15,539	15,410	12,460	2,892

***$p < 0.001$; **$p < 0.01$; *$p < 0.05$.

Note: High school diploma is reference group; survey years entered as dummy variables (results suppressed).

Table 2.6 reports analyses of a set of questions about respondents' advancements and threats on the job. The questions asked respondents if they are unlikely to be promoted in the next 5 years, if they have lost ground in their job, if their gender makes their own promotion opportunities better or worse, and if their race or ethnic background makes their promotion opportunities better or worse. These questions, in particular, would seem to capture the core idea of

TABLE 2.6. *Logistic Regressions of Policy Preferences on Advancement and Job Threat Variables*

	Favor death penalty	Courts too lenient	Spend too little to halt crime	Spend too little on law enforcement
Intercept	1.855**	0.909	0.378	0.082
	(0.565)	(0.645)	(0.685)	(0.690)
Unlikely to be promoted	0.050	−0.012	0.008	0.179
	(0.091)	(0.109)	(0.118)	(0.113)
Gender affects promotion	0.204	−0.041	0.257	−0.713**
	(0.168)	(0.207)	(0.213)	(0.223)
Race affects promotion	0.023	0.357	0.243	0.488*
	(0.175)	(0.219)	(0.234)	(0.225)
Lost ground in job	−0.207	0.158	−0.034	−0.004
	(0.146)	(0.169)	(0.179)	(0.178)
Age	−0.002	−0.001	−0.009	−0.006
	(0.009)	(0.017)	(0.012)	(0.011)
Education: less than high school	−0.076	0.214	0.069	0.316
	(0.348)	(0.430)	(0.466)	(0.396)
Education: some college or more	−0.734***	−0.159	−0.141	0.426
	(0.213)	(0.258)	(0.283)	(0.263)
Female	−0.434*	0.278	0.575	0.441
	(0.212)	(0.250)	(0.280)	(0.255)
African American	−0.818***	−0.470	−0.192	−0.109
	(0.227)	(0.276)	(0.303)	(0.296)
Ns	595	595	290	315

***$p < 0.001$; **$p < 0.01$; *$p < 0.05$.
Note: High school diploma is reference group; survey years entered as dummy variables (results suppressed).

system disturbance theory, focusing on whether the respondents were losing or gaining in the workplace, relative to their own past and to other groups.

Unfortunately, these questions were asked only during 1 year, resulting in small sample sizes. To make matters worse, during this particular year, the survey was split into three different forms. The GSS's standard questions appeared on all three forms, but the remaining questions did not. Of the sixteen coefficients in the second through fifth rows, two are statistically significant and have opposite signs. However, this disconfirming evidence should be interpreted cautiously because of the small number of respondents answering relevant questions.

As a final check, we reran the analyses reported in Table 2.6 using subsamples of males only and whites only because system disturbance theory suggests that these groups perceive themselves as victims of social change. Thus, the association between the system disturbance variables and four dependent variables should be strengthened for these groups. The pattern of correlation changes only slightly. One coefficient, associated with the variable "unlikely to be promoted" in the subsample of whites, becomes statistically significant in the direction supporting system disturbance theory. This is only slight support for system disturbance theory.

These analyses offer almost no shreds of optimism for system disturbance theory. Across many measures, the few significant coefficients in the theory's favor are overwhelmed by findings of no effect plus several coefficients with the "wrong" sign. If one poses system disturbance and crisis mobilization theories as zero-sum competitors so that evidence against one favors the other, then crisis mobilization survives these data analyses. People who support tougher penalties, compared to those who support more lenient penalties, are hard to distinguish in their degree of suffering at the hands of history.

The overall picture, then, is a very large shift in the American public's position on criminal punishment. There was a broad scale movement for greater punishment toward criminals; this element of the story is unassailable. More difficult to discern are the causal forces behind this change. The system disturbance theory appears to fold under the weight of the evidence. Some shred of supportive evidence should show up in the survey data of the American public, but none does. The crisis mobilization theory fares better. First, the prison buildup followed a tumultuous period in which the initial response was a prison builddown. On the face of it, there was a problem demanding new solutions, a fertile ground for social movements. Second, the American public, although becoming more punitive toward criminal offenders, became more, not less, tolerant of civil liberties. Finally, support for more punitive policies came from sectors of the American public that were reasonably integrated into the social fabric or, at least, they were not outcasts suffering in the economy.

Yet, perhaps these analyses entirely missed the real dynamics of the prison buildup. Another tradition sees prisons and the prison buildup as having little to do with popular social movements, rational or irrational. Rather, the prison buildup is an element in an insidious project of human domination. This perspective merits attention.

FROM FOUCAULT TO WACQUANT

Michel Foucault, a well-known French intellectual, stands our conventional concept of progress in criminal punishments on its head.[49] Normally, we think of the brutal torture of criminal defendants and public executions, common in the eighteenth century, as barbaric and the invention of the prison as a step in the march of the civilizing process. Not so, according to Foucault.[50] His view is that, although torture and physical punishment of the past damage the body, prison goes further. Prison monitors an inmate's every behavior; it imposes detailed rules for behavior; it reaches into the inmate's inner self, his or her "soul."[51] Foucault seems to favor torture's manifest brutality over the concealed power of modern punishment. Better to face an enemy square on than have him take control over who you are. This form of control is extended from prisons to other institutions of society. "Is it surprising," he asks, "that prisons resemble factories, schools, barracks, hospitals, which all resemble prisons?"[52]

Presumably, Foucault would view the prison expansion that began in the mid-1970s as a product of modern society's insatiable appetite for control. *Discipline and Punish*, however, was published in 1975, too early to detect the buildup trend. Loïc Wacquant, another French intellectual (now living in the United States), picked up where Foucault left off. In the Foucauldian spirit, Wacquant urges us to "break out of the narrow 'crime and punishment' paradigm to reckon the extra-penological role of the penal system."[53] Wacquant's approach also has much in common with *Regulating the Poor*, the famous book by Frances Fox Piven and Richard Cloward published in 1971.[54] Writing in the heyday of the Great Society's antipoverty programs, Piven and Cloward argue that the main function of welfare is, not to soften the blow of poverty, but rather to contain social unrest. When the poor become unruly, welfare payments are increased to contain and regulate. In a similar fashion, Wacquant argues that social mechanisms are needed to regulate African Americans, given the great disadvantages they are made to endure. In recent decades, this was accomplished though a vast expansion of the prison system.[55]

More broadly, Wacquant argues that mass imprisonment is the last of four historical stages in an evolving project to control and exploit African Americans, a project dating back to before the founding of the United States. Although Wacquant offers a fascinating discussion of the slavery period, the Jim Crow South, and the Ghetto North, it is the identification of a fourth stage (Hyperghetto + Prison) that is his new core point. He argues that the Hyperghetto + Prison arose in response to two changes. First, beginning in the 1970s, the economies of U.S. cities were transformed from manufacturing to information-based services. As manufacturing fled to industrial parks of the suburbs, antiunion South, and foreign locations, African Americans became economically irrelevant. Reinforcing this economic marginality were (1) an unbending housing segregation, so that blacks could not move out of their consigned living space; (2) a breakdown of urban public schools, so that blacks could not acquire the skills to participate in the new information-based economy; and (3) immigration of foreign workers, which further undermined any remaining leverage African Americans might have in the labor market. As a result, the Hyperghetto came to function as a place to store a surplus population with no meaningful role in the economy.[56] At the same time, according to Wacquant, the communal organization of the ghetto, which had developed independently of mainstream society, permitted African Americans to challenge their caste subordination.[57] The weapons of protest included the urban riots that peaked in the 1960s.[58]

The conjuncture of these two changes – the irrelevance of African Americans to the economy and their increasing political leverage arising from internal solidarity – thus required a new mode of control. The Hyperghetto + Prison arose to achieve this. Under a regime of mass imprisonment, the separation between the ghetto and the prison steadily diminished. (This corresponds to Foucault's point of the resemblance among prisons, factories, schools, barracks, and hospitals – a grand convergence downward.) On the prison end, in an earlier period, prison inmate solidarity could develop because the prison was an isolated society in opposition to the dominant institutions. Yet, under a system of mass imprisonment, the circulation from the prison to the ghetto and the ghetto to the prison became similar to passing through a revolving door. Thus, the prison became like the ghetto – tense and hostile:

> Today's prison . . . resembles the ghetto for the simple reason that an overwhelming majority of its occupants originate from the racialized core of the country's major cities, and returns there upon release, only to be soon caught again in the police dragnet to be sent away for another, longer sojourn behind bars in a self-perpetuating cycle of escalating socioeconomic marginality and legal incapacitation.[59]

Just as prisons began to resemble ghettos, so too ghettos began to look more and more like prisons. Three examples illustrate. One, seemingly harmless in itself, is that ghetto residents began to dress and express themselves in a manner that was formerly distinctive to prison. This included a resurgence of body art with prison themes, the popularity of songs with hostile lyrics, and the wearing of baggy pants.[60] A second is the "prisonization" of public housing. Wacquant notes that "Projects have been fenced up, their perimeter placed under beefed-up security patrols and authoritarian controls, including identification card checks, signing in, electronic monitoring, police infiltration, 'random searches, segregation, curfews, and resident counts – all familiar with procedures of efficient prison management.'"[61] Third, public schools have also come to appear and function similar to prisons. They lost their capacity to educate and now "operate in a manner of institutions of confinement."[62] (Again, note the Foucauldian theme.)

The transformation of the ghetto as prison and prison as ghetto, "fusion of ghetto and prison culture" as Wacquant puts it, serves a political purpose: African Americans are deprived of the leverage to protest. Whereas formerly ghetto residents could protest their conditions, in the most extreme forms through urban riots, collective protest is rendered ineffective while behind walls. Except in the most notorious prison riots, an administrative response is sufficient. "By entombing poor blacks in the concrete walls of the prison," Wacquant observes, "the penal state has effectively smothered and silenced subproletarian revolt." It is for this political purpose that America has created the "*first genuine prison society* of history."[63] So, what are we to make of this – are the regression analyses reported previously scratching the surface, missing the real grand historical theme? Maybe.

The Foucauldian position, both in its original formulation by Foucault and in its application to the prison buildup by Wacquant, is highly dispiriting. Foucault's overarching point, that modern society is subject to greater and greater controls, provides few glimmers of hope. Wacquant is even more pessimistic, if possible, than Foucault. The Hyperghetto + Prison is the most dishonorable and cowardly social arrangement one can imagine. White society is portrayed as completely self-serving, devoid of any principle of human decency. Talk of racial progress is a sham. Yet, however gloomy the message, Foucault's and Wacquant's pessimism must be rejected, if it is to be rejected, on its own terms. Gloom and doom may be simple realism.

This is more difficult than one might suppose. Neither Foucault nor Wacquant lay out the empirical grounds on which their case stands. Foucault informs his reader of his judgments about modern society in dense, obscure prose, and then leaves it up the reader to see if he or she can "get it." Foucault thankfully provides examples to illuminate points, such as a breathtakingly detailed description of a gruesome execution that occurred in 1757. However, the underlying basis for the general argument remains entirely in the mind of Foucault. We do not explore with Foucault evidence and arguments, and alternative explanations are not considered. We must wait for Foucault to reveal to us what he has seen.[64]

Wacquant claims to have discovered, not just a new feature of modern society, but a new kind of society representing an extraordinary rupture in the history of humankind. Compared to Foucault, Wacquant is less oracular, and he writes in clear prose. However, as with Foucault, evidence is used to illustrate ideas rather than test them. For example, Wacquant argues that the increasing disorder behind bars was a product of a fusion of ghetto and prison. Yet, Wacquant does not delve into the details to actually show that order behind bars has declined over time.[65] Chapter 4 takes up this empirical issue, showing that the rates of disorder have been decreasing, not increasing, during the buildup period.

Wacquant provides no explanation whatsoever as to why African Americans could not be brought into the modern economy more fully. He ignores gains by the African American middle class, and virtually assumes away any possibility that government policy could help reverse economic marginality. Furthermore, Wacquant attributes pernicious values to white people; however, he neither adduces any evidence whatsoever that such values exist nor provides a foundation around which policies are formulated. To gauge white sentiment toward African Americans, he could turn to a large body of survey data, but he does not.

Likewise, African Americans are a portrait of human helplessness. They are unable to see their own oppression, let alone do something about it. Yet, Wacquant does not explain how this hegemony is achieved, nor, again, is there any evidence that such hegemony actually exists. Are these objections at too low a "level"?

To take a step back, the thread tying Foucault and Wacquant together is the belief that established powers use imprisonment to regulate, dominate, and ultimately crush the impulse to rebel. We may believe that we are better off than our forbearers, whose modes of control were brutally manifest. Nothing could be further from the truth. Torture has been replaced by prison, and the segregation of African Americans into ghettos has been replaced by mass imprisonment – but how can these changes be called progress? From these gloomy conclusions about the state of modern society, both authors make extrapolations about what they expect to see in the world. And they find it. Highlighting anomalous low-level evidence is beside the point; such facts can be accommodated into the framework in the future. Perhaps. But these authors rely a lot on faith of the readers that, through sheer intellect, these authors got it right. We would be more insistent on evidence.

PRISON BUILDUP AS AN INSTRUMENT OF VOTER EXCLUSION

A final argument to consider, although more modest in its claims than those of Foucault or Wacquant, nonetheless paints the prison buildup as coming out of efforts to silence the political voice of the lower orders of society. The focus is on state laws that disenfranchise felons and ex-felons. Christopher Uggen and Jeff Manza, who have performed the most far-reaching work on this issue, conclude "Restricted access to the ballot box is but a piece of the larger pattern of social exclusion for America's vast correctional population."[66] Their argument is worth considering in some detail. By way of background, the U.S. Constitution delegates to the states the responsibility for determining voter eligibility. Although felony disenfranchisement laws can be traced back to the founding of the country, the major growth in such legislation occurred in the 1800s, with additional states enacting laws in recent decades.[67] Currently, forty-eight states and the District of Columbia deny prison inmates the right to vote while in prison. (The exceptions are Maine and Vermont.) Thirty-five states prohibit felons from voting while on parole, and thirty of these states disallow voting by felony probationers. Three states prohibit all felons from voting, even after they have completed their sentences, and nine others disenfranchise certain groups of felons (e.g., violent offenders in Nevada and second felony offenders in Arkansas), even after they have completed their sentences. The Sentencing Project estimates that 5.3 million Americans, or about one in forty adults, have presently or permanently lost the right to vote because of a felony conviction.[68]

Felons have interests – they are disproportionately low-wage earners, unemployed, and minority. If their disenfranchisement changes the outcomes of elections then, to that measure, their interests will lose out in the political process. To assess whether a state's felony disenfranchisement law would affect a particular election, Uggen and Manza estimate (1) the number of felons and ex-felons the state excludes from voting by law, depending on the state law's exclusion criteria and the size of the various correctional population in that state; (2) the proportion of those excluded who would otherwise vote if they were permitted to vote; and (3) the proportion of the estimated voters who are likely to vote for a Democratic candidate minus the number who could be expected to vote for a Republican candidate. Uggen and Manza scour U.S. electoral history for elections that were closely contested to determine whether electoral outcomes would have been different in the counterfactual case that felons had been allowed to vote. They do not have to go far. The low-hanging fruit is George W. Bush's victory in the 2000 election, given the very slim margin of victory. If even just ex-felons (completed sentence and not under correctional supervision) had been allowed to vote in one state, Florida, the overall outcome of the election would have been reversed. Uggen and Manza also find seven U.S. Senate races that would have resulted differently, absent the combination of correctional population buildup and felon disenfranchisement laws. During the 1990s, control of the Senate may have been in the hands of Democrats rather than Republicans. Uggen and Manza also conclude that John F. Kennedy's defeat of Richard Nixon in 1960 might have been reversed had the current level of disenfranchisement then prevailed. In short, felony disenfranchisement laws have a significant and, from time to time, decisive impact on the electoral processes, owing to the dramatic increase in the correctional population since the mid-1970s.

The difficult part of Uggen's and Manza's empirical task is to come up with reasonable estimates of what the felons and ex-felons would do if they were given the opportunity to vote. Not only are these estimates inherently uncertain because they are counterfactuals, but we do not have direct information on the political preferences of felons. To get around this, Uggen and Manza use survey data collected from inmates to pair the felon population to a similar subpopulation in the general voting population, in terms of gender, race, age, income, labor force participation, and marital status, using data from the National Election Study. This matching provides Uggen and Manza with an estimate of the likely voting decision felons would make if given the opportunity to cast a vote. They calculate that about 35% of the disenfranchised felons would have voted in presidential elections, and they would have cast about 70% to 80% of their votes for Democratic candidates, depending on the specific candidate. For example, Bill Clinton would have received 85% of the felon vote, and Al Gore would have received 69% of the otherwise excluded vote.

These estimates can be reasonably challenged. For example, felons and ex-felons may vote at much lower rates than demographically similar nonfelons. Yet, the findings of Uggen and Manza appear sufficiently robust, at least for certain elections – most notably Bush versus Gore in 2000 – that even considerably lower voting rates among the disenfranchised would have still swung the election. In short, they make a strong empirical case that, if one assumes nothing else would change, disenfranchising felons and ex-felons combined with large correctional populations has had a significant impact on U.S electoral outcomes.[69]

The larger problem is the *ceteris paribus* assumption. Uggen and Manza model only a portion of the process. Left out is the impact of the growth of the correctional population on the crime rate. If large correctional populations, especially imprisonment, were associated with lower crime rates, then the American political landscape would also be affected by correctional growth through this route. Christopher Jencks has observed, "Like rain on election day, crime is good for Republicans. . . . When the crime rates rise, liberals always find themselves on the defensive."[70] The partisan advantage of high crime rates may have weakened, or even disappeared, with falling crime rates. To the extent the buildup reduced the crime rate, it may have taken away from Republicans an election winning-issue. This *may* have counterbalanced the immediate effect of excluding felons from voting. We do not know this.

Finally, the impact of reforming felony disenfranchisement laws depends on precisely when prisoners (and other felons) are given the vote. The impact would be greatest, of course, if the franchise were extended to all felons, including those behind bars. A more modest proposal, in its effect, would be to restore inmates' right to vote after their release. This would be consistent with society's judgment that the offender, after serving his or her time, is capable of rejoining society. If an ex-offender can rejoin society, then he or she should be given (most of) the privileges that the rest of us enjoy, such as the right to vote. Richard Posner suggests a possible modification of such a reform – impose a 5-year waiting period on ex-offenders before restoring their right to vote.[71] Former felons would regain the right to vote only if they avoided trouble with the law during the waiting period. Either policy would draw a tight link between the right to vote and being a responsible member of society.

CONCLUSION

No change in the U.S. criminal justice system has been bigger – more people, more money, far-reaching consequences – than the prison buildup. Observers bring quite different approaches to explaining this buildup.

Foucault finds that "how" a society punishes its offenders reveals much about its moral character. His results concerning modern prisons are not encouraging. Prisons are systems of power, regulation, and domination, extreme versions of the systems of domination that inhere in modern schools, families, and factory floors. They epitomize the decay of modern society. Wacquant extends this analysis to the prison buildup, arguing that it, too, is driven by the goal of domination. We live in a prison society.

The moral implication of the system disturbance model is also highly negative with regard to the buildup. Popular demands for more prisons arose from issues unrelated to crime control. All would surely agree that not a single person should be imprisoned because the political establishment needs to shore up its legitimacy, citizens are bothered by the extension of civil rights to discriminated-against groups, changing gender relations, economic insecurity, or other aspects of rapid social change. To give in to demands based on such nonsensical or self-indulgent reasoning would violate the most basic moral precept to treat others as ends, not means. Justice would be a sham.

From this, it would follow that those imprisoned for extrapenological purposes deserve freedom, perhaps even reparations for injustices suffered. Surprisingly, even the most radical critics seldom draw this implication. For example, William Chambliss, who over many years has established himself as one of the country's leading leftist criminologists, expresses the standard system disturbance critique. He states that everyone knows that prison is counterproductive, and that the only interesting question is why "a policy that is irrational, inhumane, costly, and ineffective" is pursued.[72] Like others in the system disturbance tradition, he finds the answer in political elites exploiting the crime issue for their own ends, as well as the need to control and repress the unemployed and (predominantly African American) unemployable.

Yet, the political implications of this critique, as Chambliss draws them, could not be more moderate. He delineates nine policy proposals that could "make a real difference," although he cautions that the "opponents are numerous and powerful." Having braced the reader, Chambliss unleashes only the most temperate proposals for reforms. One is that "[t]he movement toward more-severe sentences for all offenders . . . must be reversed." Interestingly, writing about the same time, conservative criminologist John DiIulio called for a moratorium on the prison buildup and zero prison growth.[73] Chambliss and DiIulio seem to be in the same camp.

Perhaps, in the end, we are all pragmatists. We worry about putting too many people in prison, but we also wonder if society has benefited from the buildup. Although the critics believe that mass imprisonment does not work, at the same time they believe that a mass release of prisoners is not only politically infeasible, but also dangerously irresponsible. Neither Chambliss nor Beckett nor Wacquant calls for a return to the 1970s levels of imprisonment. As noted at the outset, in 1973, there were 96 inmates per 100,000 population; in 2005, there were 491 inmates per 100,000. Garland expresses a preference for the days when professionals determined imprisonment policy. Nowhere, however, does he ask for 91 inmates per 100,000, or 191, 291, or 391. The only exception may be Foucault, who seems not to have had a pragmatic bone in him.

The crisis mobilization approach takes seriously the formally stated goal of institutions. If the buildup was supposed to reduce crime and validate the worth of victims, then the serious issue is if these effects follow. Although the institutional mobilization position may easily fall into a Pollyannaish optimism, nothing in this framework precludes us from both asserting that the prison buildup sought to achieve crime reduction and that it failed.

We pursue the issue of actual effects in the remainder of the book.

More Prison, Less Crime?

> Cruelty turns out to be mainly the infliction of pain and suffering for a purpose. Our negative moral judgment has to do not only with pain but purpose.[1]

> Who is filling our jails and prisons? Most of the *victims* of the criminal justice system are minor offenders.[2]

> American jails and prisons are overflowing with convicts who would not have been thrown behind bars 30 years ago and who, moreover, would not be rotting there if the public were better informed about the realities of the country's penal policy.[3]

Chapter 2 ended on a pragmatic note. Commentators on the buildup – however much confidence they express when they portray the causes of the buildup – are far less certain about what we should do tomorrow. The critics may see the prison buildup as insane, they may describe prisons as overflowing with minor offenders, and they may argue that the public's ignorance about "who" goes to prison is necessary to sustain the buildup. Yet, their own sanity, good reason, and informed opinions do not lead them to demand that we tear down the walls or even make them permeable enough to return to pre-buildup levels. They despise this "cruel historical experiment,"[4] but they are not ready to reverse it, at least not all the way. How cruel could it be, in their view?

The proponents of the buildup see the quintupling of the prison population as bringing great benefits to society in the form of crime reduction. Fewer crimes mean fewer victims, and fewer victims mean less suffering. They hold this position, however, without much proof that things worked out that way. The prison buildup *was* an experiment, at least in the sense that the outcome was inherently uncertain before the fact and even difficult to ascertain after the fact. No other society has ever undertaken such an effort; the scale is unprecedented. Also, the buildup was not a *controlled* experiment, in the scientific sense of the term, allowing us to compare "treatment" and "control" observations. Moreover, the proponents harbor their own doubts about the scope of the buildup. Perhaps we have taken the buildup too far, much as dieters sometimes fall into the trap of taking weight loss to a damaging extreme. Prison expansion may have become a harmful addiction.

There are two ways to go about examining the effect of the buildup on crime. One is to look at "who" is in prison over time. If the prison buildup resulted in increasingly less serious offenders behind bars, this would suggest that the crime- reducing effect of prison has been diminished. The strength of this approach is that it captures the "incapacitation" effect of prison on crime. Offenders behind bars cannot commit new crimes against nonprisoners unless and until they are released. The disadvantage of this approach is that prison rates may affect the crime rates through other mechanisms, such as deterrence or rehabilitation. Still, a useful question is whether the proportion of truly dangerous people behind bars – for whom incapacitation is incontestably worthwhile – has diminished as the prison population doubled, tripled, quadrupled, and finally quintupled. The prison critics are right to worry that we are now imprisoning a large number of low-level offenders.

A second way is some type of regression analysis, using observed data to draw inferences about the impact of the buildup. The advantage of a regression approach to our problem is that, however prison affects the crime rate, it should capture all of the effects. In addition, the sharpest critics of the buildup worry that, not only does prison fail to inhibit crime, but it may actually generate it by having a negative impact on individuals and communities.[5] A regression approach permits us to test the proposal that high levels of incarceration increase crime because of the damage done to communities and the social networks of young men and women. The crucial issue is not whether some negative effects occur in communities; they most certainly do.[6] Rather it is whether those effects overwhelm the crime-reducing mechanisms of prison, deterrence, and incapacitation, which also most certainly occur. Regression allows us to examine this possibility. The main disadvantage of regression is that many factors affect crime rates, and statistical models are simplified representations of complex interactions. If key factors escape our thinking, cannot be measured with the resources at hand, or are incorrectly modeled, then the resulting inference will be biased.

This equivocation (shifting back and forth between advantages and disadvantages of the two approaches) suggests that we need both. It would be helpful if the two imperfect methods tell the same basic story, which, as we will see, in large measure they do.

WHO GOES TO PRISON, NOW AND BEFORE THE BUILDUP?

Efforts to find out "who" is in prison over time rely on two sorts of individual-level data. One sort of data is official records on prisoners' incarcerating crime – the most serious offense for which they were imprisoned. If these incarcerating crimes were, on average, more serious before the buildup than after the buildup, this would suggest that the buildup might have gone too far. As already noted, critics charge that the buildup came about mainly by incarcerating greater numbers of "nonviolent" offenders. There is something to this claim, although qualifications are needed and the point is often overstated.

The advantage of these data is that, for the entire buildup period, fairly consistent records have been kept on the offenses for which inmates were serving. This permits an apples-to-apples comparison between the prison populations, pre- and post-buildup. Also, the federal government's Bureau of Justice Statistics (BJS) collects these data. They can be considered valid, not only because BJS has a reputation among criminologists for the integrity of its data (as far as we know, no commentator has alleged that BJS manipulates its data to please anyone), but also because research studies have borne this out.[7] If the BJS data are found to "say" something important, that something is likely to be true.

The disadvantage is that these records fail to capture the full set of costs that prisoners would impose on society if not behind bars. A great deal of crime goes unreported, unresolved, and undetected. On average, about one-third (36%) of serious crimes are reported to the police. Within that one-third, one-fifth of them are "cleared," meaning a person is arrested and charged with committing the offense.[8] Additional crimes may go undetected, such as embezzlement or drug dealing. Those behind bars are sure to have committed more than their share of unreported, unresolved, and undetected crimes. Also, a 1997 survey of federal and state inmates found that a majority of prisoners plea-bargained down the crimes that were originally charged to them.[9] This is another reason why prisoners' officially recorded crimes will understate the true harm done by a population of prison inmates. (It is possible that some arrestees are overcharged, perhaps in anticipation of plea bargaining.) In short, the "most serious offense" data are especially helpful in allowing us to track changes in the composition of prison populations over time. Apples at time one can be compared to apples at time two. Yet, they are almost certain to understate the full extent of a prisoner's criminality prior to incarceration.

The second sort of data is survey results collected directly from inmates. Surveys can ask offenders about their criminal past, about which there may be no official record. Inmates may not admit to every crime they may have committed, and some may even exaggerate their criminal history. Experience shows, however, that inmates are surprisingly forthcoming. The key disadvantage is the limited number of surveys that have been conducted. Also, the few surveys that have been done have not been implemented in exactly the same way. The comparison among surveys conducted at different times has a bit of an apples-to-oranges quality.

Most Serious Offense, Before and After the Buildup

If the buildup critics are right, we should see a decline in the proportion of violent offenders behind bars concurrent with the prison buildup. Convictions for nonviolent offenses should account for the great majority of the increase. In examining these trends, we separate state and federal prisons because their patterns of growth, in crime types, were somewhat different.

Figures 3.1 and 3.2 report data on the "most serious" offenses of state prisoners. The hundreds of different offenses, defined by statutes somewhat differently from one jurisdiction to the next, are grouped together in four categories: violent, property, drug, and public order.[10] To provide a better sense for these aggregated categories, we list

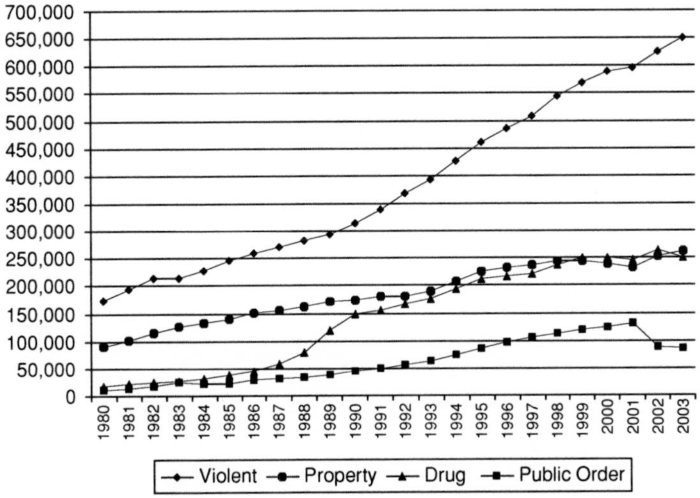

Figure 3.1. Number of state prisoners by offense type, 1980–2003.
Note: Violent offenses include murder, manslaughter, rape, sexual assault, robbery, assault, extortion, intimidation, and criminal endangerment.
Source: Bureau of Justice Statistics, "Number of Persons in Custody of State Correctional Authorities by Most Serious Offense, 1980–2003," www.ojp.usdoj.gov/bjs/glance/tables/corrtyptab.htm.

some of the subcategories in each of the four main categories, keeping in mind that the subcategories themselves have subcategories: (1) *violent offenses* include murder, negligent and nonnegligent manslaughter, rape, sexual assault, robbery, assault, extortion, intimidation, and criminal endangerment; (2) *property offenses* include burglary, larceny, motor vehicle theft, fraud, possession and selling of stolen property, destruction of property, trespassing, vandalism, and criminal tampering; (3) *drug offenses* include possession, manufacturing, and trafficking; and (4) *public order offenses* include weapons violations, drunk driving, escape/flight to avoid prosecution, court offenses, obstruction, commercialized vice, morals and decency charges, and liquor law violations. Additional distinctions can be made within each subcategory. For example, for federal prisoners, the Bureau of Prisons further classifies weapons violations crimes into nine subcategories, including "use of restricted ammunition" and "licensing, gun control act of 1978."[11] Obviously, then, a four-category classification of criminal activities is a simplification of a simplification, but it is sufficient to capture broad movements in prison populations.

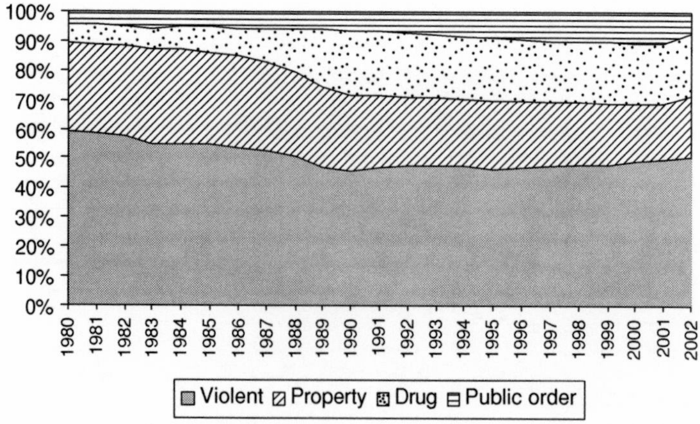

Figure 3.2. Percentages of state prisoners by offense type, 1980–2003. *Source:* Bureau of Justice Statistics, "Number of Persons in Custody of State Correctional Authorities by Most Serious Offense, 1980–2003," www.ojp.usdoj.gov/bjs/glance/tables/corrtyptab.htm.

Figure 3.1 graphs the buildup in state prisons by showing the actual numbers in each of the four categories; Figure 3.2 shows changes in the percentages in each category. Although the two figures are based on the same underlying data, they highlight different aspects of the story. Between 1980 and 2003, the number of state inmates in the custody of state prison officials increased from 304,300 to 1,221,500, a gain of nearly 1 million inmates (917,200). Figure 3.1 shows that, although the number of prisoners in each of the four major crime categories increased, prisoners in the violent crime category contributed most to buildup. Violent offenders grew by 451,600 inmates; property offenders by 163,700; drug crime prisoners by 246,000; and public order offenders by 75,100. The combined category of nonviolent offenders (property, drugs, and public order) added only slightly more inmates to the prison stock (484,800) than the single category of violent offenders (451,600). Thus, it would be fair to say that a slight majority of the state prison buildup was due to increases in nonviolent offenders.

Figure 3.2 shows each of the four categories of state prisoners as a percentage of the state prison population in custody. From 1980 to 2003, the proportion of violent offenders and property offenders declined, respectively, from 59% to 51% and 30% to 21%. Filling the

TABLE 3.1. *Number of Sentenced Federal Prisoners, by the Most Serious Offense, 1980–2003*

	1980	1985	1990	1995	2000	2003
Violent	6,572	7,768	9,557	11,409	12,973	16,688
Property	4,651	5,289	7,935	7,842	9,849	11,283
Drug	4,900	9,482	30,470	52,782	73,389	86,972
Public order	2,040	2,514	8,585	15,655	31,855	42,325
No classification*	3,595	6,293	442	970	1,263	1,158
Total	21,758	31,346	56,989	88,658	129,329	158,426

* Includes offenses not classifiable and unknown.

Source: Data for 1980 and 1985 are from Allen J. Beck and Darrell K. Gilliard, *Prisoners in 1994* (Washington, DC: Bureau of Justice Statistics, 1995); data for 1990 and 1995 are from Compendium of Federal Justice Statistics, Bureau of Justice Statistics, www.ojp.usdoj.gov/bjs/pubalp2.htm#cfjs; data for 2000 and 2003, are BJS Prisoners at Year-End, www.ojp.usdoj.gov/bjs/prisons.htm.

gap, drug offenders increased from 6% in 1980 to 21% in 2002, and public order offenders increased from 4% in 1980 to 7% in 2002. Expressed this way, the data provide mild support for the idea that the buildup caused a decline in the seriousness of the prison population. This assumes, of course, that drug offenses and public order offenses are less "serious." We turn to this issue later in the chapter. Still, the more dramatic claim, that the overwhelming majority of inmates had committed no violent crimes after the buildup, is not supported.

The data for federal prisons shows a different pattern of growth, although it should be kept in mind that state prisons hold about 92% of the country's prison population, as shown in Table 3.1. Between 1980 and 2003, the number of federal prisoners increased from about 22,000 to 158,000.[12] The most telling pattern emerges if one combines property, violent, and public orders crimes into one category, and compares that with drug crimes. From 1980 to 2003, the number of nondrug offenders increased from 13,300 to 70,300, a ratio of 5.3 to 1. This is about the same increase of state prisoners in these three categories, from 120,700 to 605,500, a ratio of 5.0.[13] Thus, the federal prisons were adding nondrug offenders at a rate comparable to state prisons.

However, although state prisons experienced a large increase in the number of drug offenders, the federal prison system experienced a huge increase in that category. In 1980, there were 4,900 sentenced drug inmates in federal prison, or 27% of the federal prisoners. In 2003, there were 86,972 sentenced drug inmates, or 55% of the federal prison population (excluding inmates not classified). For every drug offender in federal prison in 1980, there were 17.75 drug offenders in federal prison in 2003.

In summary, the data on prisoners' "most serious offenses" fail to support the idea that the prison buildup resulted in a massive decrease in the number of "serious" or dangerous state prisoners. Violent offenders account for about one-half of the increase in state prisoners from 1980 to 2003. Yet, there are differences in the criminal profiles of 2003 state inmates versus 1980 state inmates. Most strikingly, the proportion of drug offenders more than tripled, from 6% to 21%. In regard to federal prisoners, the pattern of growth of nondrug offenders is very similar to the growth of nondrug state offenders. But drug offenders increasingly filled federal prisons. This means that one's conclusion about the efficacy of the buildup depends centrally on the efficacy of incarcerating those convicted of drug crimes.

How "Serious" Are Nonviolent Offenders?

If one is willing to grant the assumption that violent offenders are "serious offenders," it does not necessarily follow that nonviolent offenders are "nonserious" offenders, a leap that the buildup critics are all too willing to make without looking. To help decide the issue, we draw on data from surveys of inmates conducted by the Census Bureau for BJS in 1997 and 2004. The surveys are based on personal interviews with a nationally representative sample of state and federal inmates. Inmates were asked to provide information about their current offense, criminal history, and other aspects of their lives prior to incarceration. Figure 3.3 breaks down the state and federal populations by self-reported crime type for 2004. It highlights the major difference between state and federal prisons: one-half of those in state prison are there for violent offenses, whereas one-half of federal inmates are there for drug offenses.

What proportion of nonviolent offenders could be considered "serious offenders"? There are no standard criteria to distinguish nonserious from serious offenders. After all, one could easily enough imagine a vigorous debate about whether a particular inmate, say one who stole

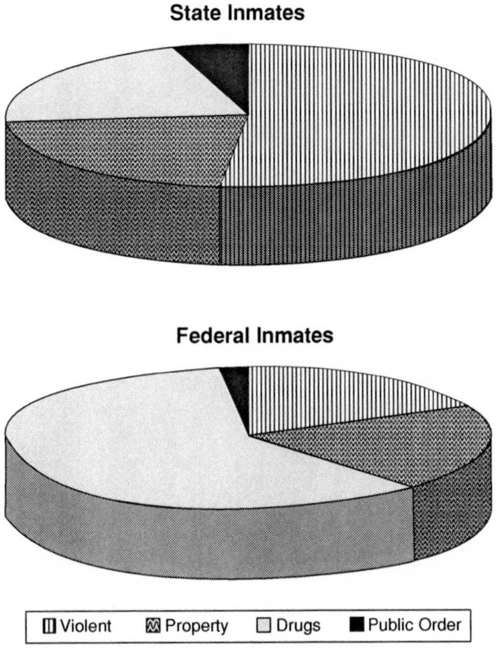

Figure 3.3. Current incarcerating offense, state and federal inmates, 2004. *Source: Survey of Inmates in State and Federal Correctional Facilities, 2004*, National Archive of Criminal Justice Data, www.icpsr.umich.edu/NACJD/.

a car or lied under oath, should be considered a "serious" offender, with any final judgment heavily influenced by one's intuitive sense of the meaning of "serious." Here we are generalizing across hundreds of thousands of inmates, using information from a research methodology that asks respondents questions in a standardized format. This suggests modesty in what we, or anyone, can claim on this score. With this qualification in mind, we use four criteria to distinguish "serious" nonviolent offenders from the "nonserious" offenders.[14] They are whether the offender carried or used a weapon in the current offense; had a prior violent conviction; committed the current offense while on probation, parole, or escape; or had two or more prior sentences.

Table 3.2 shows that, in 2004, 81% of state, nonviolent inmates, and 55% of federal nonviolent inmates, reported at least one indicator suggesting that they were serious offenders. Forty-five percent of state and 24% of federal nonviolent prisoners reported two or more serious

TABLE 3.2. *Indicators of "Serious Offender" of Nonviolent Offender, State and Federal Inmates, 2004*

	State inmates				Federal inmates			
Percent of inmates	Property offenses (%)	Drug offenses (%)	Public order offenses (%)	All nonviolent offenses (%)	Property offenses (%)	Drug offenses (%)	Public order offenses (%)	All nonviolent offenses (%)
Used weapon in current offense*	5.0	7.1	6.6	6.1	12.5	9.2	30.4	10.6
Prior violent conviction	23.1	20.8	28.1	22.6	16.6	14.9	30.9	15.7
On probation/parole/escape at time of offense	54.1	50.3	66.5	53.7	28.5	22.9	46.9	24.9
Two or more prior sentences to incarceration*	58.1	52.8	65.0	56.5	31.2	35.7	54.9	35.0
One "serious offender" indicator	83.0	77.9	89.4	81.4	55.1	53.4	86.2	54.6
Two or more "serious offender" indicators	45.7	41.5	57.3	45.0	25.7	22.4	56.7	24.1

* Excludes incarcerations for "minor" offenses (drunkenness, vagrancy, loitering, disorderly conduct, and minor traffic crimes).

Source: Survey of Inmates in State and Federal Correctional Facilities, 1997, National Archive of Criminal Justice Data, www.icpsr.umich.edu/NACJD.

TABLE 3.3. *Number of Prior Arrests of Nonviolent Offender, State and Federal Inmates, 2004*

Number of arrests prior to current arrest*	State inmates (%)	Federal inmates (%)
0	20.7	24.9
1	18.0	18.5
2	15.3	14.5
3	11.2	10.6
4 or more	34.8	31.4

* How many times have you ever been arrested, as an adult or a juvenile, before your arrest (controlling arrest date)?

Source: Survey of Inmates in State and Federal Correctional Facilities, 2004, National Archive of Criminal Justice Data, www.icpsr.umich.edu/NACJD.

indicators. A reasonable inference is that nonviolent prison inmates are largely serious offenders, although more so in state prison then federal prison. Compared to nondrug offenders, drug offenders in both state and federal prisons are somewhat less likely to have a single "serious indicator" (78% for state and 53% for federal) and multiple "serious indicators" (41% for state and 22% for federal).

Also, the arrest records of nonviolent inmates seemed to indicate serious histories of involvement in the criminal justice system. As shown in Table 3.3, for 2004, collapsing the three nonviolent crime categories, among state inmates, only 21% had not been arrested prior to the arrest for their current crime, 18% had been arrested once, 15% had been twice, and about one-third (35%) had been arrested four or more times. The arrest records of federal inmates were somewhat less serious. Almost one-fourth had not been arrested prior to their current arrest, and 31% had been arrested four times or more.

The data reported in Tables 3.2 and 3.3 should be treated with caution, especially the data on prisoners in federal prison. A large proportion of federal prisoners are drug offenders, and one need develop a more refined (or at least different) set of criteria to separate serious from nonserious drug offenders.

The Special Case of Drug Offenders: "King Pins or Mules"

Eric Sevigny and Jonathan Caulkins have undertaken an intensive effort to examine the "seriousness" of drug offenders, using the

1997 survey of state and federal inmates.[15] They partition the two prison populations based, not only on the criminal history of offenders and their weapon usage, but also on the gravity of their drug offense. The seriousness of the drug offense is seen to have several dimensions: offenders' role in the drug offense (e.g., importer, manufacturer/grower, money launderer, wholesale dealer, retail dealer, body guard/debt collector, possession); member of a drug organization or not; quantity of drugs (recoded to typical retail purchase amount); and type of drug (e.g., cocaine, amphetamines, marijuana, heroin). Sevigny and Caulkins found, on one end of the spectrum, that only 5.7% of state inmates and 1.6% of federal inmates are "unambiguously low-level" offenders. At the extreme, nonviolent, possession-only, small-quantity offenders comprise 0.2% of drug offenders and 0.06% of all prisoners.[16] In contrast, there are few "drug kingpins" in prison. Only 4.4% of state and 6.6% of federal drug offenders reported to be mid- to high-level drug participants. This is in large part because few admitted to being part of any drug organization.[17] Instead, the vast bulk of prisoners fall in between the two poles, with the median degree of seriousness depending in large measure on which factor is given greatest weight. We are back to the eye of the beholder, at least to some degree.

More Survey Results in Cost–Benefit Framework

A major drawback of the analyses discussed thus far is that they are limited to data collected on offenses for which the offender has been apprehended and convicted. Even the 1997 survey of inmates, perhaps because the federal government administered it, does not ask inmates about crimes they may have committed but for which they were not apprehended. To get around this problem, another line of survey research has queried inmates about their full range of criminal activities prior to incarceration. When these sorts of surveys have been done, researchers have typically sought to evaluate the results using a cost–benefit analysis.

Cost–benefit analysis allows us to compare things that seem very different than each other. That is, we can compare the same outcome at different times (building a bridge today vs. building a bridge in

10 years) or different outcomes (a bridge today vs. a school today). To do this, however, one must come up with criteria for measuring the value of these outcomes. Generally, the outcomes are translated into dollar terms, which then allow easy comparisons. We should not, however, overstate the precision that has been attained. We need to consider carefully the method by which these outcomes are translated into dollars. A full discussion of all the different ways this can be done is beyond the scope of this chapter. Here we describe the conceptual issues involved and our attempts to resolve them.[18]

The purpose of a cost–benefit analysis of incarceration is to calculate the social costs and benefits of prison and compare them. It is generally believed that calculating the costs of incarceration is relatively simple: just add up the costs of building and operating a cell. The range of estimates for these costs is about $20,000 to $50,000 per year. This large range reflects in part actual variation in the costs of operating an institution from one jurisdiction to the next. Also, the amortized costs of building a new prison depends on whether one assumes the prison will last 40 years or 100 years or more. For example, the Penitentiary of New Mexico, opened in 1956, was mothballed in 1998, whereas the U.S. Penitentiary (Atlanta), built in 1902, still operates today. Even more important, many social costs are left out of these numbers. By "social costs," we mean any burdens on society in addition to the resources it takes to run a prison system. They include the lost labor market productivity of inmates, the loss to families of having a member away from home, and the loss to communities of having a resident removed.

Likewise, there are a variety of positive effects. First, incarceration will incapacitate the offender so that he or she will not victimize nonincarcerated citizens during the period of confinement. Second, the incarceration of one person may serve as a deterrent to others. Moderating against these influences are the possibility that the criminal activities of inmates are picked up by other inmates (prisons as "schools of crime"), the possibility that incarcerated criminals are simply "replaced" by other individuals in the community, and the likelihood that at some point in time an offender naturally reduces his criminal activity regardless of government sanction.

The Zedlewski Study. The first serious effort to apply cost–benefit analysis to corrections was published in 1987, by Edwin Zedlewski, a staff economist for the National Institute of Justice (the research wing of the U.S. Department of Justice).[19] Zedlewski divided the yearly cost to keep one inmate in prison ($25,000 per annum, he estimated) by the product of the number of crimes the "typical" inmate would commit if on the streets (187) and the average cost of a crime to society ($2,300).[20] Simple arithmetic showed that the benefits greatly outweighed the costs, on the order of 17 to 1. The results, as interpreted by Zedlewski, strongly supported the idea of increased incarceration.

Numerous researchers challenged the 17-to-1 ratio. Zedlewski had estimated the number of crimes the "typical" inmate would commit if on the streets based on a survey of prisoners in three states (Michigan, Texas, and California) conducted by the Rand Corporation. The inmates were asked about the number of crimes they committed in the period immediately prior to their incarceration. Critics argued that Zedlewski should have used the median, rather than the mean, to calculate the number of crimes committed. A few inmates claimed an extraordinarily high rate of crimes; some of these claims may have been boasts or even deliberate jests to "put on" the researchers. Using the median would have reduced the impact on the estimate of these possibly outlandish claims. (In contrast, if the claims were real, the benefits may have been real.)

But even if one was to accept Zedlewski's calculations as 100% correct, this could not be the last word on the topic. The offense rate data were collected in late 1978 and early 1979, still in the beginning stages of the buildup. The cost–benefit ratio might depend crucially on the size of the prison system. That is, if most high-rate offenders were already in prison, then prison growth would result in the imprisonment of less and less dangerous offenders (assuming the offender population is not growing larger or more dangerous). Actually, Zedlewski thought about this possibility. In a rebuttal to two law professor critics, Zedlewski argued that the number of offenders behind bars was then low enough that expanding the prison population would not affect the inmate profile. There is, he stated, "no basis for believing that the average commission rates should decrease in the 300,000 to 600,000 inmate range under discussion."[21]

In fact, the country exceeded the upper boundary of 600,000 in 1988, the year after Zedlewski published his report. Thus, it would be natural to ask if increased use of incarceration remains cost beneficial, with a much larger inmate population.

The DiIulio, Piehl, Useem Studies. Some immediate improvement on Zedlewski could be obtained through a reanalysis of the Rand Corporation data. Merely substituting the median for mean of crimes committed provides a more realistic "average" preincarceration criminal profile. Also, a group of economists had undertaken an effort to come up with improved estimates of the social costs of crime, taking into account the pain and suffering of victims as experienced in different sorts of crimes. These estimates could now be incorporated into the analysis rather than Zedlewski's (admittedly) very rough estimate of the average cost of all crimes. However, if one wanted to know about what the buildup had done to the benefits and costs of imprisonment, new survey data would need to be collected from inmates. We undertook such an effort, in Wisconsin in 1990, in New Jersey in 1993, and in New York, Arizona, and New Mexico in 1997. The results of the Wisconsin and New Jersey surveys were published in the *Brookings Review*, and the results of New York, Arizona, and New Mexico surveys were published in a report by the Manhattan Institute.[22]

Table 3.4 displays the estimates of the costs of crime used in the several studies under consideration. The first column shows that Zedlewski used a single average for all crimes, computed by dividing the total cost of crime in a year by the number of crimes in that year. The second through fourth columns are estimates of the value of the crimes of rape, robbery, assault, burglary, auto theft, petty theft, and drug crimes. These estimates, published in a report issued by the National Institute of Justice, are based on the compensation awarded by juries to crime victims. The changes across the three columns should be seen primarily as a product of improvements in the estimates, rather than increases in the cost of crime.

The two *Brookings* papers, as had Zedlewski, excluded attributing any costs to drug crime. But there is no pure methodological reason why drug sales should not be included in this calculation. Drug sales are crimes, and they involve both direct and indirect social costs. The

TABLE 3.4. *Estimates of the Social Costs of Selected Crimes*

Crime	Zedlewski[a]	Brookings-1[b]	Brookings-2[c]	Manhattan Institute[d]
Average for all crimes	$2,300	–	–	–
Rape		–	$56,280	$98,327
Robbery		$12,060	12,060	8,830
Assault		11,518	11,518	10,624
Burglary		1,314	1,314	1,271
Auto theft		2,995	2,995	3,249
Fraud, forgery, petty theft		110	110	342
Drug		–	–	5

Source: [a] Edwin Zedlewski, *Making Confinement Decisions* (Washington, DC: U.S. Department of Justice, Bureau of Justice Statistics, 1987); [b] John J. DiIulio, Jr., and Anne Morrison Piehl, "Does Prison Pay? The Stormy National Debate over the Cost Effectiveness of Imprisonment." *The Brookings Review*, 9 (Fall 1991): 28–36; [c] Anne Morrison Piehl and John DiIulio, Jr., "Does Prison Pay? Revisited." *The Brookings Review* (1995): 21–25; [d] Anne Morrison Piehl, Bert Useem, and John J. DiIulio, Jr., *Right-Sizing Justice: A Cost–Benefit Analysis of Imprisonment in Three States. A Report of the Manhattan Institute for Policy Research Center for Civic Innovation* (New York: Manhattan Institute, 1999).

Manhattan Institute analysis attributed a cost of $5 per drug sale. Many of the social costs of drug crimes come from the violence and theft associated with the trade. These costs will be largely accounted for on their own. In addition, drug usage has its own inherent costs – they are the reason that drug use is criminalized. Thus, unless society is sorely mistaken about the costs of drug usage – and we do not believe it is – then it would be unrealistic to assign no costs to drug offenses. Thus, the $5 cost reflects a reasonable middle ground. This $5 cost should represent the social savings from incarcerating a drug offender and therefore preventing him or her from making a sale. Note that if the offender is "replaced" by another drug dealer satisfying the same customers, this estimate will be too high. The challenge of dealing with replacement of drug offenders merely reveals this issue; it is present for other crime types, just to a lesser extent.

It should be noted that, although the differences in the estimates reported in the last three columns in Table 3.4 are not trivial, in practice it turns out that they are close enough that choosing one over another does not make much difference to the policy considerations.

We tested this by substituting the different estimates in the analysis of the Manhattan Institute data that follows. The results were nearly indistinguishable.[23]

Table 3.5 shows the estimates of the social costs of property and assault crimes provided by the four studies under consideration: Zedlewski (California, Michigan, and Texas, 1978–1979); Brookings I (Wisconsin, 1990); Brookings II (New Jersey 1993); and Manhattan Institute (New York, Arizona, and New Mexico, 1997). The estimates are from the studies themselves and are not recalculated using a single methodology. The first column shows that Zedlewski found that the average inmate in the three states studied imposed $187,000 in social costs.

The studies that followed improved on Zedlewski's calculation in two key respects. Whereas Zedlewski assumed that all crimes have the same costs, the Brookings and Manhattan studies relaxed that assumption with the new costs-of-crime data in hand. Second, Zedlewski calculated a single cost for the "average" inmate. Table 3.5 reports the costs at various cutting points (percentiles). It is useful to know not only the cost–benefit ratio of imprisoning the "typical" inmate, but also that ratio for the more and less serious offenders. Thus, we ascertain various cutting points to see the proportions of inmates for whom incarceration clearly is or is not cost beneficial.

The estimates reported in Table 3.5 reflect somewhat different methodologies of the studies, but they also show true variation in the criminality of prison populations. This variation can be divided into the differences within states, the differences across state jurisdictions, and the differences across time. Additional tables help explain the three types of variation.

Differences within States. Variation within a state's prison population can be observed by focusing on the five states survey during the buildup – Wisconsin, New Jersey, New York, Arizona, and New Mexico. As is always found in inmate surveys, the social costs at the high end greatly exceed those at the lower end of the spectrum (Table 3.5, columns 4–6). Although it clearly pays on incapacitation grounds alone to incarcerate those at the eightieth percentile in all five states, it does not appear to "pay" to incarcerate those below the median.

TABLE 3.5. *Social Costs of Property and Assault Crimes*

	California, Michigan & Texas, 1978–1979[a] ($)	Wisconsin, 1990[b] ($)	New Jersey, 1993[c] ($)	New York, 1997[d] ($)	Arizona, 1997[d] ($)	New Mexico, 1997[d] ($)
Mean	187,000	369,000	1,600,000	—	—	—
80th percentile				239,000	220,000	163,000
60th percentile				79,000	38,000	41,000
Median (50th percentile)		46,000	70,000	32,000	25,000	26,000
40th percentile				14,000	11,000	11,000
25th percentile		16,000	20,000			
20th percentile				7,000	4,000	4,000
10th percentile		2,000	2,000			

Source: [a] Edwin Zedlewski, *Making Confinement Decisions* (Washington, DC: Bureau of Justice Statistics, 1987); [b] John J. DiIulio, Jr., and Anne Morrison Piehl, "Does Prison Pay? The Stormy National Debate over the Cost Effectiveness of Imprisonment." *The Brookings Review*, 9 (Fall 1991): 28–36; [c] Anne Morrison Piehl and John DiIulio, Jr., "Does Prison Pay? Revisited," *The Brookings Review* (1995): 21–25; [d] Anne Morrison Piehl, Bert Useem, and John J. DiIulio, Jr., *Right-Sizing Justice: A Cost–Benefit Analysis of Imprisonment in Three States. A Report of the Manhattan Institute for Policy Research Center for Civic Innovation* (New York: Manhattan Institute, 1999).

The estimated social costs associated with the offender at the fortieth percentile in New York, Arizona, and New Mexico are all less than $15,000.[24] The social costs associated with the offender at the twenty-fifth percentile in Wisconsin and New Jersey are less than $20,000.

Differences across States. State-to-state variation is best examined if we compare data collected among several states in the same time frame. However, it should be kept in mind that different states increased their prison populations at different rates and at somewhat different times. The Rand Corporation data were collected in three states over a 1-year period (late 1978 and early 1979), as were the Manhattan Institute data (1997).

In the Rand Corporation data, substantial differences were found across the states. For example, the median number of nondrug crimes was forty-two in California, seventeen in Michigan, and nine in Texas.[25] This is a lot of variation. Table 3.6 shows cross state variation also: at all cut points the social cost inflicted by New York inmates is higher than in New Mexico and Arizona. The median social cost in New York is about $32,000, whereas the median cost in New Mexico and Arizona is $26,000.

Another way to consider the criminality of the median offender is to look at his reported criminal acts. In New York, the $32,000 figure represents the damages associated with the commission of three assaults per year. In New Mexico, the median offender committed robberies at the rate of three per year (and no other offenses). In Arizona, the median offender committed burglaries (three per year), thefts (six per year), and car thefts (six per year).

Perhaps we should anticipate that the high incarceration states should have lower social costs per inmate because their prison systems would incarcerate relatively less serious offenders. This pattern generally holds for the surveys in 1979. As shown in Table 3.6, Texas's crime rate, especially its violent crime rate, was low compared to the rates in California and Michigan. However, Texas's incarceration rate was almost double that of California, and well above Michigan's. Because Texas was more likely to incarcerate per unit of population and per unit of crime, as compared to Michigan and California, its inmates were on average less serious than those in Michigan and California. It

TABLE 3.6. *Median Crimes, Incarceration Rates, and Crime Rates in Six States and the United States*

	California, 1979	Michigan, 1979	Texas, 1979	United States, 1980	New York, 1997	Arizona, 1997	New Mexico, 1997	United States, 1997
Inmates/100,000	99	163	196	130	386	484	256	410*
Violent crime/100,000	811	614	508	536	689	624	853	611
Property crime/100,000	6,658	5,533	5,417	4,986	3,244	6,571	6,053	4,312

* State only; excludes federal inmates.

Source: Sourcebook of Criminal Justice Statistics, 1981 (Washington, DC: Bureau of Justice Statistics, 1982); *Sourcebook of Criminal Justice Statistics, 1988* (Washington, DC: Bureau of Justice Statistics, 1989), *Sourcebook of Criminal Justice Statistics, 2000* (Washington, DC: Bureau of Justice Statistics, 2001).

appears that Texas had to reach deeper into the pool of offenders to obtain a higher incarceration rate.

This pattern, though, does not hold up for the three other states whose inmates were surveyed in the same year (New York, Arizona, and New Mexico). Here we can take advantage of the new cost estimates. New York's incarceration rate per unit of population is roughly halfway between Arizona and New Mexico; thus, that factor cannot explain New York's high offender costs. Also, the crime rates for these states (Table 3.6, rows 2 and 3) are not very helpful as explanatory factors. New Mexico has a high violent crime rate, compared to New York and Arizona. However, New York had recently experienced dramatic declines in violent crime. At the same time, Arizona and New Mexico have property crime rates nearly double that of New York. No clear pattern emerges here. But then the amount of variation among these three states is not large, at least when compared to the variation among the three states in the Rand Corporation sample.

The offenders going to prison in these three states exhibit two different patterns. Many high-rate offenders and many drug offenders take up New York's prison space. In Arizona and New Mexico, the nondrug offenders have committed, on average, fewer crimes than their New York counterparts. (The median number of nondrug crimes committed by nondrug-only offenders is sixteen in New Mexico and fifteen in Arizona, compared to twenty-four in New York.) However, compared to New York, these two states imprison fewer drug-only offenders.

Changes over Time. This variation is the most relevant to our broader concerns because it bears directly on the issue of the impact of the buildup on crime rate. The data, though, are not ideally suited to the task, however, because the several studies do not use a uniform sampling procedure. To understand these differences, it is important to take into account the distinction between going to prison and being in prison, that is, between "flow" into prison and "stock" in prison. A stock sample is a cross section of inmates incarcerated at a point in time, whereas a flow sample is a cross section of inmates who have just been admitted to prison. It is generally safe to assume that the social costs of all inmates behind bars (stock) will be higher than incoming inmates (flow). This would be true if judges assign longer sentences to offenders who inflict higher social costs – which is no doubt true. The Rand Corporation (California, Michigan, and Texas) and Wisconsin data are based on stock samples, that is, those in prison. The Manhattan Institute (Arizona, New Mexico, and New York) data are based on flow, which is to say, an admission cohort. The New Jersey inmates are halfway between flow and stock. They are stock in the sense they are in the prison population, but flow in that the sample was limited to recent arrivals (2 years or less in prison).

The overall problem is that the time order of the surveys correlates with the sampling procedure used: first, Rand Corporation (stock), followed by Wisconsin (stock), then New Jersey (stock/flow), and finally Manhattan Institute (flow).

The common metric across the six states and three time periods is the median number of crimes, as reported in Table 3.7. If we confine the analysis to stock samples only (to include the mixed case of New Jersey), the pattern provides mild support for the diminishing returns hypothesis. The median of 12 reported in Wisconsin and New Jersey was higher than the median of Texas, but less than the median of Michigan and considerably less than the median of California. If there was a strong pattern of diminishing returns, it did not show itself in these data.

The medians in New York (6), Arizona (6), and New Mexico (9) are smaller than those found in earlier studies. The extreme comparison is that California's median of 42 is six times greater than New York's and Arizona's medians of 6 each. This is consistent with the hypothesis of diminishing returns. That is, if the most serious offenders are already in prison, then prison growth requires the criminal justice system to reach deeper into the pool of prison-eligible offenders, such that increases in incarceration are less and less cost effective. Yet, the Manhattan Institute data are flow data, whereas California's data are stock data. Whether this fully accounts for the observed differences cannot be determined. Perhaps not, and somewhere in the buildup process, the "law" of diminishing returns took effect.

Conclusions on Who Goes to Prison

Arguing against the further prison expansion, at whatever level, is the principle of diminishing returns to scale. If the most serious offenders

TABLE 3.7. *Reported Crimes Committed in Self-report Surveys*

	California, 1982[a]	Michigan, 1982[a]	Texas, 1982[a]	Wisconsin, 1990[b]	New Jersey, 1993[c]	New York, 1997[d]	Arizona, 1997[d]	New Mexico, 1997[d]
Mean number of nondrug crimes	258*	222*	107*	141				
Median number of nondrug crimes	42	17	9	12	12	6	6	9

* Rand Corporation computed high and low estimates. Following Zedlewski, low estimates are reported here.

Source: [a] Jan M. Chaiken and Marcia R. Chaiken, *Varieties of Criminal Behavior* (Santa Monica, CA: Rand Corp., 1982): table A15, p. 215; [b] John J. DiIulio, Jr., and Anne Morrison Piehl, "Does Prison Pay? The Stormy National Debate over the Cost Effectiveness of Imprisonment." *The Brookings Review*, 9 (Fall 1991): 28–36; [c] Anne Morrison Piehl and John J. DiIulio, Jr., "Does Prison Pay? Revisited." *The Brookings Review* (Winter 1995): 21–25; [d] Anne Morrison Piehl, Bert Useem, and John J. DiIulio, Jr. *Right-Sizing Justice: A Cost–Benefit Analysis of Imprisonment in Three States. A Report of the Manhattan Institute for Policy Research Center for Civic Innovation* (New York: Manhattan Institute, 1999).

are already in prison, prison growth requires the criminal justice system to reach deeper into the pool of prison-eligible offenders, such that increases in incarceration are less and less cost effective. When using data on "who" goes to prison to adjudicate the issue, this argument has a strong version and a weak version.

The strong version asserts that the buildup has turned U.S. prisons into a large reservoir of low-level offenders, most of whom have little business in being there. If this were the case, we would see two major effects. First, there would be a precipitous drop in the proportion of serious offenders behind bars. "Serious" is difficult to operationalize, but one measure is having committed a violent offense. Using this criterion, there was not a huge drop in the proportion of serious offenders behind bars. A slight majority of the prison growth resulted from the addition of more violent offenders. The overall proportion of violent offenders decreased somewhat, by about 10% over a 25-year period. Although this drop is not trivial, neither does it suggest a radical change in the composition of state prisons.

A second way to measure seriousness is to use the analytic tool of cost–benefit analysis. Nonserious could be defined as when that ratio is less than one; that is, for every dollar spent on incarcerating an inmate, society gets back somewhat less than a dollar. Yet the median costs of property and assault crimes in the five buildup samples – Wisconsin, New Jersey, New York, Arizona, and New Mexico – was more than $25,000, or the estimated cost of prison.

The soft version of the diminishing returns argument – the buildup has gone too far, or at least should go no further, or is imprisoning the wrong sorts of offenders – cannot be rejected based on the data examined in this chapter. First, the median number of crimes committed decreased over several studies, although this may be partially due to different sampling procedures.

Second, the proportion of drug-only offenders rose modestly among state inmates and dramatically among federal inmates. The main effect of imprisoning drug sellers, we believe, is to open the market for another seller. Numerous students of drug policy attest to the existence of this "replacement process." Presumably, if the incarceration of drug offenders does make a dent in the drug market, we would expect to see an association between the number of drug offenders behind bars and the street price of drugs.

The evidence is not encouraging. It is probably not enough to point out, as Steven Donziger and collaborators did, that the street price of cocaine has decreased since 1980, whereas the rates of incarceration have increased.[26] One needs to know, as well, what the price of cocaine would have been in the absence of that enforcement level – and we do not. Furthermore, as Mark Moore points out, the "effective" price of a drug includes not only the drug's cash price, but also the risk of imprisonment and other inconveniences and dangers associated with its purchase. At least for some potential drug sellers and users, prisons may have priced out that activity. Still, the data suggest that the market for illicit drugs has not been disrupted by increased incarceration. Thus, at least some prison beds currently occupied by drug offenders would be better reserved for high-rate property and violent offenders.

Third, the bottom one-fourth of the inmate population among inmates surveyed in Wisconsin, New Jersey, New York, Arizona, and New Mexico are less than most estimates of the cost of incarceration. This would suggest that society would benefit by placing this one-fourth of the inmate population in alternative correctional settings.

Let's approach the same problem (the prison buildup/crime link) using a second methodology.

REGRESSION APPROACH

The major limitation of a "who goes to prison" approach is that it relies on a mental experiment: "What would be the result of not incarcerating those currently imprisoned?" The presumption is that more serious offenders behind bars today would cause fewer crimes tomorrow. But this is *only* a presumption, however reasonable. The advantage of a regression approach is that it permits us to examine actual changes in the world. We can see, quantitatively, where jurisdictions gain a measure of protection against crime by putting more of their offenders in prison.

Another advantage of a regression approach is that it allows for the buildup critics' worst fear – that the buildup actually generates new crimes. We can distinguish two hypotheses along these lines, which we call the "less-less" hypothesis and the "crime augmentation" hypothesis. The less-less hypothesis is that, as the prison system continues to grow, we should anticipate diminishing marginal returns to the crime control effect of imprisonment. Furthermore, the size of the diminishing returns will accelerate with ever-greater increases in imprisonment. We call this the less-less hypothesis because it implies the more prison, the smaller the crime reduction that results. This would be observed as the size of the statistical association between prison and crime declines with increasing levels of incarceration.

The crime augmentation hypothesis is that, beyond a certain level, additional increases in imprisonment will lead to higher levels of crime, not lower ones. Prison would be causing the problem it is meant to solve, like trying to douse a fire by throwing the most easily obtainable liquid on it, which happens to be gasoline. This would be observed as the statistical association between prison and crime shifting from negative to positive beyond some threshold level of incarceration

Regression Estimates

The research literature generally models the statistical relationship between states' incarceration rates and crime rates as an "elasticity." In the present context, an elasticity is the percentage reduction in the crime rate brought about by percentage increase in the prison rate. For example, if the incarceration/crime elasticity is found to be −0.5, this would tell us that a 10% increase in the incarceration rate would result in a 5% drop in the crime rate.

The three "best" regression studies yield similar estimates – that the elasticity of crime with regard to the prison rate is between −0.159 and −0.55.[27] That is, a 10% increase in the prison rate will result in a 1.6% to 5.5% drop in the crime rate. Specifically, Thomas Marvell and Carlisle Moody find an elasticity of –0.159, Steven Levitt finds an elasticity of –0.379 for violent crime and –0.261 for property crime, and Robert Witt and Anne Witte discovered an overall elasticity of –0.55. These three studies were conducted using similar data over similar time periods and somewhat different statistical models. The models all imposed an assumption of a constant elasticity, whereas the previous discussion suggests it is desirable to use a model flexible enough to allow for the elasticity to change with the scale of the prison population.

One researcher who directly considered a changing relationship between prison and crime is William Spelman, who argued that prisons became a *more* effective force in reducing crime under conditions of the buildup.[28] Unfortunately, Spelman's model was not sufficiently flexible. Specifically, his model was constrained to find that the effect of prison on crime would be intensified with larger prison populations. This rules out the possibility of a crime reduction effect that gets smaller as incarceration increases. A full exploration of the relationship between prison and crime would allow for a wider array of possible impacts, including the possibility of a constant effect.

If Spelman's analysis is flawed in its empirical implementation, it highlights the problem: the need to consider whether prison's effectiveness changes with the scale of imprisonment rather than to presume that it would not vary over a period during which changes were dramatic.

Liedka, Piehl, and Useem Results

In work published with Raymond Liedka,[29] we found that allowing for a nonconstant elasticity was important for drawing inference about the relationship between prison populations and crime rates. When we estimated the key relationships between prison populations and crime using state-level data from 1972 to 2000 and using models similar to those of Marvell and Moody, Levitt, and Witt and Witte, the results were within the same ballpark. From this, we conclude that the addition of another decade's worth of data on prison growth has not drastically changed the conclusions drawn in the empirical literature of the mid-1990s.

However, when we estimated a model that encompasses a nonconstant elasticity, we found that the effect of incarceration did indeed depend on the scale of incarceration, rejecting the constant elasticity framework. We found negative elasticities at low rates of imprisonment, which become less negative as the incarceration rates get bigger, eventually reaching an inflection point where the elasticity turns positive. This inflection point occurs when a state's incarceration rate is 3.25 persons per 1,000 population. This value might seem very low, but it actually corresponds to the seventy-eighth percentile of the observed state imprisonment rates.

It is harder to summarize the results of an elasticity that varies with the scale of the prison population precisely *because* the estimate is nonconstant. Here we provide just a few of the results.[30] At the median value of the state prison population, our preferred estimate indicates that a 10% increase in the incarceration rate would lower crime rates by 0.58%. However, at the twenty-fifth percentile of the state prison population, that same 10% increase would reduce crime rates by 1.12%, and at the seventy-fifth percentile, the reduction would only be 0.08%. At the highest levels of state prison population, at the ninetieth percentile and above, the prison/crime elasticity becomes positive, indicating a crime-augmentative effect. This pattern is robust to a wide range of alternative specifications of empirical models and is clearly consistent with the less-less hypothesis of diminishing *proportional* returns to the use of incarceration.

Note that these results go beyond the more typical claim of declining marginal returns. Rather, they document *accelerating* declining marginal returns, that is, a percent reduction in crime that gets smaller with ever-larger prison populations. As the prison population continues to increase, albeit at a slower rate, after three decades of phenomenal growth, these findings provide an important caution that for many jurisdictions, the point of accelerating declining marginal returns may have been reached.

In sum, at low to moderate levels of incarceration, the estimated elasticity is negative, indicating a crime control effect of imprisonment. At higher levels of incarceration, the negative elasticity gets weaker, sliding closer to zero, until it reaches a level whereupon the elasticity actually becomes positive, indicating a crime augmentation effect of further incarceration. The prison elasticity of crime declines with the scale of imprisonment. These results imply that (1) estimates from one time period cannot be extrapolated to other points in time with vastly different incarceration experience; (2) at low levels of incarceration, a constant elasticity model underestimates the negative relationship between incarceration and crime; and (3) at higher levels of incarceration, the constant elasticity model overstates the negative effect.

Finally, a caution about interpretation. An unavoidable issue in regressions of crime rates on incarceration rates is that of simultaneity bias. To interpret the estimates of a model as causal, one must view incarceration rates as exogenous to crime rates. However, it is plausible (even likely) that the process also operates in the opposite direction – that increases in crime rates eventually lead to a growth in the incarceration rate. When simultaneity occurs, the regression estimate of the effect of incarceration on crime will be understated. Although there have been attempts to solve the simultaneity problem, they have not been satisfactory.[31] Because of concerns that our estimates may in part reflect simultaneity bias, we are cautious about interpreting their precise magnitudes. However, we are fully confident of the more general point that the effect of prison on crime depends on the scale of incarceration.

CONCLUSION

We have taken a long and winding road to get to our destination – a general conclusion about the effects of the buildup on crime. The extra miles have been worth it, we believe, because they allowed us to observe the purported cause and effect through several routes. And that effect (thankfully) looks about the same from each. With some confidence, we are able to draw two broad conclusions.

First, the prison buildup has not been all folly with regard to crime reduction. As we noted at the outset, even the sternest critics of the buildup harbored the belief that prison expansion would result in lowered crime rates – otherwise, why not tear down the walls now? Their intuition seems correct. The prison expansion has not lowered the "seriousness" of offenders sent to prison, at least in any sort of blanket way. This needs to be qualified by the observation that an increasing number of drug offenders are filling our prisons, especially federal prisons. This is worrisome to the critics and to us, too. In addition, the regression results bear out that the prison buildup has lowered the crime rate. Using data from the United States over 30 years, we find strong evidence of a negative relationship between prison size and the crime rate. In a phrase, more prison, less crime.

Second, the prison buildup has not been equally effective across the buildup period. The regression results showed not just declining marginal returns but *acceleration* in the declining marginal return to scale. These results should be central to any discussion of the scale of imprisonment in the United States. As the prison population continues to increase, albeit at a slower rate, after three decades of phenomenal growth, these findings provide an important caution that for many jurisdictions the point of accelerating declining marginal returns may have set in. Any policy discussion of the appropriate scale of punishment should be concerned with the empirical impact of this expensive and intrusive government intervention.

CHAPTER FOUR

Prison Buildup and Disorder

> Turning and Turning in the widening gyre
> The falcon cannot hear the falconer;
> Things fall apart; the centre cannot hold;
> Mere anarchy is loosed upon the world.[1]

> There was in the France of 1789, the Russia of 1917, the Italy of 1922, the Germany of 1932, a vacuum of power which political nature abhors.[2]

During the course of the U.S. prison buildup and even toward its end, many criminologists predicted that the buildup would be extremely difficult if not impossible to implement, and that they expected a crisis of order exemplified by high rates of riots, violence, and escapes. Criminologist John Hagan warned that "increased imprisonment will lead to more disruptions and riots in prisons."[3] Based on this prediction, as well as a belief that prison does little to reduce crime, Hagan advocated that we should "have as few of these inherently unstable institutions as possible."[4] Similarly, Thomas Blomberg and Karol Lucken cautioned that we reap what we sow, now and into the future:

> It does not appear likely that prisons will fare any better in the future. Rather, and quite the opposite, it appears that prisons will worsen in conditions and inmate consequences. . . . Prison riots, hostage taking, gang warfare, and inmate to inmate, inmate to staff, and staff to inmate violence are all increasingly routine aspects of everyday operations.[5]

At least *during* the buildup period, no one could have known what would happen behind bars as the number of prisoners climbed toward, and eventually surpassed, the 1 million mark. As noted in Chapter 3, a prison system of this scale had never been tried in human history. One possible outcome would have been the near collapse of authority, followed by chaos and a free-for-all struggle. Small islands of inmate solidarity, in the form of racial groups and gangs, would be pitted against each other. The rates of violence would escalate, and armed rebellion would be common. This is the outcome that the critics feared.

As an analogue, increasing scholarly and policy attention is being given to "failed states," societies in which there is a partial or near total collapse of the central government.[6] Weak or failing states typically experience violent civil strife, escalating crime rates, and an inability to control nonstate actors, such as tribal warlords, terrorists, and criminal gangs. They are tense, dangerous, chaotic, and lack credibility. U.S. corrections may have features of failed states. Its 1.4 million residents would (if congregated in one geographic area) be larger than forty-five countries in population size, and its $34 billion annual spending is on a par with the national budgets of Malaysia, Taiwan, and Argentina.

Another possibility would be the imposition of the Leviathan – Thomas Hobbes's answer to the anarchy of a war of all against all. State officials, facing a collapse of authority behind bars, would impose increasingly repressive controls. We might expect that a growing proportion of inmates would be placed in maximum security, rather than in lower security, prisons. Supermax prisons, extremely high-security "prisons within prisons," would be increasingly used to solve the problem of order. Rules would be tightened in other types of facilities. To again use a societywide analogue, the core feature of a revolutionary situation is uncertainty about whom and what policies will rule in the future.[7] The Leviathan is one way to get out of a revolutionary situation, ordinarily chosen not as a matter of political philosophy, but because people are sickened by the lack of order and nothing else seems capable of restoring it. A correctional Leviathan may have been the only way to combat the chaos wrought by the buildup.

A third possibility would have been a successful transformation: the prison system would be much bigger, but no worse for it. Corrections leadership, seeing the costs of both widespread chaos and the Leviathan, may have been motivated to develop effective solutions. Perhaps they forged conditions in which the rates of prison violence might even decline. An optimistic (but perhaps wholly unrealistic) forecast would be an absolute decline in disorder, as measured by the per annum number of riots or inmate-against-inmate murders.

Has the prison system become increasingly disorderly, dangerous, and insecure under conditions of buildup? The answer to this question is crucial. In the first place, there is the human toll of those injured or killed under conditions of disorder. Perhaps more important, prisons are instruments of law. What legal institutions do (and how they do it) may signal society's underlying attitudes and establish norms.[8] If prisons themselves are lawless, their expressive value in asserting the rule of law may be lost or even in the negative. Hagan's *premise* is right: if prisons on a mass scale create high rates of disorder, then these failed institutions should be limited in scale. But Hagan and his fellow critics have not given their argument the simplest empirical test. We do this later in this chapter.

Before turning to the data, we review several studies of the conditions that produce order behind bars. This review shows that prisons are neither inherently stable nor inherently unstable institutions. Prisons can change from order to disorder, and the reverse, rather rapidly.

RESEARCH ON PRISON DISORDER

The field of prison studies is only slowly coming to understand how to create order behind bars while achieving other moral and collective goals such as the elimination of decrepit living conditions, protection of the public purse, and rehabilitation of inmates. Perhaps the fundamental insight, developed by a first generation of researchers such as Gresham Sykes, Erving Goffman, and Richard Cloward, is that prisons are a political community.[9] They are, before they can achieve anything else, a system of cooperation – although a system that is authoritarian and hierarchical.[10] Those in command – from the correctional officers in the cellblocks, up the chain of command to the prison's middle managers and the warden, to the commissioner in the state capital – decide on and judge the course of action. The subordinates, the inmates, may experience policies and procedures as unpleasant and acts of force, but they typically accept the overall legitimacy of the situation. Although inmates may perform isolated acts of resistance, some degree of voluntary cooperation on the part of inmates is necessary for prisons to operate and can be normally obtained.

The noteworthy defect of the early formulations of prison order was the position that state authorities could do little to alter the degree of political legitimacy, except by restraining their own managerial activism. This pessimism – state capacity is inherently low – was visible in Gresham Sykes's theory of prison riots. Sykes argued:

1. The legal rewards and punishments that prison authorities can offer inmates are too few to secure their cooperation. In addition, prison authorities are hampered by the fact that prisons are required to pursue two conflicting goals. The need to maintain security interferes with efforts to rehabilitate inmates, and vice versa.
2. Given these difficulties, prison officials obtain inmate cooperation by a system of illicit rewards. Correctional officers allow contraband to circulate and disregard petty infractions by inmates. Inmates accept these minor illicit benefits, in return for which they keep the order. Inmate leaders, although never more than the best of a bad lot, help the administration to preserve order by restraining the more violent inmates.
3. From time to time, prison officials attempt to regain control over the prison by eliminating corruption and strictly enforcing rules. The reassertion of custodial control disrupts the inmates' incentives to cooperate and undermines the established inmate leaders. Unstable, riot-prone inmates fill the power vacuum.
4. Ironically, the harder prison officials try to manage "by the book," the less stable the system. Writing better procedures or hiring and training better managers are not effective options because of the inherent defects in prison: "The system breeds rebellion by attempting to enforce the system's rules."[11]

The central policy lesson of Sykes's analysis, on which John Hagan draws for his pessimistic buildup prediction, is that prison officials can do little to limit disorder once it is underway. The system is inherently frail. If too many more people are behind bars, personal violence and the threat of rebellions may crush the social order.

Research since the mid-1980s has sustained the basic insight that prisons are political communities requiring cooperation before they can achieve anything else. Prisons cannot operate by force alone. However, it has also shown that the degree of cooperation (1) varies from one prison to the next, from one correctional system to the next, and from one time to the next; (2) cannot be predicted based on abstract principles of prison social organization; and (3) depends on the will, strategies, and resources of the political community and correctional leadership. Studies advancing these points include the following.

Prison Governance in Three States

John DiIulio's *Governing Prisons* was born in polemic opposition to the argument that prison governance structures can do little to improve, and much to harm, prison order.[12] DiIulio examined prison management and the quality of prisons in Michigan, Texas, and California. Prison quality was measured using three criteria: *order* (rates of assault, murder, and riots); *amenities* (availability of wholesome food, clean cells, and recreational opportunities); and *services* (availability of vocational training, education, and work opportunities). These three outcome measures clustered together. Some prisons and prison systems were safe, humane, and treatment oriented, whereas others were tense, dangerous, and unproductive in changing inmates. This variation was observed: (1) among prison systems, by comparing Michigan, Texas, and California (intersystem variation); (2) between prisons within a single state, by comparing two California prisons (intrasystem variation); and (3) across time, by comparing Texas prisons at time "t" to Texas prisons at "t + 1" (historical variation).

The nonfindings were significant. The intersystem, intrasystem, and historical variations in amenity, service, and order could *not* be explained by these factors: the dangerousness of inmates, per-inmate spending, crowding levels, inmate-to-staff ratios, length of officer training, ethnic and racial composition of inmate population or correctional officers, and newness of prison and equipment. There was no evidence that prison disturbances were associated with efforts to tighten administration and eliminate corruption. Instead, the quality of correctional management appeared to be the key factor that could account for the variation. Specific features of "good management" included leadership by a strong, stable set of correctional executives; commitment to a well-specified organizational mission; effectiveness in dealing with relevant outside actors, such as key legislators and community activists; and management in a security-driven manner.

Finally, whereas Sykes and coworkers had argued that prison's task to rehabilitate inmates was undone by the need to maintain security, DiIulio's findings suggest the opposite. Prisons with high levels of service and amenities provide more effective programming. This is because (1) order, amenities, and service share a common cause in effective management; (2) prisons with high levels of order can provide more effective programs; and (3) programming facilitates order by providing an opportunity for inmate–staff communication.

Governing Prisons paints a negative picture of judicial intervention in prison management, holding it partly responsible for a breakdown in institutional order in Texas prisons.[13] Leo Carroll's study of Rhode Island's maximum security prison, *Lawful Order*, challenges DiIulio's specific point about court intervention, while affirming his general position that the prison performance rests largely on the quality and strategy of management.[14]

Governing Rhode Island's Maximum Security Prison

From 1972 to 1977, Rhode Island's only maximum security prison, Adult Correctional Institutions (ACI), experienced chaos and near-total collapse.[15] A federal court had intervened, undermining the patriarchal authority that had previously been the basis of order. This was followed by a sharp upsurge in the level of inmate assaults against other inmates and staff, security lapses, and collective disorders. In September 1972, four inmates escaped, followed by a report that found security incredibly lax. In April 1973, inmates rioted, taking six hostages and causing $1 million in damage. By July 1975, almost 20% of the inmates were in protective custody. The chaos was made public through press reports: "scarcely a day passed without a major story in the newspapers concerning disorder in the prison.... Disturbances, riots, escapes of dangerous convicts, murders and job actions by correctional officers kept ACI in the headlines."[16]

These conditions of disorder were instrumental in causing, and were caused by, a deep division within the correctional polity. Correctional officers, organized in a strong union beginning in 1971, believed the administration to be weak and given to inmate appeasement. As officers saw it, they had little choice but to take security into their own hands. For their part, the administration attributed their inability to restore order to the usurpation of management prerogatives by the union. For example, the union controlled the assignment of officers to their posts, allowing the most experienced officers to choose assignments with the least amount of contact with inmates. From time to time, tensions boiled over. In October 1975, correctional officers expressed outrage when the administration punished, lightly in their view, an inmate who had assaulted a correctional officer. Officers walked off the job and defied an order from the governor to return to work. The National Guard was brought in to run the unit for 2 days. Later the same month, four inmates brutally beat two other inmates with baseball bats. The incident occurred in the presence of ten officers, who refused to intervene out of fear that they might be assaulted. The administration took the position that it "is impossible to discipline and control inmates until you can discipline and control employees," with the latter unattainable given the protections afforded to officers by their union.[17]

Order began to be restored in 1978, again associated with a major legal intervention. In this period, however, the administration and the courts worked in alliance. Under new departmental leadership, staff training was increased, talented middle managers were recruited, and lines of authority and responsibility were strengthened. Old facilities were renovated. The leadership – judicial and correctional – took a strong stand with correctional officers. Those accused of brutality were suspended and indicted. When job actions followed, the courts issued injunctions and, when disobeyed, found the officers and unions in contempt. Eventually, the relations between management and labor were stabilized. All measures of disorder plummeted. By 1990, ACI was "remarkably safe and secure."[18]

To conclude, federal court intervention was a constant feature in Rhode Island's correctional system from 1970 to 1990. In the first half of that period, ACI had features of a failed state. In the second half, a unified, mission-driven management effort, now including the federal courts, restored order.

Prison Riots as Revolution

In two essays, Goldstone and Useem argued that a state-centered theory of revolution, developed to explain revolutions in entire societies, could also help account for prison riots.[19] Specifically, prison riots were hypothesized to occur when prison administrators are unable to balance external demands imposed by state and national governments with internal demands from staff and inmates regarding conditions within prisons. This imbalance, in turn, is a by-product of five factors: (1) state, national, or judicial authorities impose new or increased demands on prison administrations without augmenting prison resources; (2) dissension and alienation among correctional staff, often resulting in high absenteeism and turnover, failure to follow prison routines, or harsh confrontations between officers and administration; (3) grievances among inmates that the conditions of their confinement are far worse than they should be, according to broadly visible and externally validated standards; (4) spread of inmate ideologies that undercut the legitimacy of the prison and unite inmates by providing them a common framework for opposition and justifying rebellion; and (5) actions by prison administration that inmates see as demonstrating the administration's injustice, ineffectiveness, and vulnerability to inmate challenges. The two essays tested this argument against sixteen instances of prison riots, drawing on existing case studies and newly collected data.

The first essay examined thirteen riots that occurred in medium and high security prisons from 1952 to 1993.[20] Although the case studies were not a random sample, they provided a reasonable variety in terms of type of facility and geography. They include the most notable riots of that 40-year period, such as those at State Prison of Southern Michigan (1952), Attica (1971), Penitentiary of New Mexico (1980), Camp Hill, Pennsylvania (1989), and Lucasville, Ohio (1993). Operational indicators were developed for each of the five key variables. Using these indicators, the conditions were rated in the thirteen prisons immediately prior to the riot and during a more stable time period some years before the riot. Quantitative analysis found that the five conditions were not equally present in all riot cases. However, in no case did a riot occur without at least three of the five conditions being present.

The second essay used the five-variable model to explain two cases of prison reform in the 1990s with widely divergent results.[21] In the 1990s, the state of New Mexico privatized several prisons, and two prisons soon experienced riots. At about the same time, the New York City Department of Correction (NYCDOC) brought about reforms that ended many years of extremely high rates of individual and collective violence.

New York City Department of Correction. Although NYCDOC is a jail system, rather than a prison system, it held as many as 20,000 inmates in the mid-1990s, larger at that time than thirty-five state prison systems. The majority of inmates are housed on Rikers Island, located on the East River. From 1990 to 1995, the department had failed state features. Inmate stabbings and slashings were routine occurrences, averaging 137 incidents per month for the first 6 months of 1990. Correctional officers and inmates alike described conditions as extremely dangerous. Graffiti covered the walls, and the quality of medical and other services was abysmal. As a low-level indicator, correctional officers found it necessary to dry clean their uniforms often because they would absorb the prison's foul odor. A major riot occurred in August 1990, precipitated by correctional officers blocking the only bridge to the island. They were protesting the administration's overly restrictive (at least in their eyes) use-of-force policy and lenient treatment of several inmates who had assaulted an officer.

Starting in 1995, a new prison administration turned this around. The number of assaults decreased by more than 90%, and the fears of riot turned from rampant to nearly nonexistent. The quality of services improved dramatically. The transformation was achieved by the actions of the new administration attacking the root causes of disorder by (1) successfully balancing resources and demands on the administration and ending conflict with the city and the courts; (2) requiring wardens to be accountable for order in their prisons, which, in turn, won the support of middle managers and correctional officers; (3) clamping down on inmate violence and gang membership, while improving medical and other services; (4) undercutting an inmate ideology that the system is out of control and therefore anything goes; and (5) skillfully managing the implementation of these reforms, so that both inmates and officers perceived the restoration of order as in their interests.

Privatization of New Mexico Prisons. As a result of the 1980 riot at the Penitentiary of New Mexico, New Mexico's prisons were some of the most expensive in the United States, despite the state's ranking near the bottom on most economic indicators. To control costs, the state decided to build new private prisons in 1998. This effort led to two major riots in the private prisons under state authority. The efforts faltered for these reasons: (1) state government was divided over the legitimacy of putting state inmates in private correctional facilities; (2) staff loyalty in the private facilities was low because corrections staff were newly recruited and given less pay and less training than were officers in public prisons; (3) inmates in private prisons, as a matter of state policy, were afforded fewer amenities than inmates in state prisons; (4) in one prison, Native American inmates developed an ideology that the private prisons were illegitimately interfering with their religious practices. The ideology was reinforced by the state legislation giving Native American inmates specific religious rights. In both prisons, an ideology of deprivation was amplified by continuing debate over the legitimacy of privatization; and (5) prison authorities and state officials were lax in responding to provocations and violent behavior by inmates.

Goldstone and Useem argued that prisons have characteristics of societies, a point retuning to Sykes and his colleagues. In contradiction, however, they asserted that prison order could be deliberately forged, without turning power over to inmates, by addressing the five conditions for stability.

Crowding, Inmate Transfers, and Rioting

On April 24, 2007, a riot broke out at a prison in Indiana, which, like the most recent ones in New Mexico, occurred in a privately managed prison. As background, in 2006, California held 172,000 inmates in a space designed for 100,000. To help relieve the overflow, California contracted to transfer inmates to Indiana, where there were more cells than inmates. A California state court, however, prohibited the transfer.[22] Arizona was in a similar predicament and sought the same solution. Its prison population was increasing at a rate of 160 inmates per month, but the state had funded for a growth rate of only 100 inmates per month.[23] With a shortage of beds in the thousands, requiring the state to take measures that included setting up tent units and placing two inmates in cells designed for one, in March 2007, Arizona contracted with Indiana to transfer 1,260 medium security prisoners. The transfer began without court intervention.

Soon after the first 630 Arizona inmates arrived in Indiana, a major riot broke out at the private facility housing them, the New Castle Correctional Facility (NCCF).[24] The riot began when a group of inmates defied orders to wear their prison-issued uniforms before entering the mess hall. They pushed their way through staff. Meanwhile, inmates in a housing unit, hearing the commotion, broke through security windows and locked doors to join the disturbance. In all, about 500 prisoners overwhelmed correctional officers and took over a portion of the facility. The facility's emergency response team formed a skirmish line, firing warning shots to contain the disturbance. About 2 hours later, an assault team retook the prison with little inmate resistance.[25]

The disturbance appears to have conformed to the pattern of prison riots identified in earlier studies.[26] Consistent with DiIulio's nonfindings, the NCCF was relatively new (it opened in April 2002); the inmates were selected for transfer by Arizona because they were considered nonviolent, low-threat inmates; and crowding in the Indiana prison was not an issue (almost one-half of the NCCF facility had been unused). Consistent with other work on prison riots, the events flowed from action of state and prison officials, which created widespread prisoner grievance regarding administrative actions, not just imprisonment per se. Specifically, the following factors appear to have contributed to the disturbance: (1) Arizona offenders were not informed that the conditions in Indiana would be harsher than their home state, nor were they told that efforts were underway to increase programming and privileges; (2) Arizona prisoners were not only being forcibly transferred a great distance away from their home communities, as they did not volunteer to move to Indiana, but this transfer was done very rapidly, increasing the shock.[27] Many inmates were unable to say goodbye to family and friends[28]; (3) At least in recent years, many correctional practitioners assert that locating prisoners in prisons near their homes increases the chances of successful prisoner reentry, casting doubt on the legitimacy of inter-state transfers;[29] (4) a large number of NCCF staff were inexperienced, including some in key managerial positions. Also, during the 6 weeks prior to the riot, Arizona sent five different staff members to act as monitors at NCCF, contributing to a sense of instability; and (5) the prison's security doors and windows were below correctional standards for strength for the classification of the inmates being housed, allowing inmates to penetrate them.

In summary, the transfer of inmates from one state to another inevitably imposes new hardships on inmates. In this instance, efforts to explain and justify those hardships, in both words and programming, although underway, were not sufficient to forestall a rebellion. If the transfer was to be done with "all deliberate speed" the emphasis was on speed.

RESEARCH SUMMARY

Since the mid-1960s, researchers have made significant gains in understanding the social dynamics of prisons. We believe that this body of research yields several insights that are helpful for thinking about the effect of buildup on prison order.

First, prisons are systems of cooperation. Those in power – a line of authority running from correctional officers on prison floors, through the warden, to the commissioner in the state capitol, the governor, and, ultimately, to free citizens – make decisions and evaluate the course of events. Their subordinates, the inmates, may find those decisions unpleasant, but accept their legitimacy most of the time. Inmates recognize that they would do little different if they were in power. When legitimacy declines – when inmates come to believe that they would do things differently if in power – individual and collective resistance may mount. Resistance may further impede, disrupt, or even threaten to destroy the system of cooperation.

Second, there is a great deal of variation in the degree of order achieved by U.S. prisons. At one extreme, some prisons are a Hobbesian world of unrelenting strife. Like failed states, these prisons are tense, unpleasant, and dangerous. Buildup critics were well founded in their concern that the buildup would produce mass disorder. Things fall apart. At the other end, some prisons are safe, orderly, and productive. Things may come together; the center holds. It is possible that the correctional and political leadership may have met the challenge posed by the buildup.

Third, the causes of disorder do not lie in the inherent defects of prison, unalterable "structural" conditions, or even the violent nature of inmates. This is implied by the fact that prisons and prison systems can turn from order to disorder, or the reverse, fairly rapidly. Agency looms large: people running prisons can change the conditions that produce order. It can be created, or destroyed, by altering the relationships among prison management, staff, inmates, and outside authorities.

Finally, two big questions can be asked about order behind bars. One is what causes variation in order from one prison (or prison system) to the next. Researchers answer this question by identifying the factors that distinguish prisons (or prison systems) that have high rates of disorder from those that have low rates. A second question (not reducible to the first) is whether corrections as a whole has become safer, or more dangerous, over time. This can be answered by tracking indicators of order over time, which is our next task.

To summarize, buildup critics suggested that prisons would collapse under the weight of more and more prisoners. In our view, this position does not take advantage of the empirical work on the conditions of prison order or on broader theories of societywide disorder. Although this work emphasizes variation in state capacity, it offers no specific prediction about whether order will decrease or increase with a substantial population increase. Rather, it suggests that the outcome will depend on institutional leadership and whether it can solve the problems that the buildup poses. This research also predicts that various measures of order should track together because of the operations of a causal variable of broad scope. We first consider the incidence of prison riots, and then turn to individual-level indicators of order.

WHAT IS A PRISON RIOT?

Dual power – having two political blocs claim sovereignty over the same territory – is the core feature of a revolutionary situation.[30] Likewise,

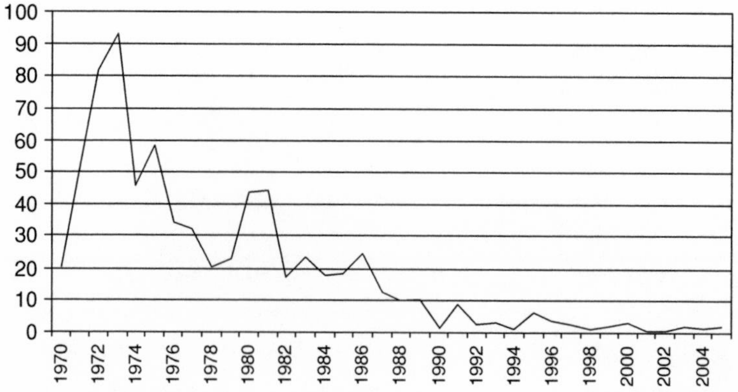

Figure 4.1. Prison riots, 1970–2005. *Source: New York Times, Washington Post, Chicago Tribune,* and *Christian Science Monitor.*

the central feature of a prison riot is dual power: inmates claim to control prison territory, at least for a time. Accordingly, we use the following operational definition: a prison riot occurs when prison authorities lose control of a significant number of prisoners in a significant area of the prison for a significant amount of time. The task of prison authorities is to end the institutional confusion with a minimum of casualties for all parties and other costs to the state. The task of prison rioters is to perpetuate their control, at least until they are exhausted or have achieved their collective or personal goals.

We used the following indicators to identify prison riots that occurred from 1970 to 2005. A prison riot is an incident (1) involving thirty inmates or more, (2) lasting 30 minutes or longer, (3) resulting in serious injury or significant property damage, and/or (4) involving inmates taking hostages or using force to expel correctional authorities from a section of the prison. The data are from four major newspapers that are indexed over the relevant period: the *New York Times,* the *Washington Post,* the *Chicago Tribune,* and the *Christian Science Monitor.*[31]

The prediction that society should expect an escalation in the number of prison riots with the buildup could hardly have done worse. Both the absolute number of riots and the ratio of inmates to riots declined, as shown in Figure 4.1. By the twentieth century's end, prison riots had become increasingly rare.[32] What explains this?

The simplest explanation is demographics: the buildup brought increasingly less violent offenders into the prisons. Such inmates, in turn, are less likely to riot. Although there may be something to this explanation, it does not get us very far. From Chapter 3, we know that while the *proportion* of inmates who had committed violent offenses declined somewhat over the buildup period, this group grew in absolute numbers more than any other category.[33] If demographics were the driving force, there would have been a large increase in the absolute number of riots and a modest decline in the ratio of riots to total inmates. In fact, the decline in the number of prison riots was steep, and the decline in the ratio of riots to inmates was even steeper. In the period under consideration, there is a strong *negative* association between the frequency of prison riots and the imprisonment numbers, however denominated.

An alternative hypothesis is that riots declined because prison and state authorities improved their political and management capability to meet the buildup challenge.[34] If prison riots are a sign of state disorganization, then the declining incidence of riots suggests greater political capability. It would be impossible to measure, at least retrospectively, political and management capability across the many jurisdictions and many years involved in the buildup analysis. Here, however, we can rely on the earlier studies cited previously. A key finding of this work is the existence of covariation between riots and individual rates of disorder. This is because they share a common cause: the quality and degree of government. At one end are prisons as failed states; at the other are prisons led by a coherent stable, effective management team supported by external political authorities. If indeed, we observe that the incidence of riots and rates of individual disorder change together over time, this would suggest the operation of this common cause. This interpretation will gain credibility if we can rule out alternative explanations for the covariation.

INDIVIDUAL-LEVEL DISORDER

Critics of the buildup argued that the buildup would cause increases in both the rates of collective disorder and signs of individual-level disorder. The figures and tables in this section test this position, by showing the trends in the rates of inmate homicides, inmate suicides, staff homicides, escapes, and inmates in protective custody. The denominator in all five rates is the prison population of the reporting jurisdictions. (Some states have missing data for some years.) We believe that this is the right denominator for the purposes at hand, even though the prison population became somewhat less violent in this period.

First, the critics argued that the buildup would result in a prison population that is ungovernable. Loïc Wacquant, for example, reports that prisons have become an "often unsafe and violent social jungle," characterized by "increased levels of interpersonal and group brutality."[35] This position implies that prison life was becoming degraded, on average, across all inmates. Second, the purpose of these performance measures is to capture whether prison authorities can govern the prison populations assigned to them, whatever their size and composition. If the relevant question is whether prisons are doing what they have been asked to do, this is best measured by the ratio of incidents to total population.

Crime researchers, when they are especially concerned about the validity of their data, typically turn to homicide as the best measured crime.[36] Figure 4.2 shows a 94% decline in the rate of inmate homicides over three decades among state inmates. In 1973, there were 63 homicides per 100,000 state inmates. In 1990, there were 8, and in 2003, the homicide rate dropped further to 4. The chances of being murdered behind bars decreased, not increased, with the buildup. To highlight the magnitude of the change, in 1973, the homicide rate in prison (63 per 100,000) was seven times the homicide rate of the U.S. resident population (9 per 100,000). During 2003, the homicide rate in prison (4 per 100,000) was lower than for the U.S. resident population (6 per 100,000).[37] This decrease in prison homicide could not be accounted for by prison demographics. Although the drop in the inmate homicide rate was large, the change in the composition of inmates was small.

Prison suicide rates also dropped sharply. Figure 4.2 shows that, in 1980, there were 34 inmate suicides per 100,000 inmates. This rate decreased to 16 suicides per 100,000 in 1990, and has remained stable since then.

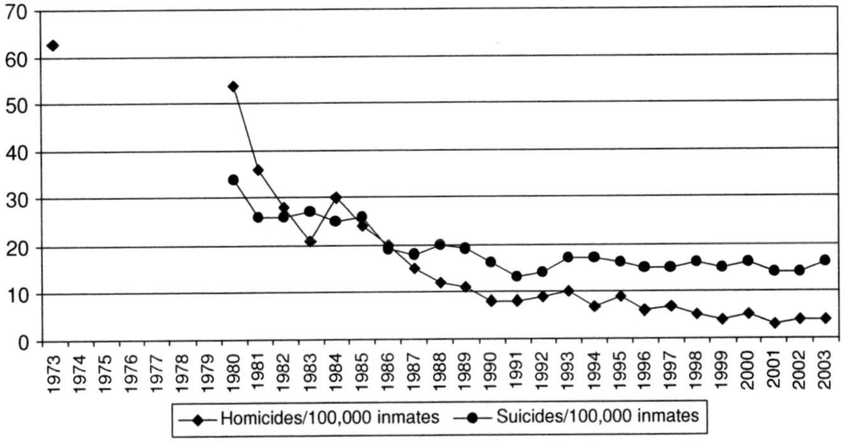

Figure 4.2. Homicide and suicide in state prisons, 1973–2003. *Source:* The 1973 figure is from Sawyer F. Sylvester, John H. Reed, and David O. Nelson, *Prison Homicide* (Jamaica, NY: Spectrum Publications, 1977); Other years, Christopher J. Mumola, *Suicide and Homicide Rates in State Prison and Jails* (Washington, DC: Bureau of Justice Statistics, 2005).

Figure 4.3 reveals a similar drop in the number of staff killed by inmates. In 1982, nine staff were murdered, or a ratio of 22.3 murders per 1,000,000 inmates. There followed an almost steady decline. By 1999, there were two staff murders, or a ratio of 1.6 murders per 1,000,000 inmates. In 2000 and 2001, inmates murdered no staff. To

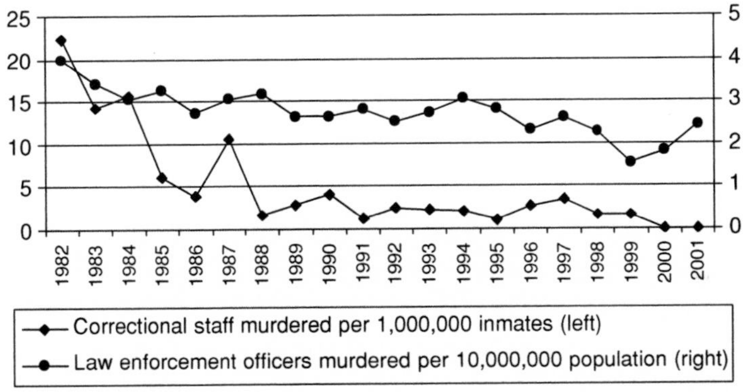

Figure 4.3. Correctional staff and law enforcement personnel killed, 1979–2001. *Source: Corrections Yearbook* (South Salem, NY, and Middletown, CT: Criminal Justice Institute, annually, 1983–2002); *Sourcebook of Criminal Justice Statistics*, 2002, table 3.57, "Law Enforcement Officers Killed."

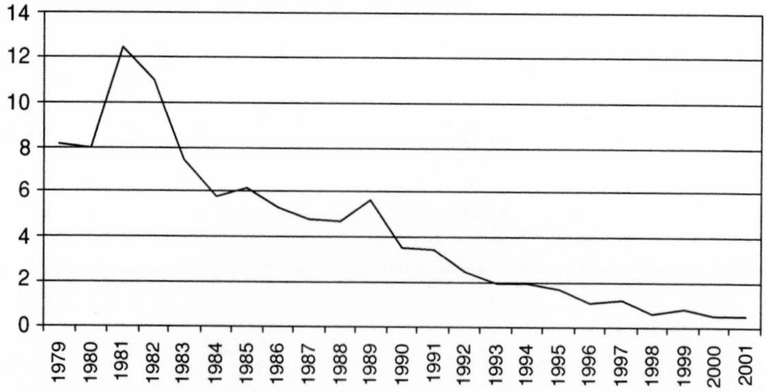

Figure 4.4. Number of escapes per 1,000 inmates, 1979–2001. *Source: Corrections Yearbook* (South Salem, NY, and Middletown, CT: Criminal Justice Institute, annually, 1980–2002).

put the decrease in a broader context, Figure 4.3 also shows the number of sworn law enforcement officers killed per 10 million resident population over the same period. Between 1982 and 2001, this ratio was cut by one-half. Although a significant decline, it does not compare to the decline in corrections.

The same pattern holds for escapes, an obvious indicator of weak security. Figure 4.4 shows that, in 1981, there were 12.4 escapes per 1,000 inmates in U.S. prisons. By 2001, the ratio had declined to 0.5 escapes per 1,000 inmates.[38] Figure 4.5 shows the proportion of inmates in protective custody.[39] In 1980, there were 27 inmates in protective custody per 1,000 inmates. By 2001, there were 8 inmates in protective custody per 1,000 inmates.

As a final check on these trends, Table 4.1 reports data collected by the U.S. Bureau of the Census for the BJS. These data have been collected in 5- or 6-year intervals. Although the first Census of Prisons was conducted in 1974, disorder data were first gathered in 1984. The 1984 census collected data from state prisons only, so we exclude data from federal prisons, which were not collected until 1990 – well into the buildup.

The first two rows of Table 4.1 show that although the number of inmate assaults against other inmates and staff increased with the buildup, the ratio of assaults to inmates declined. In 1984, there were 43.0 assaults on inmates per 1,000 inmates; this declined to 28.8 by

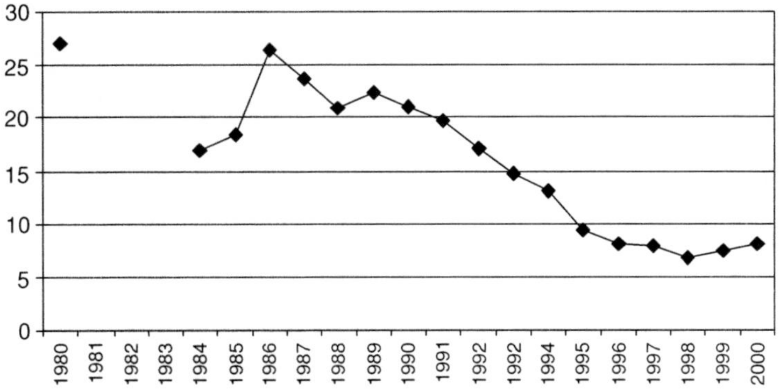

Figure 4.5. Inmates in protective custody per 1,000 inmates, 1980–2001. *Source: Corrections Yearbook* (South Salem, NY, and Middletown, CT: Criminal Justice Institute, annually, 1980–2002).

2000. The number of assaults against staff declined slightly, from about 17 per 1,000 inmates to about 15 assaults per 1,000 inmates.

The third row of Table 4.1 reports data on the incidence of predominantly low-level collective disorders. We collapse together three categories of disorders: (1) "major disturbances" or "riots" (incidents involving five or more inmates that resulted in serious injury or significant property damage),[40] (2) arson incidents (deliberately set fires that resulted in damage exceeding $200), and (3) "other disruptions" (e.g., hunger strikes, work slowdowns). We believe that because the BJS defined "riot" so broadly, it is sensible to use the more inclusive

TABLE 4.1. *Inmate Violations in State Confinement Correctional Facilities, 1984–2000*

	1984	1990	1995	2000
Assault on inmates/assaults	15,320	21,184	23,654	30,219
per 1,000 inmates	43.0	33.0	27.3	28.8
Assaults on staff/assaults	6,018	10,562	12,730	15,650
per 1,000 inmates	16.9	16.5	14.7	14.9
Disturbances and arsons/	2,821	6,587	2,748	1,494
disturbances and arsons per 1,000 inmates	7.9	10.3	3.2	1.4

Source: U.S. Department of Justice, Bureau of Justice Statistics, Census of State Correctional Facilities, various years, data holdings, National Archive of Criminal Justice Data.

category of disturbances. For example, a brawl among a half-dozen inmates would qualify as a "riot" under the BJS definition, yet this is not an event that we would normally recognize as a riot. Although some of the events captured by this category will be full-fledged riots, the vast majority will not be. In any case, there was a substantial increase in the number of disturbances and arsons between 1984 and 1990. This growth was more than reversed, however, by 1995. In 2000, the ratio of incidents to inmates was about one-fifth of its 1984 level.

To conclude, all measures point in the same direction – away from the position that the prison buildup caused increasing rates of individual-level and collective-level disorder. In fact, most measures show that prisons became safer and less likely to experience riots and disturbances. This trend, in turn, suggests that correctional leadership and management became more effective in organizing their activities. We should consider alternative explanations.

LESS-THAN-LETHAL VIOLENCE

A recent report, issued by the Commission on Safety and Abuse in America's Prisons, acknowledges that the rates of lethal violence in U.S. prisons have declined in recent years. The report, however, goes on to point out that there may be significant unmeasured nonlethal violence and abuse occurring behind bars.[41] They raised this possibility based on two sorts of considerations.

One was testimony given to the commission, as they held hearings in four regions of the country, by current and former corrections officials, policy makers, academic researchers, community activists, and a small number of ex-prisoners. They also received written submissions from interested parties. Some correctional officers reported that they were in near constant fear of being assaulted, and ex-prisoners and prisoner family members described patterns of gang violence, rape, beatings by officers, and illegal strip searches.[42] For example, the mother of a deceased inmate stated that her son "was a human being who got less [medical] treatment than the dogs receive at the local animal rescue center."[43] These are deeply troubling observations. Still, there may have been a selection bias, in which potential witnesses or writers who did not perceive a pattern of abuse would not take the trouble to

TABLE 4.2. *Inmate Safety from Assault: How safe do you feel from being hit, punched, or assaulted by other inmates?*

	State (%)	Federal (%)
Unsafe	12.0	5.9
Somewhat unsafe	8.5	4.0
Neither safe nor unsafe	10.4	7.7
Somewhat safe	20.4	17.6
Safe	48.6	64.8

Source: Survey of State and Federal Inmates, 1997, data holdings, National Archive of Criminal Justice Data.

express their views. The commission's approach was not designed to measure general patterns of behavior.[44]

Second, the commission argues that "to precisely measure the . . . universe of non-lethal violence is practically impossible given how we collect data today."[45] This is certainly true, but "precisely measure" is an exceptionally high standard. Several crude measures are available, which may allow us to see whether the buildup has given rise to more violence behind bars.

The 1997 BJS *Survey of Inmates* asks a representative sample of federal and state inmates two relevant questions: (1) "How safe do you feel from being hit, punched, or assaulted by other inmates?" and (2) "How safe is it here compared to the streets around where you lived?" Tables 4.2 and 4.3 separately report the results for both state and federal inmates. If fear is widespread, we should expect to see large majorities of inmates reporting that they do not feel safe from other inmates and that their home streets are much safer than prison. This expectation is not borne out.

TABLE 4.3. *Prison Safety versus Streets: How safe is it compared to the streets around where you lived?*

	State (%)	Federal (%)
Here is safer	26.5	26.4
Streets are safer	44.6	39.5
About the same	32.7	34.1

Source: Survey of State and Federal Inmates, 1997, data holdings, National Archive of Criminal Justice Data.

TABLE 4.4. *Proportions of State Inmates Guilty of Charges of Assaults, 1991, 1997, and 2004*

	1991	1997	2004
Physical assault on a correctional officer or other staff member	9.9	7.7	5.9
Verbal assault on a correctional officer or other staff member	25.2	21.4	16.6
Physical assault on another inmate	32.1	25.7	25.7
Verbal assault on another inmate	8.2	9.3	10.0

Note:
1991: Since your admission, were you found guilty of:
1997: Since your admission, have you been written up or formally charged with:
2004: Since your admission, have you been written up or been found guilty of:
Source: Survey of State Inmates, 1991, 1997, 2004, data holdings, National Archive of Criminal Justice Data.

Table 4.2 shows that about one in five state inmates and one in ten federal inmates report feeling either unsafe or somewhat unsafe from assault by other inmates. Although this lack of personal security is worrisome, almost 70% of state inmates and more than 80% of federal inmates report that they feel "safe" or "somewhat safe." In Table 4.3, we see that a significant minority of state inmates and federal inmates, 45% and 40%, respectively, consider the streets to be safer than prison. This leaves a majority in both systems who report that the state and federal prisons are safer or about the same in safety as the streets. It would be helpful to see how these questions track over time, but those data are unavailable.

A second sort of indicator is the proportions of inmates who report that they have been charged with, or been found guilty of, assaulting other inmates or staff. The BJS *Survey of Inmates* began to ask a set of questions along these lines in 1991, repeating them in roughly the same form in 1997 and 2004. We limit our consideration here to state inmates. The first column in Table 4.4 shows that, in 1991, almost 10% of state inmates reported that they had been found guilty of a physical assault against a correctional officer, 25% had been found guilty of a verbal assault against a correctional officer, 32% had been found guilty of a physical assault on another inmate, and 8% had been found guilty of a verbal assault on another inmate. These figures suggest a lot of contention and interpersonal aggression, reinforcing the commission's concern of a hostile environment behind bars.

The second and third columns in Table 4.4 show the results of nearly the same set of questions being asked in 1997 and 2004, although the wording has been broadened to include both those found guilty of assaults and those "written up" for assaults. By 2004, the proportion who reported that they had been *written up* (the broader category) or found guilty of physical assault against a correctional officer had declined to 6%; verbal assault on a correctional officer, 17%; physical assault on another inmate, 26%; and verbal assault on another inmate, 10%.[46]

The *Corrections Yearbook* provides an alternate source of data on the number of inmate assaults against staff and other inmates for the years 1986 through 2001.[47] However, for the years 1986 through 1993, the *Corrections Yearbook* did not maintain consistent criteria for classifying an event as an assault.[48] It standardized its criteria for assaults starting with the collection of the 1994 data, reporting (as it had in 1986) the total number of assaults against staff and inmates. In 1994, there were 16.1 total assaults against staff per 1,000 state inmates and 28.5 total assaults against inmates per 1,000 state inmates. By 2001, these rates had declined slightly to 15.1 total assaults against staff per 1,000 state inmates, and 26.7 total assaults against inmates per 1,000 state inmates. For what it is worth, in 1986, there were 25.5 total assaults against staff per 1,000 inmates, and 36.6 total assaults against inmates per 1,000 inmates.

The *Corrections Yearbook* warns readers to interpret its assault data cautiously because agencies may count assaults differently. For our purposes, this is less problematic than if agencies change their criteria for what constitutes assault over time. Taking these caveats into account, the data can nonetheless be read as showing no substantial increase in the level of assaults associated with the buildup, at least in its later stages.

In sum, nonlethal violence does not appear to have escalated along with the prison buildup. That is a somewhat different question than whether its level is acceptable. The Commission on Safety and Abuse argues that it is too high. We agree that greater efforts should be made for *additional* gains.

TABLE 4.5. *Percentage of Inmates in State Confinement Facilities by Security Level of Facilities, 1974–2000*

	1974	1979	1984	1990	1995	2000
Maximum security	44.5	51.7	43.7	38.0	38.9	38.4
Medium security	37.6	37.4	44.3	49.2	49.6	46.8
Minimum security	17.9	10.8	11.8	11.5	11.5	14.8

Note: The early-year censuses excluded federal prisons. To achieve comparability, federal prisons are excluded for all years.
Source: Law Enforcement Assistance Administration, *Census of Sate Correctional Facilities, 1974. Advance Report* (Washington, DC: U.S. Department of Justice, LEAA, July 1975); Bureau of Justice Statistics, *1984 Census of State Adult Correctional Facilities* (Washington, DC: U.S. Department of Justice, Bureau of Justice Statistics, August 1987); James J. Stephan, *Census of State and Federal Correctional Facilities, 1995* (Washington, DC: U.S. Department of Justice, Bureau of Justice Statistics, August 1997); National Archive of Criminal Justice Data for 2000.

CREATING ORDER THROUGH THE LEVIATHAN

We noted at the outset that one solution to the problem of order is to create an increasingly repressive prison system. The rates of disorder may have declined over the buildup period, not because of improved governance, but because prison authorities imposed increasingly repressive circumstances, a correctional Leviathan.

One step toward the Leviathan would be to increase the proportion of inmates in maximum security facilities. Table 4.5 shows a modest trend running in the reverse direction. In 1974, about 44% of the inmates in state confinement facilities[49] were housed in maximum security prisons; by 2000, this percentage declined to about 38%. It would be incorrect to argue, from these data alone, that U.S. prisons were becoming *less* repressive; the shifts may reflect the changing character of the inmate population. The relevant point, however, is that there is little evidence of a correctional Leviathan as the instrument achieving order.

Another indicator of repressiveness is the proportion of inmates in administrative segregation. The trend is in the wrong direction to support the idea that order was achieved through repression. As shown in Figure 4.6, in 1982, there were 5.4 inmates per 100 inmates in administrative segregation. By 2001, this proportion had dropped slightly to 5.2.[50]

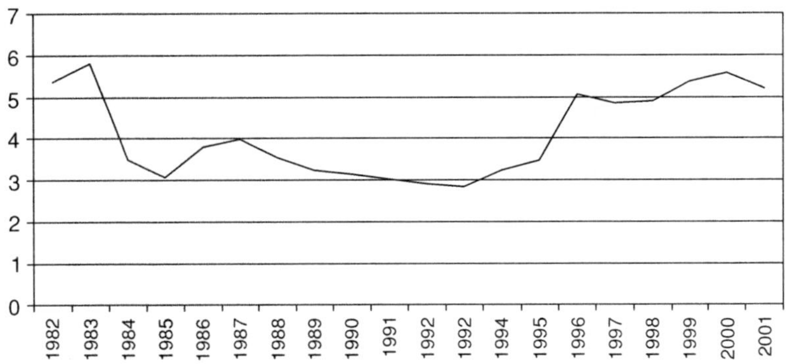

Figure 4.6. Inmates in administrative segregation per 100 state inmates, 1982–2001. *Source: Corrections Yearbook* (South Salem, NY, and Middletown, CT: Criminal Justice Institute, annually, 1980–2002).

Finally, we need to consider the proliferation of super maximum security prisons (or "supermaxes") in the late 1980s and 1990s as an explanation for the decreasing rates of disorder. Supermaxes are extremely high security facilities, in effect, prisons within prisons.[51] Inmates typically spend 23 hours a day locked in their cells and have little or no contact with other inmates. Services to inmates, such as food and medical care, are provided to inmates in their cells. When inmates are taken out of their cells, they are usually handcuffed, shackled, and escorted by a four-person team. Inmates most often are allowed to exercise in a small fenced-in yard.

Supermax prisons have become common in U.S. corrections. In 1984, the U.S. Penitentiary in Marion, Illinois, was the only supermax prison in the country. By 1999, thirty-four states and the Federal Bureau of Prisons had supermax prisons, holding just more than 20,000 inmates, or 1.8% of the total prison population.[52] How much of the decline in disorder in U.S. prisons can be attributed to the proliferation of supermaxes?

Supermax prisons certainly incapacitate those so confined, and they may deter general population inmates from committing in-prison crimes, trying to escape, or starting prison riots. This is their organizational mission. Conversely, some have argued that supermax prisons may actually increase disorder and prison riots. This position has been developed most fully by Leena Kurki and Norval Morris.[53] They state that prison order is achieved by engendering a sense of justice among inmates, a point (as argued previously) supported by the evidence. But, according to Kurki and Morris, inmates see supermax prisons as unjustly harsh. Hence, rather than creating order, supermaxes paradoxically undercut it. Similarly, Roy King hypothesizes that, "ever more repressive response to violence – of which supermax is but the latest expression – sets up a vicious circle of intolerance which is doomed to make matters worse."[54] Hans Toch notes that supermaxes may brutalize correctional officers by having them treat inmates as objects rather than people.[55] Jesenia Pizarro and Vanja Stenius attack supermaxes from a somewhat different angle: they damage inmates' mental health, making order more difficult to achieve.[56] Jonathan Simon likewise comments, "inmates held for long periods under 'supermax' style regimes are at greater risk for behavioral abnormalities."[57] Although these authors provide little systematic evidence to support their arguments that supermaxes have *negative* effects on order, they are convincing that it should not be taken for granted that supermaxes have *positive* effects on order.[58]

To date, Chad Briggs, Jody Sundt, and Thomas Castellano have conducted the only test of effect of supermaxes on order in correctional systems.[59] They selected four correctional systems to study, based in part on the availability of reliable data on violence over time. Three of the systems (Arizona, Illinois, and Minnesota) had opened a supermax in the time period covered. A fourth system (Utah) had not, providing a comparison system. They asked whether inmate-against-inmate and inmate-against-staff violence declined, systemwide, after a supermax facility opened. A formal data analysis found little effect. Specifically, the opening of a supermax did not reduce the level of inmate-against-inmate assaults. Inmates were no safer after the opening of a supermax than before. The opening of supermaxes had mixed effects on inmate-against-staff violence. The opening of a supermax left unaffected inmate-against-staff assaults in one prison system, decreased it in another, and increased it in a third.

This study, based on a small number of states, cannot definitely answer the question of whether supermaxes have a negative effect on prison violence. Not only is the number of cases studied small, but also the states implementing supermaxes are unlikely to be a random sample of states, and the timing may be nonrandom as well. Far-sighted correctional administrators may open a supermax when they anticipate an increase in violence. Thus, the finding that inmate-against-inmate violence did not change after supermaxes are introduced may be because they suppressed otherwise increasing rates of violence. Yet, even if supermaxes do have a negative effect on violence, which somehow Briggs's study did not pick up on, that effect would be small. If supermaxes were a major causal force in the broader trend toward order, some trace of that effect is likely to have shown up in Briggs's excellent analysis.[60]

Other Developments during the Buildup

The case studies of correctional reform cited previously, from Sykes to DiIulio to Carroll and Goldstone and Useem, all suggest that the quality of prison moves with the quality of prison leadership and management. In this section, we elaborate on this point in the context of the prison buildup.

Prison Buildup and Judicial Intervention. A great deal of work has been done on court intervention in prisons during the buildup period. Courts get involved in regulating or even taking control of a prison or prison system in response to inmate litigation, which can be filed by an individual or on behalf of a class of inmates. Sometimes this litigation addresses a limited concern, whereas in other cases the list of concerns is so broad that the court may attack the "totality of conditions." In these broader situations, courts attempt "structural reform" of a prison or set of prisons. Inmate suits may be filed in state or federal courts; there are many, many inmate suits filed each year, most of which are dismissed. Those that proceed may result either in a settlement before trial or in a court judgment.

Two excellent studies are by Malcolm Feeley and Edwin Rubin, who examine prison reform cases that occurred between 1965 and 1980, and by Margo Schlanger, who reports on more recent experiences.[61] Without delving fully into this impressive body of scholarship, several points can be made about it with regard to the issues at hand.

First, surprisingly little headway has been made on the issue most relevant to us, whether judicial intervention as a whole has been a major independent variable causing the prison system to transform itself. This lacuna is forthrightly noted by Feeley and Rubin, who, in a recent essay, comment about their earlier book, "We did not . . . advance any claim about whether judicial policy making, either in prison reform cases or in general, is actually effective."[62] Feeley and Rubin go on, in this recent essay, to try to fill this gap, but the evidence adduced focuses on the effectiveness of specific interventions, rather than the impact of judicial intervention on corrections as a whole. Indeed, Feeley and Rubin comment, after describing the effectiveness of a particular intervention (Arkansas Department of Corrections), "prisons throughout the United States remain brutal institutions, permitting inmates to be subjected to sexual predators and violence."[63] They provide no aggregate evidence on this point.

Second, the main thrust of Schlanger's study is that "litigation is about compensation for injured parties."[64] That is, the proof is whether the judicial system allows inmates to express their legitimate grievance in court and receive a fair hearing. Schlanger assesses whether 1996 legislation intended to reduce frivolous litigation, the Prisoner Reform Litigation Act (PRLA), achieved its purposes or has had perverse consequences. She provides considerable quantitative and qualitative data to show that the PRLA reduced (by about 40%) inmate litigation, but failed to distinguish meritorious from bad cases.[65]

Schlanger goes on to consider the broad effect of inmate litigation on the correctional system. She argues that inmate litigation has had two major effects on the prison system. One is to require prison officials to govern in a more rational manner, rather than exercising rule arbitrarily and according to whim. She asserts that prisons improve their performance when they must follow written rules, stated policies, and procedures for accountability.[66] Second, inmate litigation deters prison officials from violating rules and engaging in other acts that would otherwise damage inmates. Prison officials seek to avoid litigation, if only because of its monetary costs, which causes them to straighten up their act. Schlanger, however, does not directly address the issue most relevant to this chapter, the aggregate effect of litigation on prison order over time. For what it is worth, the correctional officials she interviewed, on a whole, told her that inmate litigation is effective "mostly around the edges."[67]

To conclude, Feeley and Rubin and Schlanger, as well as many other scholars, make a strong argument – richly detailed in case studies, augmented by some quantitative evidence – that judicial intervention has been a progressive force in transforming the prison system during the buildup period. Prisons have improved because inmates sue and judges take control over them when conditions are egregious. This position, however, is consistent with the one developed here – the crucial role of correctional leadership – *if* one broadens the concept of "correctional leadership" to include the judiciary in its role in managing prisons.

This is a reasonable broadening. It is supported by Leo Carroll's case study of the transformation of the Rhode Island maximum-security prison. Order and safety came to the prison system only when an alliance was struck between the judiciary and correctional officials. Feeley and Rubin's extended case study of the transformation of the Arkansas Department of Corrections also supports it. They observe that the judges in this case became thoughtful, skilled administrators.[68] They learned to break complex problems into manageable component parts, used both carrots and sticks to prompt sluggish corrections officials to act, required detailed reports to establish progress and accountability; and infused the change process with a sense of moral worth. Judges became part of the extended correctional polity, and some were quite skilled in that role. Whether this level of competence can be relied on is another matter. Judges are not trained as correctional administrators. Their knowledge of correctional operations, at least coming into the situation, is likely to be quite limited.[69]

Prison Buildup and Changing Prison Architecture and Physical Security Measures. Another set of factors that may have caused a decline in prison disorder in the buildup period is improvement in the conditions of plants, architectural designs, and physical security measures. John DiIulio notes that "correctional officials are in uniform agreement that architecture matters a great deal, and some believe that it 'makes or breaks' the operation."[70] DiIulio argues that his evidence contradicts a position of "architectural determinism."[71] For example, included in his sample of prisons in three states, the Huron Valley Men's Facility (HVMF) in Michigan was newly opened, small in size, organized into a progressive college campus design, not overcrowded, and had the advantage of a low inmate-to-staff ratio. Even though accredited by the American Correctional Association, HVMF experienced major riots and frequent stabbings and escapes.[72] The Huntsville prison in Texas, in contrast, achieved a high level of order "despite a decrepit physical plant, inhospitable to security."[73]

Other case studies, in contrast, suggest that prisons may be made safer through stricter security measures and architectural designs. Howard Bidna examined efforts by the California Department of Corrections to lower inmate violence through new operational procedures.[74] They included additional gun coverage, canceling evening activities, tighter controls on visitation, and a reconfiguration of offices and shops to enhance security. He compared, before and after the reforms, stabbing rates of inmates against inmates and stabbing and assault rates against staff. Bidna found a significant decline in inmate-against-inmate assaults, but reforms did not lower the rate of assaults against staff.

Useem and Goldstone, in their study of the NYCDOC, found the 90% decline in prison violence had little to do with changes in Rikers Island's underlying architecture or physical plant. Stricter security measures were implemented, including special red-colored identification cards for violent inmates; more frequent searches and pat-downs of inmates, especially of those with red identification cards; greater separation of violent inmates in housing areas and on transportation vehicles; and the use of metal detectors to monitor the movement of inmates. However, these reforms were part of a larger effort to bring order, safety, and better services to inmates. Significantly, following major riots in 1986 and 1990, the official investigations called for major reforms, including tighter security.[75] These reforms appear not to have been implemented, and the rates of violence remained high through the mid-1990s. The improvements in security measures were achieved only as part of a more comprehensive managerial reform.

To conclude, this body of research suggests that improvement in the physical characteristics of prisons and tighter security may reduce prison violence. Unfortunately, no work has sought to isolate the effect of this set of factors across many prisons during the buildup period. Moreover, the physical and operational conditions of prisons may be best thought of as elements of correctional leadership and management.

Rehabilitation Programs and Prison Buildup. The central conclusion of this chapter is that the U.S. correctional regime has not caved in to the pressures of prison growth. This is no small accomplishment, and not one predicted by criminologists. Yet, we have considered a narrow set of measures of order. Most would agree that prison should offer programs that would provide the opportunity for self-improvement. And it is possible that other aspects of correctional practice suffered during the buildup in order to allow for improvements to physical security. To return to the failed state analogue, although a state's first responsibility is to provide security, a strong state will deliver a full range of high-quality services to its citizens.[76]

Although a detailed analysis of the range of potential and actual program offerings (or other services) is beyond the scope of this chapter, it is essential to consider the issue in general terms. It is controversial whether many offerings have lasting beneficial effects for the majority of inmates. Still, some programs (especially education) appear to have positive effects for the general population and, if appropriately targeted, benefit subsets of the population. Were efforts to provide educational programming, substance abuse treatment, and other services curtailed during the buildup a consequence of the effort to maintain and improve security?

Whereas order can be straightforwardly measured, the aggregate effectiveness of programs is difficult to measure. This is in part because the quality of services varies greatly from one prison to the next. For example, Ann Chih Lin studied rehabilitation programming, including educational programs, in five medium security prisons.[77] All five prisons had mandatory GED classes for inmates without a high school education. Real education took place in three of the prisons, but in the two others, classes amounted to little more than required attendance and busywork. In the latter, according to Lin, staff's first priority was to protect one another, especially from inmate assaults and manipulation. Any relaxation of this culture of solidarity, which might be fostered by staff–inmate communication, threatened to initiate a spiral toward disorder. Although staff was obligated to provide inmates with programs, it was up to inmates to take advantage of those opportunities. The staff culture in the former (the prisons that provided effective programming) emphasized fluid staff–inmate communication. Although there was never doubt about the social divide, staff sought to understand inmates' problems and dilemmas. Staff felt responsible that inmates took advantage of programs. To reach these conclusions, Lin observed and attended meetings for 10 to 12 hours per day for 3 weeks in each of the five prisons studied.

Although we cannot measure program quality over time for many jurisdictions involved in the buildup, we can track the proportion of inmates who receive various programs while in prisons, although the data do not provide good indications of the quantity of services. Joan Petersilia has observed that participation in prison programming has declined in recent years.[78] She, however, looks at changes over a relatively short period, from 1991 to 1997, more than halfway through the buildup period. For data on program participation, Petersilia draws on the *Survey of Inmates* data collected by BJS. Petersilia's overall conclusion is that the "data suggest that U.S. prisons today offer fewer services than they did when inmate problems were less severe, although history shows that we have never invested much in prison rehabilitation."[79]

The data reported in Table 4.6 are also from BJS *Survey of Inmates*, but provide a longer time frame. In addition to the 1991, 1997, and 2004 surveys, conducted in both state and federal prisons, surveys of state-only inmates were conducted in 1974, 1979, and 1986. Table 4.6 reinforces the observation of declines in programming in recent years. From 1991 to 2004, in both state and federal prisons, the proportion of inmates receiving academic training decreased by about 10%, from 46.4% to 28.6% in state prisons and from 56.3% to 35.4% in federal prisons.

TABLE 4.6. *Participation in Education Programs Since Most Recent Incarceration and Current Work Participation*

	State						Federal		
	1974 (%)	1979 (%)	1986 (%)	1991 (%)	1997 (%)	2004 (%)	1991 (%)	1997 (%)	2004 (%)
In prison education*									
Academic	20.9	27.0	45.0	46.4	35.8	28.6	56.3	37.0	35.4
Vocational	25.8	30.9	–	31.2	31.4	27.4	29.4	28.2	31.6
ESL	–	–	–	–	1.2	1.0	–	5.5	2.3
Work assignments									
In prison	72.1	72.6	65.9	62.0	60.2	60.1	91.2	87.1	90.9
Work release	5.3	8.8	10.5	9.6	10.4	7.5	0.4	4.2	1.7

* Category "other" excluded.
Source: Survey of Inmates in State and Federal Correctional Facilities, various years, National Archive of Criminal Justice Data, www.icpsr.umich.edu/NACJD.

Although these declines are significant, it should be pointed out that the long-term trend has an inverse U shape, at least with regard to state inmates. In 1974, before the onset of the buildup, only 20.9% of the inmates received academic training. The proportion increased through 1991, reaching a peak of 46.4% in that year. The trend in vocational training is far more even and shows no recent drop off. Over a 30-year period, the proportion of inmates receiving vocational training has been about 31% in both state and federal prisons.

Table 4.6 shows a long-term decline in the proportion of inmates in work programs. In 1974, 72.1% of state prison inmates had work assignments. In 2004, only 60.1% of the inmates had such assignments. In federal prisons, the proportions, in the 3 years for which we have surveys, are higher and more stable. In 1991, 91.2% of the inmates had work assignments; in 2004, 90.9% of the inmates did. The percentage of state inmates participating in work release increased almost two-fold, from 5.3% in 1974 to 10.4% in 1997, but then declined to 7.5% in 2004. A similar pattern occurred among federal inmates. For these inmates, work release among federal inmates increased from 0.4% in 1991 to 4.2% in 1997, and then declined to 1.7% in 2004.

It is a caveat that we cannot assess the content or intensity of these efforts. It is possible that relative effort in parts of the correctional environment other than physical security deteriorated even more than is suggested by these statistics.

CONCLUSION

Critics of the buildup were certain that the country had embarked on a self-destructive course. This was not a naive prediction – based on simple extrapolation of current trends into the future – but instead based on a theoretical argument. The prison system would collapse under its own weight because of the flaws inherent to prisons. With the very unfair advantage of hindsight – buttressed by reasonably good data – we now know they were wrong. The prison buildup has been associated with a sharp decline in chaos behind bars. Compared to an earlier period, prison riots have become rare, the homicide and suicide rates have declined dramatically, and a smaller proportion of inmates are held in segregation and protective custody. Escapes are less common. If we want to have mass-scale imprisonment, we can have it without out-of-control conditions behind bars. This is the central empirical conclusion of this chapter.

What caused the trend toward greater, rather than less, order? The data are consistent with the position that the political and correctional leadership made the institution more effective. This consistency has a number of aspects. First, a substantial body of evidence, based on in-depth case studies, shows that level of order depends crucially on the quality of political and correctional leadership. If this is fundamentally true, then the incidence of riots, homicides, escapes, and the like are all sensitive indicators of managerial effectiveness. Second, although changing demographics of the inmate population might account for a small portion of the decreasing ratio of homicides to total inmates, it cannot account for the large drop in the absolute number of prison riots and the even larger drop in the ratio of riots to inmates. Third, the proliferation of supermaxes might account for some portion of the decline in violence, but the best evidence suggests that this is a minor factor. It is quite possible that there were many negative social consequences of the buildup, but diminished prison order was not one.

No effort has been made in this chapter to present new evidence on the features of effective correctional leadership and competent management. The data do not lend themselves to this task. Case studies, such as those by DiIulio and Carroll, provide examples of effective correctional agencies and leadership playing a constructive role. However, these case studies provide useful clues, rather than a comprehensive picture, of the core features of good correctional governance. Our understanding of "good management" and creative, forward-looking leadership is still a work in progress.

CHAPTER FIVE

The Buildup and Inmate Release

What are we doing about all the people coming out of prison?[1]

A natural consequence of the prison buildup is the record number of inmates released from the nation's prisons, now on the order of 670,000 per year.[2] Political leaders, criminal justice practitioners, and researchers from diverse policy areas have raised alarm about the effects of this flow on communities.[3] As we discuss in this chapter, inmate release is interconnected with crime, the number and characteristics of those incarcerated, and with prison conditions, the consequences of mass incarceration considered in previous chapters.

Studies consistently show that almost two-thirds of the prisoners released from state and federal prisons are rearrested, and two-fifths are reincarcerated within 3 years of release.[4] In tandem with the concern for public safety is a concern for quality of life in the poor and disadvantaged neighborhoods where prisoners return in large concentration.[5] Diseases such as HIV, hepatitis, tuberculosis, and mental health problems among prisoners constitute a sizable percentage of all cases in the U.S. population.[6] Ex-prisoners crowd homeless shelters and have intertwined education, employment, housing, family, and health needs that tax government agencies, as well as the private and nonprofit organizations that provide services in these areas.[7]

Encouraged by $100 million in grants issued by the federal government in 2002, initiatives are being mounted across the United States to improve prisoner reentry.[8] Research has described the social and economic costs of poorly prepared and poorly supervised ex-prisoners.[9] Research has also highlighted the policies that impede successful reentry, including legal restrictions on employment, employer resistance to hiring those with criminal records, and public housing rules, among others.[10] This work appropriately characterizes the difficult environment faced by inmates exiting prison and points out the challenges for improving outcomes. Several teams have folded this research into proposals for optimal prisoner reentry systems.[11]

A close look at prisoner reentry, however, reveals as much about the prison buildup as it does about the release of inmates per se or how to best address it as a policy problem. We begin this chapter with a brief review of the facts about inmate release, and we then turn to the ways in which the prison buildup has constrained the options for managing inmate release more effectively.

DIMENSIONS OF PRISONER REENTRY

The number of inmates released from prison each year lags by several years the number admitted. During the late 1980s and early 1990s, the number released fell somewhat behind the number admitted as the latter surged. The number released per year has approximately quadrupled since the late 1970s, to about 670,000 leaving state and federal prisons in the United States in 2004. The number would be far higher if we were to include those leaving jails, where stays are typically much shorter, but the same issues are faced.[12]

Characteristics of Released Inmates

Not surprisingly, those released from prison have characteristics that are associated with minimal success in the broader society.[13] Inmates are disproportionately poor, minority, and from poverty-stricken communities. They typically have low levels of education, are less likely than the general population to be married, and are much more likely to have relatives who have also been incarcerated. They are likely to have health, dental, and mental health liabilities and, more often than not, substance abuse histories. As discussed in Chapter 4, when one takes the long view, beyond creating safer and more orderly conditions, prisons have not improved their responsiveness to inmates' needs. In-prison programming has fallen off, especially relative to inmate needs, as fiscal pressures have squeezed discretionary line items such as program budgets.[14]

Those leaving prison have increasingly long criminal histories. A substantial fraction of those released from prison return within a short time, either for a violation of parole or for a new crime. This group accounts for an increasing share of prison admissions. The process of rapid, repeated movement from incarceration to civil society has been termed "churning" by several analysts.[15] The churning process also affects the parole population. Those released from prison and entering parole supervision are increasingly likely to have previously exited prison during the same criminal sentence. From 1985 to 2001, the number of rereleases from prison entering parole increased from 45,200 to 176,800 – a nearly 300% increase – whereas the number of new releases entering parole increased only 100% from 126,300 to 252,600 in the same time period.[16]

The high rate of recidivism and the large number of reentrants have implications for crime. In the past few years, crime rates have fallen dramatically. If it is true, as many communities believe, that those recently released from prison are responsible for an increasing fraction of the crime problem, this consequence of mass incarceration may require adapting both models of law enforcement on the street and postincarceration supervision to respond to the changing crime dynamic.

Release of Inmates and Subsequent Supervision

Most prisoners released from correctional facilities receive some form of postrelease supervision, generally called parole. Which inmates are supervised, the release decision-making process, the supervising correctional agencies, and the supervision practices have changed significantly over time and vary widely from state to state. There are more than 750,000 adults currently on parole. Although this number is high, it belies the tremendous flow of individuals entering and exiting parole and the 60% turnover of the census in the course of a year. The large number of released prisoners on parole reflects the growth of the prison population, although the growth of parolees has been smaller. In 2005, the prison population was 4.5 times its 1980 level and the parole population was 3.5 times its 1980 level.

Historically, discretionary parole served as the principal release mechanism by which prisoners left correctional facilities, accounting for 69% of state prison releasees in 1977. In a system that allows discretionary release, a parole board assesses inmates' likelihood of reoffending by considering their criminal history, institutional conduct, and remorse and motivation to live law-abiding lives postrelease. For those inmates deemed to pose a minimal risk of reoffending, the board may grant a parole date and allow them to leave prison to complete their original sentences under terms of conditional release spelled out by the board and monitored by parole officers in the field. "Indeterminate" sentences provided a large gap between the minimum and maximum term (e.g., "2–20 years"), with the actual release date to be determined by the behavior of the inmate during incarceration. Under such sentences, the possibility of parole encouraged inmates to participate in prison-based education and treatment programs and also served to balance out disparities in sentences across offenders convicted of similar crimes.[17] Parole usually followed actions by an institutional correctional agency to "step" down inmates to lower security and prerelease programs. Daniel Glaser's influential 1964 study, "The Effectiveness of a Prison and Parole System," demonstrated the common understanding at the time that these correctional institutions and agencies operated together to form the prisoner reentry system.[18]

The late 1970s, 1980s, and 1990s ushered in new "get-tough" sentencing and correctional practices that, in some states, led to diminished use of indeterminate sentences and institutional prerelease programs. By the end of 2000, sixteen states had abolished discretionary release and, with the exception of Maine and Virginia, introduced mandatory postrelease supervision.[19] Among those states retaining discretionary release, many significantly curtailed its use.[20]

In 1994, federal legislation tied funds for prison construction and expansion to the adoption of state "truth-in-sentencing" legislation, supporting states that require violent offenders to serve 85% of their nominal sentences.[21] It had its desired effect: by 1998, twenty-seven states had such laws. Several other states passed legislation that was similar in spirit, but they did not meet the federal threshold (because they chose different minimum sentence threshold percentages and/or applied them to a different set of offenses).[22] The reforms induced by the "truth in sentencing" legislation further restricted the extent to which discretion governed the timing of inmate release. The shift from discretionary release to mandatory release has been dramatic. Of the inmates serving sentences of more than 1 year leaving state prison in 1980, 55% left by a decision of a parole board. By 2003, the percentage was 22%. Over the same period, the percent receiving mandatory parole increased from 19% to 36%.[23]

In addition to parole, probation plays a substantial role in supervising adults following release from prison. An estimated 320,000 adults were supervised by probation following incarceration, which constituted 8% of the almost 4 million adults on probation at year-end 2002.[24] This use of probation to provide postincarceration supervision represents a historical shift away from using probation as a sentencing alternative to prison, putting pressures on probation agencies because of the generally more criminally entrenched population.[25]

Variation in State Practices

Table 5.1 provides some indication of the varying scale and character of supervision across states.[26] Using year-end data from 2001, the first column reveals that five states (California, Texas, Pennsylvania, New York, and Illinois) supervise more than 60% of all parolees nationwide. Column (2) reports the number of inmates released from prison in 2001. In some cases, the number of people released in a year exceeds the number on parole; in other cases, it is far smaller. The discrepancy is accounted for by a combination of factors: the proportion of those released who have a term of parole (versus another form of supervision or none at all) and the speed at which parolees leave parole supervision by returning to prison or completing the terms of supervision. Glancing down columns (3) and (4), it is obvious that states vary greatly in the extent to which inmates are released to supervisory authorities (mostly parole, but also probation and other programs). Tremendous state-level variation underlies all general characterizations of prison release in the United States. Column (5) shows the percentage of those released by a discretionary decision of a parole board, with the timing of release for the remainder having been determined by the sentence and any "good time" earned in the institution. ("Good time" refers

TABLE 5.1. *Parole and Release Data by State, 2001*

	(1) Number of parolees	(2) Total released	(3) % Releases unconditional	(4) % Releases conditional	(5) % Releases discretionary
Alabama	5,484	7,617	47.2	52.8	26.7
Alaska	525	2,029	32.6	67.4	1.4
Arizona	3,474	8,933	22.3	77.7	3.1
Arkansas	8,659	6,515	11.3	88.7	74.0
California	117,647	126,409	2.8	97.2	0
Colorado	5,500	6,439	27.7	72.3	34.4
Connecticut	1,868	6,007	53.8	46.2	23.0
Delaware	579	2,019	74.2	25.8	0
Florida	5,982	23,527	63.0	37.0	0.4
Georgia	21,556	15,658	31.7	68.3	45.0
Hawaii	2,504	1,187	13.7	86.3	84.9
Idaho	1,409	2,521	18.5	81.5	37.2
Illinois	30,196	35,980	18.2	81.8	0.1
Indiana	4,917	11,771	10.7	89.3	0
Iowa	2,763	4,786	19.0	81.0	46.7
Kansas	3,829	4,243	26.5	73.5	70.4
Kentucky	4,614	8,034	48.2	51.8	36.1
Louisiana	22,860	14,851	6.5	93.5	8.5
Maine	28	701	36.2	63.8	0.3
Maryland	13,666	9,969	11.8	88.2	27.2
Massachusetts	3,703	2,453	75.7	24.3	24.3
Michigan	15,753	11,636	14.1	85.9	82.4
Minnesota	3,072	4,237	10.9	89.1	0.1
Mississippi	1,596	5,414	50.0	50.0	15.0
Missouri	12,563	13,782	12.7	87.3	40.9
Montana	621	1,226	21.2	78.8	40.9
Nebraska	476	1,730	59.1	40.9	40.4
Nevada	4,056	4,450	42.6	57.4	57.4
New Hampshire	944	1,026	21.0	79.0	64.8
New Jersey	11,709	15,839	33.8	66.2	61.5
New Mexico	1,670	3,182	41.6	58.4	49.9
New York	57,858	27,771	10.7	89.3	60.9
North Carolina	3,352	8,827	62.8	37.2	0
North Dakota	110	711	42.1	57.9	27.4
Ohio	18,248	24,797	34.9	65.1	22.0
Oklahoma	1,825	8,188	42.2	57.8	28.3
Oregon	17,579	3,409	0.4	99.6	98.3
Pennsylvania	82,345	10,083	30.9	69.1	69.1
Rhode Island	331	2,806	84.0	16.0	16.0
South Carolina	4,378	8,335	42.2	57.8	36.8
South Dakota	1,481	1,374	26.6	73.4	68.5

(continued)

TABLE 5.1 *(continued)*

	(1) Number of parolees	(2) Total released	(3) % Releases unconditional	(4) % Releases conditional	(5) % Releases discretionary
Tennessee	8,093	12,631	32.0	68.0	25.6
Texas	111,719	63,790	19.7	80.3	50.2
Utah	3,231	3,137	18.2	81.8	81.8
Vermont	867	1,065	17.6	82.3	36.3
Virginia	5,148	9,743	71.6	28.4	7.4
Washington	160	6,853	29.5	70.5	0.6
West Virginia	1,112	1,121	55.8	44.2	44.2
Wisconsin	9,923	6,979	9.7	90.3	26.8
Wyoming	514	716	40.1	59.9	19.7
Totals	647,829	566,507	23%	77%	25.7%

Source: Column (1) "Probation and Parole in the United States, 2001" (Washington, DC: Bureau of Justice Statistics, 2002); columns (2)–(5): calculations from National Prisoner Statistics 2001, Bureau of Justice Statistics, Washington, DC (unpublished data).

to incentives offered to inmates in many prison systems to encourage participation in work, training, and/or educational programs.)

Table 5.2 attempts to summarize the widely varying postrelease parole and supervision policies by state. It indicates which states have "truth-in-sentencing" requirements and which have retained discretionary parole for sentences. The last four columns describe the different ways states have chosen to organize postrelease supervision by branch and level of government. Whereas all states except Oregon and Pennsylvania place parole as an executive agency, sixteen states have chosen to keep probation as an arm of the judiciary at the local level. In four states, parole is also organized at the local level. Probationary technical violations processed within the court system often require a judge to make a final dispositional decision, which can lead to significant delays. Executive supervising agencies can typically process violations more swiftly.

Summary

This description of the problem of inmate release shows several dimensions of complexity. The needs of inmates are varied and serious. State policies and practices vary enormously in release policies, the extent of supervision, the specific requirements for those under supervision,

TABLE 5.2. *Parole and Probation Policies and Governing Institutions by State*

	Current truth-in-sentencing requirement[a]	Year in which state abolished all parole[b]	Whether state abolished parole for violent offenders[b]	Branch of government overseeing parole supervision*[c]	Branch of government overseeing probation supervision[c]	State/local probation supervision[c]	State/local parole supervision[c]
Alabama	None			Executive	Executive	State	State
Alaska	Other			Executive	Executive	State	State
Arizona	85%	1994	X	Executive	Judicial	Local	State
Arkansas	Other			Executive	Executive	State	State
California	85%		X	Executive	Judicial	Local	State
Colorado	Other			Executive	Judicial	Local	State
Connecticut	85%			Executive	Judicial	State	State
Delaware	85%	1990	X	Executive	Executive	State	State
Florida	85%	1983	X	Executive	Executive	State	State
Georgia	85%		X	Executive	Executive	State	State
Hawaii	None			Executive	Judicial	State	State
Idaho	100%			Executive	Executive	State	State
Illinois	85%	1978	X	Executive	Judicial	Local	State
Indiana	50%	1977	X	Executive	Executive	Local	State
Iowa	85%		X	Executive	Executive	Local	State
Kansas	85%	1993	X	Executive	Judicial	Local	State
Kentucky	Other			Executive	Executive	State	State
Louisiana	85%			Executive	Executive	State	State
Maine	85%	1975	X	Executive	Executive	State	State
Maryland	50%			Executive	Executive	State	State
Massachusetts	Other			Executive	Judicial	State	State
Michigan	85%			Executive	Executive	State	State
Minnesota	85%	1980	X	Executive	Executive	Local	State
Mississippi	85%	1995	X	Executive	Executive	State	State
Missouri	85%			Executive	Executive	State	State
Montana	Other			Executive	Executive	State	State
Nebraska	50%			Executive	Judicial	State	State
Nevada	100%			Executive	Executive	State	State
New Hampshire	100%			Executive	Executive	State	State
New Jersey	85%			Executive	Judicial	Local	State

(continued)

TABLE 5.2 *(continued)*

	Current truth-in-sentencing requirement[a]	Year in which state abolished all parole[b]	Whether state abolished parole for violent offenders[b]	Branch of government overseeing parole supervision*[c]	Branch of government overseeing probation supervision[c]	State/local probation supervision[c]	State/local parole supervision[c]
New Mexico	None			Executive	Executive	State	State
New York	85%		X	Executive	Executive	Local	State
North Carolina	85%	1994	X	Executive	Executive	State	State
North Dakota	85%			Executive	Executive	State	State
Ohio	85%	1996	X	Executive	Judicial/Executive	Local	State
Oklahoma	85%			Executive	Executive	State	State
Oregon	85%	1989	X	Judicial	Judicial	Local	Local
Pennsylvania	85%			Judicial	Judicial	Local	N/A
Rhode Island	None			Executive	Executive	State	State
South Carolina	85%			Executive	Executive	State	State
South Dakota	None			Executive	Judicial	State	State
Tennessee	85%		X	Executive	Executive	State	State
Texas	50%			Executive	Judicial	Local	Local
Utah	85%			Executive	Executive	State	State
Vermont	None			Executive	Executive	State	State
Virginia	85%		X	Executive	Executive	State	State
Washington	85%	1984	X	Executive	Judicial	Local	Local
West Virginia	None			Executive	Judicial	Local	Local
Wisconsin	Other	1999	X	Executive	Executive	State	State
Wyoming	None			Executive	Executive	State	State
Totals	50% (4) 85% (28) 100% (3) None (8) Other (7)	(14)	(20)	Executive (48) Judiciary (2)	Executive (33.5) Judiciary (16.5)	State (34) Local (16)	State (45) Local (4)

* Parole boards still have discretion over inmates who were sentenced prior to the effective date of the various states' parole abolition laws.

Source: [a] *Paula M. Ditton and Doris James Wilson, Truth in Sentencing in State Prisons (Washington, DC: Bureau of Justice Statistics, 1999);* [b] William J. Sabol, Katherine Rosich, Kamala Mallik Kane, David P. Kirk, and Glenn Dubin, *The Influence of Truth-in-Sentencing Reforms on Changes in States' Sentencing Practices and Prison Populations* (Washington, DC: Urban Institute, Justice Policy Center, 2002); [c] Peggy B. Burke, *Policy-Driven Responses to Probation and Parole Violations* (Silver Spring, MD: Center for Effective Public Policy, 1997).

and how these efforts are organized. Because of these differences, generalizing about prisoner reentry must be done with great care. At the same time, there are several truths about the buildup that appear in sharp relief when considering prisoner reentry.

THE PRISON BUILDUP THROUGH THE LENS OF PRISONER REENTRY

It is tautological that the prison buildup affected prisoner reentry by increasing the size of the release cohort. However, there are several ways in which the buildup influenced inmate release.

Sentencing Reform

In many states, beginning in the mid-1990s, sentencing reforms greatly reduced the scope for supervision of former inmates.[27] Some states set a high threshold for the proportion of the imposed sentence that must be served behind the walls before release is considered, dramatically reducing the scope for discretionary release to parole, with the result that more prisoners were released without supervision. Some states abolished discretionary release altogether.[28]

One consequence of these changes is a reduction in the incentive provided inmates to conform to expectations of nondisruptive behavior and rehabilitative efforts while in prison. Because the scope for parole was reduced, inmates had less reason to adapt their behavior to the desires of the parole board in anticipation of review of their case for discretionary release. A new analysis of policy changes in Georgia documents that possibility of discretionary release substantially improves inmate behavior.[29]

Mandatory minimum sentencing laws for various crimes further reduced the scope of a variety of mechanisms to aid prisoner reentry. In practice, sentencing under mandatory minimum laws makes it unlikely that there will be any criminal justice supervision following release because inmates must be released on the expiration of the sentenced term of confinement. One way to look at the potential scope for discretionary release is to compare the minimum sentence to the maximum sentence. If there is a large gap between the two, the parole board uses its discretion to determine the actual release date. The magnitude of the impact of mandatory sentencing can be seen in the experience of Massachusetts. Among those sentenced to state prison for offenses other than mandatory drug offenses in fiscal year 1999, 31% had minimum and maximum release dates that were less than 1 month apart. In fiscal year 1994, only 2% of such offenders had such little scope for discretionary release. For those sentenced for drug offenses under mandatory minimum sentencing laws, 57% had less than 1 month between the minimum and maximum.[30] For these offenders, Massachusetts has effectively joined those states that have legislatively eliminated or gutted postrelease supervision. In effect, the get-tough stance on prison sentences has resulted in a go-easy stance on postrelease supervision.

Restrictions on Programming

Many state legislatures further passed laws (mostly in the 1980s and 1990s) prohibiting inmates with particular offenses from participating fully in probation, parole, furlough, work release, and earned good time for particular offenses. Together, these restrictions constrain even the well-intentioned efforts of correctional administrators to prepare inmates for release. At the same time, departmental policies also restrict their own efforts to effectively address inmate release. A glimpse at a correctional population shows that these constraints can be surprisingly far reaching.

These restrictions operate through classification, the institutional process that determines where inmates reside within an institution and which programs they receive. Ideally, the process determines institutional placement by balancing the risks and needs of the inmates. Inmates who are suicidal, who have "enemies" within the institution, who are disruptive, and who fall within a number of categories, are generally placed in specialized living units. Most inmates, though, are placed in general population living units and receive an institutional service plan that requires them to participate in a variety of education, treatment programming, and work assignments. The plan is often a wish list of activities because the institution does not offer enough programs to engage fully the whole inmate population at any point in time. The classification status of an inmate is reviewed periodically, and the

TABLE 5.3. *Eligibility for a Prisoner Reentry Program, Suffolk County House of Correction*

	Male inmates (%)	Female inmates (%)
Eligibility		
Eligible	8	10
Potentially eligible	15	49
Ineligible for prerelease status	67	41
Placements		
Among those eligible	27	43

Source: Jamie Watson, *Community Corrections Programs at the Suffolk County House of Correction: Strategies for Optimizing Use While Minimizing Risk* (Cambridge, MA: Kennedy School of Government, Harvard University, 2002).

inmate is rewarded for following his or her plan by placement in living units of lower security with greater privileges (e.g., more recreation time, greater access to visits, better institutional jobs, opportunities to earn time off their sentences). In this way, the institution provides incentives for good behavior and steps inmates down from higher- to lower-custody living areas.

Tables 5.3 and 5.4 show the results of an analysis of various legal and policy restrictions on a program to help inmates prepare for release at the Suffolk County (Boston) House of Correction.[31] This particular

TABLE 5.4. *Factors That Affect Prerelease Eligibility*

Criterion	Eligibility status	Male inmates (%)	Female inmates (%)
Parole or probation violation	Review	67	61
Felony warrant/open case	Ineligible	56	40
Sentence less than 30 days	Ineligible	16	16
Misdemeanor warrant/open case	Review	12	16
Assault and battery w/ deadly weapon	Review	14	9
On and after sentence	Ineligible	10	1
Active restraining order	Ineligible	10	6
Disciplinary reports within 90 days	Ineligible	27	4

Source: Jamie Watson, *Community Corrections Programs at the Suffolk County House of Correction: Strategies for Optimizing Use While Minimizing Risk* (Cambridge, MA: Kennedy School of Government, Harvard University, 2002).

facility may not be representative of all local correctional facilities. It is a large urban facility with a mix of short-term inmates and those with longer sentences; in Massachusetts, sentences of up to 2.5 years are served in local correctional facilities. Nonetheless, the results are instructive because the processes within corrections are generally impervious to researchers studying broad trends such as prisoner reentry. Yet, as we will see, these internal processes determine the practicality of programmatic and policy reforms.

The Suffolk County study analyzed a cohort of inmates released in January 2001 to determine how many of them qualified for placement in the department's prerelease program based on criminal history and institutional conduct data, and how many of them actually were placed in these programs. As shown in Table 5.3, 67% of male inmates were ineligible for placement to the prerelease setting, 15% may have been eligible subject to an additional risk assessment review, and only 8% of the cohort were eligible for placement outright. For female inmates, the comparable percentages were 41% ineligible, 49% eligible pending review, and 10% eligible outright. Furthermore, Table 5.4 presents a breakdown of the effects of the specific classification criteria on eligibility. It reveals that external factors, such as the fact that many inmates in prison continue to have open and unresolved cases pending in addition to the convicted offense for which they are serving time, rule out 56% of male inmates and 41% of female inmates. Criteria concerning institutional conduct – inmates cannot be placed in prerelease programs if they have had a major disciplinary report 90 days prior to the classification review – excluded 27% of male inmates, yet only 4% of female inmates. Finally, even among those who were eligible for the program, the majority was not assigned to it although it was undersubscribed (see the bottom of Table 5.3): only 27% of outright eligible male inmates and 43% of outright eligible female inmates were placed in the halfway house where the program was provided.

Thus, the analysis produced two significant findings: (1) most inmates were not eligible for halfway house placement because of classification criteria that reflected internal and external circumstances, and (2) the institution – perhaps because of inefficient practices – failed to place a large number of eligible inmates into these programs.[32]

Tensions in the Goals of Law Enforcement

In recent decades, parole has moved from social service to largely surveillance,[33] although finding the right balance between supervising agents' emphasis on assistance and on control has long been an issue of inquiry.[34] The same rhetoric that drove changes in law and practice that led to the prison buildup was behind changes in law and practice toward discretionary release, mandatory postincarceration supervision, and conditions of supervision.

Although the "nothing works" cynicism is mostly past, researchers and practitioners often discuss the support functions for ex-offenders as qualitatively distinct from the surveillance functions. In a recent article, Anne Morrison Piehl and Stefan LoBuglio argue against drawing a strict dichotomy between support and surveillance.[35] The threat of surveillance can be an aid to compliance with activities to support the transition, such as substance abuse programming and employment assistance. Likewise, the support activities can provide the structure and meaning to day-to-day life that allows people to avoid situations in which they tend to get in trouble. In one sense, these activities can be "incapacitating." Inmates who choose to waive parole often explain that it is easier for them to do prison time than meet the requirements of parole. This argument extends to parole supervision the theoretical underpinning of innovations in other areas of law enforcement.[36]

If supervision is efficacious, clearly it is possible to have too little of it. Increasing its intensity, expanding its reach to more ex-offenders, or extending the length of terms could be called for. Some argue that funding for supervision relative to the number of inmates being released from incarceration has declined dramatically since the mid-1970s. This may be the case, but the detailed expenditure information needed for solid estimates is unavailable. Less frequently discussed is the possibility of providing too much supervision, either by supervising people who are very unlikely to reoffend after a term in prison or by having so many requirements that they get in the way of obtaining or retaining employment, actually impeding successful reentry. Just like with the size of the prison population, it is essential to get the scope of postincarceration "right."

Society asks all law enforcement agencies to carry out multiple goals, sometimes without much guidance when they conflict. As an example, consider the effect on corrections departments of the surge in interest of reentry. Prison systems have few incentives to worry about inmates when they leave their facilities. The challenges of providing care, custody, and control of inmate populations are considerable enough, but eminently achievable within the authority of a prison system. In comparison, the success of prisoner reentry programs depends on difficult collaborations with other agencies and also on the highly uncertain and unpredictable actions of ex-prisoners. Why would a prison system expand its mission, raising expectations for performance measurements over which it may exercise little control? From a jailer's standpoint, institutional rehabilitation programs such as education, vocation, substance abuse, and anger management can serve an important custodial function to improve the orderliness of the institution, but how and whether they reduce recidivism is of secondary concern. Programs that transition offenders gradually from confinement to release pose additional risks of prisoner escape, jeopardizing one of the core functions of prisons. Failures in prisoner reentry (escape or return to custody) are also more likely to receive outside attention than successes. These failures can impose substantial costs on correctional authorities. That correctional institutions take on prisoner reentry at all testifies to the commitment of the practitioners.

Even when a correctional agency decides to take on reentry, incentives may affect the effort's target population. For some segments of the inmate population, there will always be a tension between what has the best chance of long-term success and the short-term interests of a supervising agency not having visible "failure" on its watch. Agencies must confront such realities in program design.

This is the same tension faced by parole boards when considering an inmate for discretionary release. Decisions to grant discretionary release have an impact on individual inmates, of course, but also on the community into which they are released. Parole boards are in the position of deciding whether someone should serve the final part of his or her sentence in the community under supervision, not whether he or she is eventually to be released. Discretionary release allows parole boards to impose particular conditions on a released offender. If the inmate is released to the street unconditionally at the expiration of his or her term, the opportunity to craft an individualized program is lost. Finally, the extent to which parole boards grant discretionary release provides incentives to current and future inmates to take full advantage of their time incarcerated to improve their chances of parole release. Thus, the existence and use of a paroling authority can have an important impact on the success of rehabilitative programming within correctional facilities, and therefore on the rate of successful inmate reintegration.

Given that parole boards are responsible for inmates and for the communities into which they are released, it is not surprising that actual practice changes somewhat over time. During the same period when the number of inmates eligible for parole consideration declined, parole boards across the United States have reduced the rate at which they granted discretionary release. This change may reflect a change in public sentiment, a new view of the role of discretionary release within criminal justice, and a new fear among public officials of being seen as responsible for the release of criminal offenders. The competing tensions involved in these decisions remain the same, but different judgments have been made as to how to resolve them.

DOES PAROLE WORK?

A research report from the Urban Institute posing the question "does parole work?" has generated a spirited debate, including a symposium of reactions in *Perspectives: The Journal of the American Parole and Probation Association.*[37] The goal of the Urban Institute report was to provide the "big picture" about parole in America, using reliable information on a representative sample of inmates, collected in 1994 by the Bureau of Justice Statistics from state and federal law enforcement agencies. The study compared the recidivism rates of those released from prison to supervision (either through mandatory or discretionary release) to the recidivism rates of those who were released without postprison supervision. The Urban Institute researchers found that those parolees released under mandatory programs did no better than those inmates without supervision. Parolees released on discretionary parole were less likely to be rearrested, but this difference largely disappeared once demographic characteristics of the offenders and their criminal histories were taken into account. From these results, they concluded that "the public safety impact of supervision is minimal" for most offenders.

The Urban Institute study ambitiously tried to discern policy lessons from the available data, but the quality of the extant data defies even a sophisticated analytic approach. The report begins by distinguishing between two factors that may affect parole outcomes: the type and timing of release, and the type and extent of supervision. However, much more work is necessary before we can claim to understand the different dimensions of these two factors, especially because they frequently interact. As was hinted at previously, across the United States, requirements for those under community supervision include a mix of elements, often crafted for individual offenders. Some states leave many released from prison unsupervised, whereas others require supervision of nearly all of those released. Within states, some ex-inmates may have terms under supervision that are decades long; others may be supervised for only a few months. In addition, what constitutes supervision at any given point is subject to interpretation. Intensive supervision in one state may mean monthly contact between a parolee and an agent in a regional parole office; in another, it may mean 24-hour electronic monitoring with officers in the field checking compliance of daily itineraries. In some systems, for some inmates, a continuum of supervision sanctions exists, allowing for progressive sanctioning for offenders in noncompliance with their terms of conditional release.

The bottom line is that these differences in supervision are so great, and their application so little understood, that a research design using variation in type of supervision compares apples to oranges and finds that they are different. Knowing that the outcomes are different by supervision status is provocative, but hardly definitive. Especially in light of the fact that parole boards exist precisely to select those offenders that are "better bets" to succeed following release. Much more, or different, basic research is necessary before policy conclusions can be drawn.

Parole Success

The Urban Institute report takes one definition of effectiveness of parole: reducing recidivism. This is clearly a goal of parole supervision, but there are additional ways to operationalize the idea. Several recent reports on parole and prisoner reentry have developed the concept of parole "success" rates.[38] This statistic is defined as the number of parolees who completed their terms of supervision without having their parole revoked, being returned to jail or prison, or absconding, divided by the total number of parolees leaving parole in a given year. The success rate for the United States as a whole has hovered at just higher than 40% since the mid-1990s.[39] Those released for the first time on the current sentence are much more successful than rereleases, and discretionary releases are substantially more successful than mandatory releases.[40] These nationwide figures mask the tremendous variation across states. Massachusetts was one of two states with the highest "success" rates (83%), and California had the lowest (21%).[41]

The BJS report notes that many factors affect measured "success" and cautions that factors other than program efficacy may explain observed differences in this statistic. "When comparing State success rates for parole discharges, differences may be due to variations in parole populations, such as age at prison release, criminal history, and most serious offense. Success rates may also differ based on the intensity of supervision and the parole agency policies related to revocation of technical violators."[42] Despite these qualifications, these "success" numbers have gained a fair bit of currency in the discussion of prisoner reentry. For example, Jeremy Travis and Sarah Lawrence use the same measure to rank states, and Joan Petersilia uses them to support an argument in favor of discretionary release.

Although these authors note that there are other factors one would like to examine in order to make sense of these numbers, the qualifications have not received the same attention as the raw numbers, although they are arguably more important. Kevin Reitz criticizes these measures for being more a reflection of state policies than measures of behavior of those supervised:

> In any jurisdiction the number and rate of revocations depends to some degree on the good or bad conduct of parolees, to be sure, but it also depends at least as much on what might be called the 'sensitivity' of the supervision system to violations. Sensitivity varies with formal definitions of what constitutes a violation, the intensity of surveillance employed by parole field officers, the institutional culture of field services from place to place, and the severity of sanctions typically used upon findings of violations.[43]

If parole outcomes largely reflect policy differences in how violations are construed, then they cannot be used to evaluate the effect of policies. To assess the effectiveness of parole, we must be able to identify which part of the observed difference is the result of behavior – of those supervised and of those doing the supervising. This is a terribly difficult research challenge.

Success, as defined previously, may well be a reasonable outcome measure for a supervising agency when used with other statistics to evaluate performance. One could argue that parole agencies that improve their success rates are likely to have improved their operations. However, comparing these measures across agencies is likely to lead to large errors. For example, it is likely that a thorough analysis of Massachusetts' stellar performance on this measure is largely driven by its limited reliance on postincarceration supervision. In fact, that state is working to broaden its use of parole because officials were worried that too many inmates were released with no community supervision, the result of determinate sentencing practices, reductions in the granting of discretionary release, and inmates deciding to finish out their terms rather than seek parole hearings.[44]

Release Type and Supervision Outcomes

A similar approach has been used to assess the efficacy of different approaches to prison release, comparing the "success" of those released by a discretionary release process to the outcomes of those released at the completion of their sentences. The fundamental problem with this inference is that it does not account for how individuals are assigned to release status. That is, inmates who are released at the discretion of a parole board are likely to have a lower risk of recidivism than inmates whom a parole board chooses not to release.[45]

Further complicating matters is the variety of statutes that govern whether inmates with given criminal histories are eligible for discretionary release; differences in these laws across states will affect average success measures by release type. Research on this topic does not generally investigate whether discretionary release was available for those who were released at the expiration of their sentences.

Given that it is not straightforward to compare the effect of release type on the effectiveness of supervision in controlling the criminal behavior of those released from prison, what can be said about the connection between release policy and supervision? Mandatory release may or may not lead to a period of postincarceration supervision.

Discretionary release generally leads to supervision for at least several months, or the parole board would not take time to hear the case. When faced with an inmate who appears to pose risk for public safety, a parole board must trade off the benefits and costs of discretionary release, as well as the supervision opportunities it provides, against the benefits and costs of keeping the inmate incarcerated until the maximum release date. For better or worse, under a policy of mandatory release, these tradeoffs are not considered on a case-by-case basis. Inherently, discretionary release works against the notion that those least equipped to reintegrate should be subject to a period of postrelease supervision from prison. Mandatory release polices not only provide a greater certainty that these individuals will receive supervision, but they also raise a secondary resource allocation question. Certainly, if supervising all prisoners dilutes the intensity of supervision of high-risk offenders and needlessly interferes with the reintegration process of low-risk offenders, it could prove costly and counterproductive.

Critics of mandatory release call for a return to discretionary release in order to increase the incentives to encourage rehabilitative behavior among prisoners and to balance disparities in sentences across offenders and jurisdictions.[46] In the end, the issue of whether discretionary release is preferable to mandatory release has many dimensions in addition to its relationship to successful reentry following release from prison. From the perspective of reentry and public safety, release policy is important both to how parole outcomes are interpreted and to how other aspects of reentry and supervision are designed. Most states have some people released under the discretion of a parole board and others at the end of their sentences. This situation is a direct relic of the prison buildup. Our current prisoner reentry policy problem cannot be addressed without either developing a way to support reentry in a system that contains multiple release types or reconsidering some of the legislation that led to these conditions.

Measuring the Impact of Supervision

An ideal test of whether postrelease supervision of recent inmates reduces the probability of criminal reoffending would be based on the random assignment of a pool of soon-to-be released prisoners to either a treatment group that would provide postrelease supervision or a control group that would have no supervision. With random assignment, a simple comparison of the rates of criminal activity between the two groups would seem to provide definitive evidence on the effect of supervision. Unfortunately, there is a problem even with this research design: the outcome – recidivism – is intrinsically linked with supervision. In practice, increased supervision will likely lead to the detection of more rule violations and new criminal offenses. Even if a parole officer emphasized treatment and downplayed supervision, he or she could not easily ignore observed crimes or serious rule infractions. Furthermore, in nonexperimental studies comparing the postrelease criminal activity of offenders released under discretionary parole with those released under mandatory parole or released without supervision, selection bias proves problematic in drawing a reliable inference. Parole boards will generally grant parole to those offenders who pose the least risk of reoffending and would be expected to have fewer arrests, on average, than those offenders who were turned down for parole and those who received mandatory parole. This follows from parole board members doing their jobs as charged.

Another challenge to research in this area comes from difficulty in comparing offenders in prison to those under supervision. No matter how effective supervision services are, the risk to public safety will always be greater if an individual is supervised in the community rather than in prison. Studies of offender supervision typically compare offenders under different intensities and mixes of surveillance and treatment services. Necessarily, some behavior will be sanctioned by additional time behind bars. If there is any difference in the extent to which alternative programs rely on incarceration, then the outcomes are incomparable. Without a way to adjust for the differences in risk of further criminal activity or even violating conditions of supervision, it is impossible to credibly compare alternative supervision schemes over a substantial period of time.

In their review of the literature on the effectiveness of parole supervision, Piehl and LoBuglio found several instances of randomized research designs.[47] In the 1950s, Richard McGee, a noted penologist and then-director of the California Department of Corrections, initiated a number of randomized research studies to determine the effectiveness of early parole as a function of offender risk and parole officer caseloads in California. From a cost–benefit perspective, McGee concluded that intensive supervision was effective for offenders who were on the margin of choosing between criminal and law-abiding behaviors and not effective for either low-risk offenders who may not have needed additional supervision to succeed or high-risk offenders who probably would have failed regardless of the nature of the supervision.[48]

The 1980s saw a resurgence of states' interests in intensive supervision programs (ISPs), efforts to increase the intensiveness of community supervision as a relatively low-cost intermediate alternatives to vastly overcrowded prisons. From 1986 to 1991, the National Institute of Justice funded the Rand Corporation to conduct a large randomized experiment of ISP programs in fourteen sites in nine states to assess their cost effectiveness. As reported by Joan Petersilia and Susan Turner, who designed and oversaw the implementation of this evaluation, at the end of the 1-year follow-up, 37% of the ISP treatment group had been rearrested as compared to 33% of the control group. Sixty-five percent of ISP offenders experienced a technical violation compared to 38% of the controls. Also, 27% of ISP offenders were recommitted to prison compared to 19% of the controls.[49]

There are two ways to interpret these findings: either the program led to increased criminal behavior of those under heightened supervision (in the opposite direction of the anticipated effect) or the increased surveillance led to an increased probability of detection. If the latter is true, it is impossible to know whether there was in fact a deterrent effect that was overwhelmed by the surveillance effect. Also, the researchers speculated that the ISP might have sanctioned these infractions more harshly in an effort to shore up the credibility of the program. This, too, would obscure any true deterrent effect.

Although the evaluation could not provide any definitive evidence that increased supervision intensity provided public safety benefits, the highly elevated rate of technical violations for those in the treatment group suggests that the surveillance did in fact increase the rate of detection. Then the interesting question becomes whether technical violations are a proxy for criminal behavior. Experience in Washington State in the mid-1980s from a program that decreased the average number of conditions of release for probationers and deemphasized the sanctions for technical violations does not support this hypothesis.[50] Specifically, the legislature required that courts only impose conditions of supervision that were related to the offenders' past criminal behaviors. This policy change led to a drop in the number of conditions, a drop in the number of revocations due to technical violations, and no increase in the arrest rate.[51]

Despite the experience of hundreds of intensive supervision programs in the United States and many studies, albeit few experimental, we still know little about the effectiveness of these programs to reduce prison overcrowding or to reduce crime in detectable ways. The same issues that hinder our learning from many criminal justice practices are at work here. There is no consistency in the design and implementation of ISP programs; their surveillance and monitoring practices, caseloads, and their incorporation of rehabilitative requirements vary significantly both within and between programs. Some researchers have found that judges begin filling ISPs with lower-risk offenders who are not prison-bound – so-called "net widening" – and believe that the investment of additional supervision resources for this population can backfire and lead to increased rates of violations and reincarceration. However, if ISPs serve to enforce release conditions that were not previously being enforced under standard probation, and the detected infractions were directly or indirectly related to criminal activity, there could be a public safety benefit. Similarly, ISPs may serve to ensure the quicker detection and apprehension of violations by higher-risk offenders. Also, as McGee found, it is entirely possible that these programs may deter criminal offending from those offenders who are at the margins of choosing between licit and illicit behaviors. However, the bottom line is that the public safety benefit of these intensive supervision programs relies on two mechanisms that have yet to be proved: the deterrence value of supervision and the value of technical violations to prevent crime.

More than in most arenas, the study of prisoner release confounds the usual research designs. There are ways, however, to respond to this challenge. We could systematically collect information that does not depend so heavily on policy differences, such as reports of behavior and whether it is sanctioned in a particular jurisdiction. We could systematically collect and aim to understand those very policy differences that we observed in the studies discussed in this chapter. We could also much more effectively use the money that is available for experimentation and research in this field, rather than allocating it for political reasons.[52]

THE CHALLENGE OF PRISONER REENTRY

Mass incarceration produced the current problem of prisoner reentry – a policy problem of how to successfully incorporate nearly 700,000 released felons each year into American community life that owes its size and character to the prison buildup. Those leaving the nation's prisons have stubbornly high rates of recidivism. Those who "churn" through prison and parole are increasingly large proportions of both systems.

At the same time, the changes to the prison system that caused and accompanied the buildup constrain our ability to effectively address prisoner reentry. The sentencing reforms, along with changes in practice toward greater caution (of parole boards, governors, corrections commissioners, and others), mean that what were once viable options for aiding the transition from prison to civilian life are no longer available. One example of this is that many reentry programs are undersubscribed despite their small size relative to the prison population.

The previous discussion noted many challenges in taking the research findings on prisoner reentry to policy recommendations. However, the growing literature on prisoner reentry and the many local, state, and federal initiatives to address it, has succeeded at highlighting the myriad consequences of the prison buildup. Arguably, its impact has been greater than that of the literature directed to the buildup itself. Pragmatism has been paramount.

We have also observed great variation in reentry programs and policies from one state to the next. One way to understand this variation is as an instance of democratic experimentation, in which subnational governments try out different programs and strategies. These experiments will generate new knowledge about what works best. Another way to understand the variation is that parole remains in the earliest stages of a learning curve. No single model has yet proved itself superior. Over time, a consensus may emerge, mainly through trial and error. Repeated errors can be minimized through careful evaluation.

CHAPTER SIX

Impact of the Buildup on the Labor Market

> The population of offenders is a relatively permanent part of American society – an "underclass" problem group that will not disappear naturally.[1]

The U.S. economy has performed extraordinary well since the mid-1990s, in regard to unemployment. In April 2000, the unemployment rate dropped to less than 4% for the first time in 30 years.[2] Gains for African Americans have been especially impressive. In January 1985, the black jobless rate was 15.2% compared to a white jobless rate of 6.3%, a gap of nearly 9 percentage points. In August 2007, the unemployment rate was 4.2% for whites and 7.7% for blacks. The racial gap of 3.5 percentage points is far below its 1985 level.

Recently, a number of researchers have begun to suspect a link of considerable magnitude between the declining unemployment rate and the increased use of imprisonment during roughly the same period.[3] A related literature deals with the impact of imprisonment and wage inequality between whites and African Americans.[4]

Labor force statistics (including the unemployment rate) play a central role in the development of formal and informal judgments about the performance of the economy and the society. Yet, these statistics exclude the institutionalized population. Incarceration rates vary greatly across geography, time, and demographic group, so whether the incarcerated population is included in these calculations can affect comparisons across these dimensions. If a population or a demographic subpopulation is incarcerated at a high rate, then the calculated unemployment rate will overstate the degree to which the population or subpopulation is successfully engaged in the legal economy. Moreover, because groups doing poorly in the economy are likely to have higher than average incarceration rates, estimates of cross-group inequality in unemployment will likewise be understated.[5] For example, in the United States, African Americans' reductions in unemployment may be a product of their increasing imprisonment rather than a genuine improvement in employment. The same phenomenon occurs when unemployment rates are used to compare nations' economic performances. Rankings of countries that have incarcerated an increasing proportion of a difficult to employ subpopulation, such as the United States, may be misleading.[6] The United States may appear to be doing well in keeping down its unemployment rate, but this may be only because increasingly large numbers of the otherwise unemployed are behind bars.

In this chapter, we consider the quantitative importance of such concerns. How much, in fact, has the buildup contributed to the apparent performance of the U.S. economy? We find that the literature has overstated the magnitude of the effect of the prison buildup. More realistic estimates of the proportion of inmates who would be working if they were not incarcerated reduce the impact of including inmates in the unemployment statistic. Our estimates are approximately midway between the Bureau of Labor Statistics (BLS) unemployment rates (the standard ones, as cited previously) and the values reported in other studies. We further conclude that although these thought experiments draw attention to the inmate population, they are of limited value for assessing criminal justice or economic policy. At first glance, these recalculations seem startling, but there is less to them in substantive significance then initially meets the eye.

We then turn to another impact of the buildup: the causal impact of incarceration on the employment of ex-inmates. There are several reasons to think that this is negative. Whether it is because prisons are "schools for crime," because confinement leads to a decay in human capital and the social networks used to find jobs, because of the negative labeling of ex-prison inmates, or because of legal prohibitions on postconviction occupations, an individual's subsequent employment is predicted to be lower than it would have been without the period of incarceration. However, many of those incarcerated have few labor market skills, so perhaps these factors do not translate into substantial effects. Or perhaps these negative effects occur in the first several years after release, but then dissipate. Although the provision of prison-based programs has been criticized previously in this book as being too meager, these opportunities are intended to improve labor market outcomes of inmates who participate in them. It is also conceivable that incarceration affects unemployment at the aggregate level. If a state or region had particularly high incarceration rates and consequently a reduced availability of low-wage labor to the legal sector, it might be less attractive as a business locale. Thus, criminal justice policy could affect economic development.

To assess the impact of incarceration on aggregate employment, we review the studies that use individual-level data to assess the impact of prison on the labor market and then provide fresh evidence on the effect of incarceration on unemployment using aggregate, state-level data from the United States. This allows us to take advantage of the substantial cross-state variation in both incarceration and economic outcomes. Because of concerns about the measurement issues discussed as follows, we seek to explain both unemployment rates and employment-population rates. Also, because it is possible that the short- and long-run impacts of incarceration on economic measures are different, we pay particular attention to issues of timing throughout the empirical work.

The results of our regression analyses of state-level panel data reveal that neither the exclusion of inmates from the employment statistics nor a long-run negative relationship between incarceration and employment are discernible in aggregate data. We conclude that there are other important general equilibrium relationships to be considered when evaluating the economywide effects of incarceration on employment.

SHOULD EMPLOYMENT STATISTICS INCLUDE PRISONERS?

In a period of stability in the relative size and composition of the prison population, how inmates are incorporated into the calculation of unemployment statistics is unlikely to be of much practical importance. However, in a time of change in the prison population, and especially in a time of rapid change, the details of the calculation of aggregate statistics could potentially introduce large biases for some of the uses of the statistics. If policy decisions or popular judgments are informed by the reported numbers, it is possible for a seemingly technical issue of measurement to have real world consequences. Reformers are inclined to fix only things that appear to be "broken." Therein lays the importance of getting unemployment measured "right."

The official unemployment rate is calculated by the U.S. Department of Labor each month for each state using data collected by the Current Population Survey (CPS) from a representative sample of 50,000 households.[7] The unemployment statistic is a measure of "slack" in the labor side of the economy and attempts to capture the proportion of the population available for work but not currently employed. To do this, the CPS survey questions are designed to ascertain who is "in the labor force," meaning those currently working plus those not working but currently available and actively looking for work. The number available and actively looking for work is used as the numerator for the unemployment rate; the denominator is that group plus those working. Given that prison and jail inmates are not available to start work immediately, they (and other institutionalized populations, such as people in long-term care hospitals and nursing homes) are omitted from the calculation of the official unemployment rate.[8]

The designation "in the labor force" is sometimes seen as problematic because it may not capture the full size of the population that might be willing to work under the right circumstances. For example, a weak economy may discourage workers from seeking work. However, these discouraged workers might be immediately available if employment prospects and working conditions improved. To remedy this potential bias, another statistic is often used. The "employment-population ratio" is the number of employed people divided by the number of noninstitutionalized individuals in the population. The disadvantage of this latter statistic is that certain groups may genuinely withdraw from employment.[9] They may instead choose to raise children, return to school, or care for elderly parents, for example.

Over time, the unemployment rate has achieved the status as a summary measure of the health of the economy. It is for this reason, we believe, that various authors have become interested in recalculating its value to account for incarceration. For example, Bruce Western and Katherine Beckett undertake such a recalculation to compare the performance of the U.S. versus European economies.[10] Any recalculation is a thought experiment that attempts to provide the numerical value of the statistic if it were to be conceived in a different way. But before recalculating the unemployment statistics to incorporate incarceration, it is useful to distinguish more carefully among the questions the unemployment rate is asked to answer.

As noted previously, the question the traditional unemployment rate is designed to answer is "what is the supply of potential labor?" To answer this question, it seems appropriate to omit those behind bars from the numerator and denominator because inmates are unavailable to begin legal sector work in response to an increase in demand for workers.[11] Given that slack in the economy is generally measured relative to the size of the economy, reporting the number of unemployed relative to those in the legitimate labor force also argues for keeping inmates out of the denominator of the unemployment statistic.

One question posed by the literature on incarceration and unemployment statistics is "what would the unemployment rate be in the absence of incarceration?" Answering this question requires making assumptions about how many of the current inmates would be in the labor force, and how many of them would be employed, if they were not incarcerated. There are a number of reasonable approaches one could take to estimating that value, as we discuss later in this chapter. In general, research of this type compares the official unemployment rate to a rate adjusted to account for prisoners. The difference between these two rates is then taken as a measure of the amount of economically productive labor that is lost because of imprisonment.

A second question raised in this literature is "how well are all citizens integrated into the society and economy?" This question expects the unemployment rate to proxy for a much broader phenomenon than do the other formulations. One strand of research, for example, seeks to link high rates of unemployment to participation in social movements and collective violence.[12] In any case, answering this second broader question requires a somewhat different treatment of inmates in the recalculation of the unemployment rate.

We now consider several efforts to assess the impact of incarceration on unemployment. One strategy is to recalculate the unemployment rate based on different notions about how best to incorporate prison inmates into that recalculation.

Using the Unemployment Rate to Compare the United States to Europe

In an important paper, Bruce Western and Katherine Beckett compared the unemployment rate in the United States to other advanced economies without such heavy use of incarceration, using the traditional unemployment rate and two adjusted measures.[13] For the United States and thirteen other Organisation for Economic Co-operation and Development (OECD) countries, they calculated two different counterfactuals: they (1) used the proportion of prisoners who were unemployed prior to their imprisonment to estimate an adjustment to the numerator and denominator of the official unemployment rate, yielding a measure of the "unemployment rate that would be obtained if the incarceration rate was zero"[14]; and (2) added all prisoners to the denominator of the official unemployment rate, yielding a measure of the "unemployment rate that would be obtained if the definition of unemployed were extended to include [all] those incarcerated."[15] When these calculations are done, the currently low U.S. unemployment rate is raised toward the level found in the other OECD nations because the United States imprisons a much higher proportion of its population. The implication drawn is that the western European economies are doing just as well as the U.S. economy, despite the stronger system of welfare protections in the former.

The raw comparison of unemployment rates to incarceration rates across countries is startling. As reported by Western and Beckett, in European countries, the ratio of unemployed males-to-male inmates runs between 20:1 and 50:1. In the United States, this ratio was less than 3 to 1.[16] Thus, it is not surprising that adding the number of inmates in prison to both the numerator and the denominator, as they did in constructing the second counterfactual, raises the unemployment rate substantially in the United States, but not in European countries. Using this comparison, the U.S. unemployment rate does not fall consistently below the European average until 1992, when the "raw" unemployment rate had crossed in 1984.[17]

What is less remarked on by Western and Beckett is that the first counterfactual leads to a much less dramatic alteration of the standard picture given by unadjusted unemployment rates. The unemployment rate adjusted to reflect the extent to which inmates are more likely to be unemployed closely mirrors the "raw" rate and, in fact, the Europe–America differences using the two statistics are quite close to each other in the 1990s.

Given the dramatic findings from the second counterfactual, we need to consider what has been gained by this new measure of unemployment, now taking into account the incarcerated population in both the numerator and the denominator. Such a statistic is best viewed, it seems to us, as a measure of the "loss of productive capacity" of a society. This notion is much broader than "unemployment," even though the unemployment rate is often used as its proxy. If one were to define a statistic to measure that broader notion, it is unlikely that the end product would be their proposed measure because there are many people who are not captured in "the labor force" who by all rights ought to be considered for inclusion. They would include the disabled, those discouraged from seeking work, homemakers caring for young children, and capable retirees. In addition, some of the officially employed may be underused.[18]

It is useful to compare the Western and Beckett results to other efforts to assess the productive loss due to incarceration. One recent effort to measure the productive loss due to incarceration for the United States is provided by Jeffrey Kling and Alan Krueger.[19] Their analysis focuses on the loss to the gross domestic product (GDP) of restrictions on inmate labor. At least in principle, all or nearly all inmates could have day jobs, although this would require changes in federal law that severely restrict inmate employment and would have to get around security problems associated with inmate labor. Nonetheless, Kling and Krueger provide another benchmark from a question similar in scope to Western and Beckett's. They conclude that "permitting inmate labor would likely increase national output, but by less than 0.2% of Gross Domestic Product."[20] Because of the assumptions made to perform the calculations, this number is likely substantially overstated. For example, it assumed that no inmates currently work and that all inmates would work if policy were changed. Yet, the calculated contribution to GDP is still quite small.

In summary, direct assessment of the numbers of inmates in the United States reveals them to be large, in absolute terms, in comparison to historical rates of incarceration and in comparison to the experience of other countries. At the same time, the various calculations of the unemployment rate to account for this large incarcerated population are not very informative. Unless extreme assumptions are made (and sometimes, even then, too), the calculations reveal that the population incarcerated is not so large that it has a great impact on statistics representing the total population or the aggregate economy.

Using the Unemployment Rate to Assess the Strength of the U.S. Economy

Two other papers, by Bruce Western and Becky Pettit[21] and Lawrence Katz and Alan Krueger,[22] raised the concern that the omission of prisoners from the statistics overstates the recent strength of the U.S. economy. Western and Pettit were particularly concerned that cross-group comparisons understate the labor market disadvantage of African Americans. To analyze this, they took an approach similar to the second of the counterfactuals from the Western and Beckett cross-country analysis,[23] adjusting the CPS data to reflect the incarceration experience of various subpopulations. Their adjustments involved revising the employment-population ratio by adding estimates of the number of inmates falling into certain demographic categories to the subpopulation denominator.

Western and Pettit concluded that standard "labor force surveys overestimate the incidence of employment and underestimate employment inequality."[24] They recalculated employment-population ratios for various groups of the population. Because the likelihood of incarceration is not distributed uniformly, the adjustments are larger for some groups than for others. Furthermore, as the incarceration rate has increased over time, the adjustments have increased as well. They concluded that the omission of incarcerated populations understates the black–white employment gap for young high school dropouts by 45%, more than double the adjustment for the period before 1990.[25]

Given the extent to which incarceration risk is concentrated among particular demographic groups, this analysis provides a useful and valid caution to those who would use employment statistics to make broad judgments about social progress.

However, the Western and Pettit exercise ignores the employment propensity of those behind bars. Rather, their numbers include all prisoners in the potential labor force, similar to the Western and Beckett exercise that led to a change in the cross-country comparisons.[26] Katz and Krueger,[27] in contrast, used an approach that emphasizes the fact that inmates are at higher risk of unemployment, and, therefore, high rates of incarceration will credit the economy with strength it does not deserve, but this credit is moderated by the fact that prisoners are below-average employees.

Katz and Krueger were particularly concerned that the time-series improvement in unemployment is overstated in traditional statistics.[28] For their counterfactual, Katz and Krueger used an estimate of the unemployment rate of inmates if they were not incarcerated of 0.65. This is obviously much higher than the civilian unemployment rate. Katz and Krueger incorporated this estimate into adjusted unemployment rates for a range of possible labor force participation rates for inmates. With a labor force participation rate for inmates near 0.4, their incorporation of inmates into the statistics yields little change from the official numbers. If the labor force participation rate were 0.7, as our reading of the data suggests, the adjusted unemployment rate was 0.073 in 1985 and 0.052 in 1998. These should be compared to the reported rates of 0.070 in 1985 and 0.044 in 1998. Using the adjusted numbers, the decrease in the unemployment rate over this period is 0.021, which is 15% lower than the improvement one would have concluded with the reported (unadjusted) numbers.

For their estimate of the unemployment rate of inmates, Katz and Krueger relied on the preincarceration employment rates reported by Jeffrey Kling, a less than optimal choice, because his sample consists only of defendants in federal criminal cases in California.[29] Yet, numbers from nationally representative samples of both federal and state prisoners are available in surveys conducted approximately every 5 years by the BJS. Furthermore, "employment" in Kling's study is defined as nonzero earnings recorded by the California

Unemployment Insurance system.[30] There are many reasons that unemployment insurance records underestimate the extent of employment: mobility across state lines, self-employment, employment in sectors not covered by unemployment insurance, etc. The same inmate surveys mentioned previously contain self-report information on employment status prior to incarceration. As such, this source is reasonably comparable to the CPS.[31]

Western and Beckett relied on the surveys of inmates of prisons and some additional surveys of inmates of jails to arrive at their estimate of the proportion of inmates unemployed.[32] Rather than the 0.65 unemployment rate used by Katz and Krueger, they read the surveys to provide a best estimate of 0.36. When they adjusted the U.S. data in 1995 using this figure, they found the unemployment rate increased by 0.5 percentage points, which is a 9% increase in its value.

RECALCULATING THE UNEMPLOYMENT RATE

It is possible to improve on the estimates of both studies. As mentioned previously, the inmate surveys provide more representative information than the Kling sample. Furthermore, the inmate surveys asked inmates if they had been unemployed and whether they were looking for work. Therefore, one can construct a measure of labor force participation so one can arrive at a measure of unemployment for inmates that comes quite close to the one used in the statistics for the civilian population. If the purpose is to adjust unemployment statistics, comparing apples to apples is a virtue.

For our own illustrative calculation, summary statistics are derived from the 1991 *Survey of State Inmates* conducted by the BJS, and used in previous chapters. That survey reported that 67% of inmates were employed at the time of arrest for the crime for which they were imprisoned. Among the 33% who were not employed, nearly one-half were looking for work.[33] The unemployment rate is then $0.155/(0.155 + 0.67) = 19\%$. Although much higher than the civilian unemployment rate, this number is substantially lower than the estimates used by both Katz and Krueger and Western and Beckett.[34] Table 6.1 reports some simple recalculations using our more realistic number for the unemployment rate for inmates. We report here consistently calculated

TABLE 6.1. *Adjustments to U.S. Male Unemployment Rate to Incorporate the Incarcerated Population*

					Adjusted unemployment rates		
	No. employed	No. unemployed	No. incarcerated	Civilian male unemployment rate	Western and Beckett ($p = 0.36$)	Katz and Krueger ($p = 0.38$)	Our estimates ($p = 0.19$)
1985	59,891,000	4,521,000	692,600	0.070	0.073	0.073	0.071
1995	67,377,000	3,983,000	1,583,046	0.056	0.062	0.063	0.059
1998	70,693,000	3,266,000	1,715,730	0.044	0.051	0.052	0.047
Change: 1998–1985				−0.026	−0.022	−0.022	−0.024

adjusted male unemployment rates using three different assumptions for the unemployment rate for inmates: (1) the Western and Beckett assumption, (2) the Katz and Krueger assumption, and (3) our own assumed value of 19%, as calculated previously. We report revised calculations for 3 years: 1985, 1995, and 1998. In 1998, the official civilian unemployment rate was 4.4%. The recalculations using the approaches of Western and Beckett and Katz and Krueger yield revised statistics of 5.1% and 5.2%, respectively. Our revision is 4.7%. This shows that more realistic estimates of the proportion of inmates who would be working if they were not incarcerated changes the magnitude of the effect, although, of course, not the direction. Our estimates are approximately midway between the BLS unemployment rates, on the one hand, and the values reported in Katz and Krueger and Western and Beckett, on the other hand.

More recent data show even higher employment rates for inmates. In the 2004 *Survey of Inmates*, 72% report they were employed in the month prior to their current arrest and, as in previous years, nearly one-half of those without jobs were looking for work. This yields a 14% unemployment rate for inmates. Adjusting the civilian unemployment rate for men with these figures would increase measured unemployment from 5.6% to 5.8%, again a modest increase.

Value of Recalculating the Unemployment Rate

Importantly, these various exercises are thought experiments and nothing more. They are worthwhile reminders that when we use labor force statistics to assess how we are doing, we are omitting a large segment of the population. They also call attention to the fact that incarceration involves the loss of a great deal of productive capacity. Other sorts of "social productivity," such as volunteer work, may be lost as well. However, by themselves, these thought experiments do not recommend any particular course of action, a point sometimes missed in the literature. In addition to those behind bars, the unemployment rate also omits children, persons who are elderly, persons with disabilities, and their unpaid caregivers. Yet, any policy implications of these exclusions depend on the other values and interests that are being served by those exclusions. For example, concurrent with the prison buildup has been a large increase in the numbers of workers receiving

Social Security Disability Insurance (SSDI), after Congress loosened the standards in the late 1980s and early 1990s.[35] SSDI takes workers out of the officially counted labor force, and because many who qualify are already not working, a liberal SSDI policy lowers the unemployment rate. Whether this change "artificially" lowers the unemployment rate depends on the legitimacy of the purpose being served.[36]

Moreover, although thought experiments can, by fiat, exclude extraneous (to the researcher) considerations, real policy changes cannot. In the present context, it would seem necessary to consider the effects on crime of any change in the imprisonment rate – just as the policy recommendation to include children, homemakers, or people who are elderly in the labor force would have a host of effects to consider. Western and Beckett dismiss this concern by asserting that prison is not "about" crime control. They contend that, because crime rates and imprisonment rates do not covary over time, imprisonment rates cannot be "about" crime control. ("U.S. incarceration trends are only loosely connected to the level of criminal activity."[37]) Yet, this position must be rejected because the effect of prison rates on crime rates is under contention, with at least some studies finding a modest negative effect, as does Chapter 3. Moreover, these studies are concerned with marginal increases in the number of prisoners – not the release of the most serious offenders. The effect of the thought experiment, if actually carried out, would be to vastly increase the crime rate because the most serious offenders would be included in the mass release.

Recalculations of the unemployment rate to include the incarcerated population can be quite important in a period of changing rates of incarceration, or when the distribution of the risk of incarceration is quite skewed, *but only to the extent that the unemployment rate is being used as a gauge of the state of economic or social standing of the population.* As a result, recalculations of official statistics can be illustrative. However, it is not clear to us that these scenarios have any direct implications or suggestions for public policy that are not contained in the raw numbers themselves. That is, it is useful to know the unemployment rate calculated in the standard manner and then, as a separate issue, discuss whether it is wise or unwise to force or induce into the economy homemakers, prisoners, persons with disabilities, or workers in the first several years past the standard retirement age.

DO HIGH RATES OF PRISON LEAD TO HIGH RATES OF UNEMPLOYMENT?

A related question is what effect incarceration has on aggregate unemployment in the longer term. If there are labeling effects due to a prison record, or scarring effects due to negative experiences while in prison, or if the time out of the labor market degrades prisoners' abilities to find jobs through social networks on release, unemployment rates will increase because there are more and more ex-prisoners in the population. Thus, the omission of inmates from unemployment statistics makes the short run look somewhat rosier than it should and, furthermore, masks the negative long-run consequences for unemployment.

Individual-Level Evidence on Unemployment and Incarceration

This line of argument is stated briefly in Katz and Krueger and is more fully developed by Western and Beckett (in an article) and Western (in a recent book), who claim to test it empirically.[38] The empirical strategy involves the use of data from a longitudinal data set of American youth (the National Longitudinal Survey of Youth [NLSY]) to estimate the long-term effects of imprisonment on unemployment. The results presented by Western and Beckett are less supportive of the theory than their text indicates, although a more recent calculation by Western suggests that the effects may be stronger. In the Western and Beckett calculation, only juvenile, not adult, imprisonment has a substantial, negative effect on long-term future employment, meaning that juveniles who are incarcerated will do far less well than their cohorts who are not. With regard to adult offenders, there is a bit of evidence that employment is lower after release from adult incarceration. However, the early negative effects, those that occur in the first and second years after release, could easily be incapacitation given the imprecise nature of the variable proxying incarceration. The "long run" they identify is year 3 and maybe year 4, and here imprisonment has a measurable but very small impact on employment. As Western and Beckett put it, the negative effects of adult incarceration on employment "decay within three to four years of release."[39] Because Western and Beckett's key arguments all pertain to adult corrections, there is little in this set of results that supports their position. Moreover, juvenile corrections has not experienced the growth that adult corrections has experienced,[40] further undercutting the dynamic that Western and Beckett propose drives the nexus linking incarceration to more unemployment. The findings do not justify a strong conclusion that prison has a long-term negative impact on employment.

Western's more recent publication finds stronger effects of prison on future earnings. He conducts two analyses. In the first, Western breaks out NLSY survey respondents who, at age 27 years, had been incarcerated.[41] He then calculates their hourly wages, number of weeks employed, and annual earnings per year, both before and after incarceration. These calculations are done separately for whites, Hispanics, and blacks. The negative effects of imprisonment on wages appear modest, depending in part on race/ethnicity. Wages decreased from $10.25 to $9.25 per hour for blacks and from $12.30 to $10.31 for Hispanics. For whites, there was a tiny increase, from $11.40 to $11.80. However, incarceration effects on annual employment (number of weeks worked per year), and thus annual earnings, are quite large. The drop in the number of weeks worked was largest for whites, from 37 to 23. (This may explain the slight increase in white wages because only the "better" white employees stay in the labor force.) For Hispanics and blacks, the number of weeks worked decreased, respectively, from 35 to 24 and 35 to 21. Annual earnings, a more general measure of standard of living, dropped from $13,340 to $7,020 for blacks, from $13,290 to $9,140 for Hispanics, and from $13,700 to $9,760 for whites. It would be useful to know whether the annual earning penalty persists over time, or decays for those not reimprisoned, but Western does not report this. (Interestingly, across racial groups, those who will be imprisoned in the future have roughly equal annual earnings: $13,340 for blacks, $13,290 for Hispanics, and $13,700 for whites.)

In the second analysis, Western identified a group of NLSY respondents who had been involved in crime at an early age, but had never been sent to prison. This comparison group either had trouble with the law as juveniles or spent time in jail but was not later incarcerated. This research design presumes that the comparison group is similar to those who would ultimately serve time in prison, permitting Western to isolate the independent effect of incarceration. To account for any difference in the two groups that did exist, a regression analysis to predict career outcomes controlled for several other factors, including education, work experience, drug use, and education. Separate analyses were conducted for whites, Hispanics, and blacks. The effects of imprisonment appear quite large on hourly wages, weeks worked per year, and annual income. For example, black ex-offenders were paid 12.4% less than crime-involved but not incarcerated respondents, and had their annual income reduced by 36.9%. For Hispanics, incarceration reduced their hourly wages by 24.7%, and annual incomes were reduced by 32.2%. Finally, for whites, wages were reduced by 16.3%, and annual income was lowered by 35.8%. Although Western controlled for many factors, if ex-inmates are really different than those not sent to prison in temperament, abilities, presentation of self, and disposition to commit future crimes, control factors may not be able to pick up these differences. Comparing prisoners to those individuals with troubled pasts but who did not go to prison may still be comparing apples and oranges, even in the presence of those control variables that are available.

Jeffrey Kling's research, in contrast, finds that those who are incarcerated for longer terms suffer no adverse employment outcomes relative to those incarcerated for shorter terms.[42] Kling has a better research design than the earlier studies because he is able to use the random assignment of criminal cases to judges to ensure that the effect of incarceration he identifies is the result of sentence length and not some other characteristic that differs between the comparison group and the treatment group. At the same time, he obtains a reliable estimate of the effect of more prison time, not the effect of going to prison versus some lesser sanction. Interestingly, although Kling finds "no substantial evidence of a negative effect of incarceration length on employment or earnings"[43] for as long as 9 years after release from prison, he finds some short-run positive impacts. In the first year or two after release, employment and earnings are higher for those with longer sentences, an effect that is partially explained by conditions of corrections such as time in a work release center. These results provide a strong counterpoint to the earlier findings of a negative impact of incarceration and are consistent with other results in the literature documenting that inmates tend to have poor employment outcomes both before and after release from prison.[44]

In summary, the work in this area has failed to establish large negative effects of incarceration on individual-level employment outcomes. Before we turn to the evidence regarding mass incarceration's impacts on the overall economy, one other set of studies merits review.

Measuring the Impact of Imprisonment on Unemployment through Gauging Acts of Discrimination

If released prisoners have no special difficulty finding a job, this would undercut the claim that prison damages inmates' future economic opportunities. The unemployment rate of ex-prisoners is high, ranging between 25% and 40%,[45] which suggests that ex-prisoners may face discrimination in the labor market. However, ex-prisoners have below-average marketable skills and education, and often return to communities with disproportionately high unemployment rates, poverty, drug addiction, and gang activity.[46] They typically have extensive criminal records before the arrest that resulted in their imprisonment. For example, among *nonviolent* offenders released from state prison, 95% had an arrest prior to their imprisoning arrest, 80% had a prior conviction, one-third had been arrested for violent crimes, one-fifth had been convicted of a violent crime, and 8% had used a weapon during their current offense. The average number of prior arrests was 9.3, and the average number of prior convictions was 4.1.[47] Thus, the high rates of unemployment among ex-prisoners may be a product of "who" they are and their returning communities, rather than a product of the imprisonment experience per se or possible discrimination against prisoners.

Measuring Directly Offender Discrimination, Racial Discrimination, and Their Interaction

If it is not entirely clear what effect prison has on the careers of ex-inmates, still another strategy for gauging this is to look at the attitudes and behavior of employers. Putting employers, rather than inmates, under the microscope may provide new information. In one study, Harry Holzer, Steven Raphael, and Michael Stoll, in 2001, surveyed 619 firms in Los Angeles County, asking respondents if they would be willing to hire a job applicant who had a "criminal record."[48] It was left open whether the offender had served time in prison. In addition, Holzer and colleagues asked the respondents if they checked the criminal backgrounds of job applicants. Just more than 40% stated that they would "probably not" or "definitely not" hire an applicant with a criminal record. Less than half that number, about 20%, said that they would definitely or probably consider hiring an applicant with a criminal history. Thirty-five percent of the employers, the modal response, said that their willingness to hire an applicant with a criminal history depended on the crime. To add perspective, Holzer asked similarly worded questions about the employers' willingness to hire other groups of low-skilled and (potentially) negatively stereotyped groups. Ninety-three percent of the employers said they would definitely or probably hire former welfare recipients, and 66% indicated they would probably or definitely hire workers with spotty work histories. Clearly, then, individuals with a "criminal record" face discrimination in the labor market. Holzer and colleagues draw this inference from the data, "From the view point of employers, a criminal history record may signal an untrustworthy or otherwise problematic employee. Employers may avoid such workers due to a perceived increased propensity to break rules, steal, or harm customers."[49] Because prison inmates are a subset of individuals with "criminal records," sorted out for the most serious crimes and history of criminal offending, presumably employers would be even less open to hiring ex-prison inmates.

To establish trends on employer checking of criminal backgrounds, Holzer and colleagues supplemented the 2001 data with data they had collected in 1992 and 1994 on this issue.[50] One finding is that criminal background checks rose substantially in the 1990s, perhaps as a result of the Internet. Of greater substantive significance is a second finding: employers who conduct criminal background checks are far more likely to hire African Americans than employers who do not conduct such checks (11.2% vs. 3.3%). Holzer and colleagues conclude that "the more information available to employers about the criminal histories of individuals, the less likely the potential discrimination against black men, even if there will be greater reluctance to hire individuals with criminal records under these circumstances."[51]

Holzer and colleagues *asked* employers what they would do in future hypothetical situations, raising the problem that attitudes correlate imperfectly with behavior. Survey respondents may say that they will treat job applicants evenhandedly, but discriminate in actual situations. To get around this problem, Devah Pager arranged for pairs of black and white males to apply for advertised positions in Milwaukee.[52] The pairs were matched in physical appearance and credentials, except one member of each pair was randomly assigned a fictitious criminal record (having served 18 months in prison for a felony drug conviction for possession of cocaine with the intent to distribute). This design allowed Pager to isolate the effect of race and prison record, with everything else held constant. The dependent variable was the proportion of applicants who were called back by employers for potential employment. If an applicant was offered a position on the spot, this was counted as a positive "callback."

Before turning to findings, we note that degree of discrimination might depend on the crime scripted. Pager chose cocaine possession with the intent to distribute, which is neither a violent felony nor a low-level drug crime. At least drug possession, and perhaps even drug sales, can be considered a "victimless" crime, in the sense that the primary "costs" of the crime are borne by the drug users themselves. However, some (perhaps most) employers would worry that a former distributor of cocaine might become a future user or seller on the job. It would be informative to see if differently scripted crimes would produce different results. Still, not everything can be found out in a single experiment, and this is an excellent effort as far as it goes.

The strongest effect in the audit study was racial discrimination.[53] Among applicants without criminal backgrounds, 34% of the whites received callbacks compared to 14% of the black applicants. In addition, applicants with prison records were at a disadvantage relative to those without prison records. Only 5% of the blacks with prison records received a callback, compared to 14% of blacks without criminal records. For whites, 17% of those with a criminal record received a callback, whereas 34% of whites without records were called back. Finally, an interaction effect appears to have occurred between race discrimination and offender discrimination, although the interaction effect was not statistically significant. For whites, the ratio between callbacks of nonoffenders to offenders was 2 to 1, whereas the ratio for blacks was 3 to 1. In other words, the effect of a criminal record was 40% larger for blacks than for whites. From these findings, Pager concludes that the prison buildup has harmed many and that African American citizens have been *more* than doubly disadvantaged.

Three key points come out of these works. First, employers are averse to hiring ex-offenders and ex-prison inmates. Pager argues that this finding of discrimination against ex-prison inmates constitutes double jeopardy – punishing the same individual twice for the same crime.[54] Still, from the point of view of any particular employer, ex-prisoners may indeed be a bad bet. How much weight, then, should be given to ex-prisoners' status, *legitimately*? We believe it unrealistic to argue zero, which, at least in principle, could be achieved by making criminal background checks and criminal job interview questions illegal, or 100%. Something in-between seems reasonable. That something arguably coincides with Pager's finding that offenders experience some discrimination in the job market, but are not excluded from it. However, it is only arguably because we have no real standard for "legitimate" discrimination against ex-prisoners.

Second, both sets of findings suggest that the issue of racial discrimination cannot be fully disentangled from the discrimination against criminal offenders. Holzer finds that racial discrimination lessens when employers are assured that applicants do not have a criminal background. Pager finds evidence of racial discrimination against blacks, discrimination against offenders, and an interaction effect that exacerbates the disadvantage.

Third, Holzer finds evidence of discrimination against criminal offenders; Pager finds discrimination against ex-prison inmates. From these findings, it is not clear how much discrimination would be reduced if the numbers behind bars were reduced, but the level of criminality remained the same. Employers may use prison experience as a proxy for serious crime; eliminating the proxy may provide no net benefit. The "discrimination" problem may not be too much prison but rather too much crime.

Finally, these two designs, as informative as they are, do not provide the sort of information needed to address the additional issue of the aggregate effects of the buildup on unemployment. For there to be an aggregate effect of discrimination on unemployment, prison must not only negatively label an offender, moving ex-inmates to the end of the employment queue, but also damage their employability in an absolute sense. Employers would have to be willing to choose no one over an ex-inmate. Unemployment rates cannot be inferred from the outcomes of individual offenders released from prison. We address this issue empirically in the next section.

In what follows, we take seriously the possibility that heavy use of incarceration has negative consequences for the aggregate economy. We test this idea using state-level panel data, considering the unemployment rate and the employment-population ratio as dependent variables. Before we turn to the data and results, it is helpful to specify the hypothesized relationships among these variables.

Empirical Results

The previous discussion of the unemployment statistics excluding those who are incarcerated implies that in the short run, increases in the use of prison will lead to decreases in measured unemployment *regardless* of the causal impact of incarceration on an individual's employment prospects. Furthermore, this effect is expected to be linear: the larger the increases in prison population, the more imprisonment will "hide" unemployment. The alarm sounded by Western and Beckett concerned the situation in which a rapid expansion of the prison population ends and the prison population levels off or falls.[55] Under such conditions, there will no longer be a short-run effect to make unemployment appear smaller than it is and, at the same time, the cumulative effects of the previous expansion will result in higher unemployment.

Along these lines, a recent contribution to the literature on the effect of incarceration on employment is by Freeman and Rodgers, which evaluated the relationship of aggregate incarceration on microlevel employment.[56] They found that "[a]reas with the most rapidly rising rates of incarceration are areas in which youths, particularly African American youths have had the worst earnings and employment experience, and where men aged 25–64 have also done poorly." In this setting, the short-run effect of incarceration cannot make unemployment rates artificially low (because incarcerated individuals are not in the data set). Therefore, the estimated relationship must represent the long-run effect. Of course, this relationship could result from either individual-level effects (e.g., the negative effect of a criminal record on employment opportunities) or through macrolevel mechanisms (e.g., prison damaging the local labor market).

Clearly, this theory requires that one consider carefully the timing of the two relationships between incarceration and unemployment. In any given year, the unemployment rate is affected by both current and past corrections policy. Therefore, any statistical model must allow for short-run and long-run effects that may be of opposite signs.

The test of the theory, then, is whether the once lagged (i.e., the previous year's) change in the state prison population has a negative relationship to the unemployment rate, reflecting the suppression of the appearance of unemployment in the year following a prison expansion. We refer to this concern of Western and Beckett as the "definitional" effect. In the longer run, 3 to 4 years out, the theory implies that increases in imprisonment rates should be associated with increases in the unemployment rate because in the long run the causal effect of incarceration on the economy will prevail, no longer masked by the definitional effect. Thus, the third and fourth lags of the change in prison population would be expected to have positive signs. We have no prior expectation for the sign of the second lag of the change in state prison population because it may include both short- and long-run impacts.

We study the relationship between incarceration and employment outcomes in a panel of U.S. states.[57] Although most of the prior discussions illustrate their arguments by comparing nations, which in most cases means the United States versus other industrialized societies, nothing in the theory precludes it from being applied to subnational units, such as states. Several empirical advantages exist in doing so. First, only one country (the United States) has had sufficient prison buildup over time to allow the long-run effect of a major buildup to occur. Second, U.S. state-level data are both more available and more consistent than data across countries. Third, the number of observations using state-level data (fifty observations times 24 years) is greater than the number of observations using cross-country data. Finally, the state is a useful unit of analysis because much criminal justice policy is set at the subnational level. Texas, for example, has a much higher incarceration rate than does Minnesota. This research design takes advantage of that variation.

TABLE 6.2. *Descriptive Statistics*

	Mean	Standard deviation (overall)	Standard deviation of state averages	Standard deviation of year averages
Unemployment rate	5.994	2.226	1.318	1.452
Employment population ratio	52.328	3.348	2.894	0.968
Male prison inmates per 1,000 population (SPP)	5.711	3.050	2.276	1.824
% Change in SPP (×100)	5.546	10.132	10.551	3.077
Gross state product (GSP) per capita ($1998)	17,597.21	8,173.84	3,456.17	7,477.17
% GSP in mining and manufacturing	20.130	7.866	6.808	3.420
% Male population ages 16–19 years (×100)	6.330	0.681	0.368	0.475
% Male population ages 20–24 years (×100)	7.952	1.129	0.474	0.958
% Male population ages 55 years and older (×100)	18.588	2.397	2.370	1.992
% Black population	9.641	9.238	9.314	0.339
% Metro population	66.635	21.201	20.907	3.395

Note: There are fifty states and 24 years (1981–1998), for a total of 1,200 observations.

Descriptive statistics are presented in Table 6.2 for two alternate dependent variables (the percentage of unemployed for males 16 years of age and older in the labor force and the percentage of employed males 16 years of age and older relative to the male population) and a set of control variables. It is useful to distinguish between the variables for which there are greater variation across states or across time, as seen in the standard deviation of state means or yearly means. The two dependent variables are quite different when viewed this way; there is much greater variance from state to state in the employment population ratio than the unemployment rate. Male prison inmates per 1,000 male population vary more across states than over time within states. Of particular note is the relative variation across states or across time of real gross state product per capita. The variation across time is about twice as great as the variation over states. Finally, the proportion of a state's population that is African American or living in metro areas is nearly constant over time, but varies highly across states.

In the results reported in Table 6.3, the dependent variables are the logit of the male unemployment rate and the logit of the employment ratio. The logit was taken because the underlying statistics are decimal variables empirically bounded by 0 and 1.[58] We use state and year fixed effects in some models and random state and year effects in other models to control for unmeasured effects particular to each state and each year. The first two models in Table 6.3 are the fixed effects models for the logit of the unemployment rate and the logit of the employment ratio. The third and fourth models are random effects models.[59]

The "definitional" impact of incarceration on the economy should be observed as a negative coefficient for the lagged change in state prison population in regressions with the unemployment rate and a positive coefficient for regressions using the employment ratio. However, none of the estimated effects for this variable are statistically significant in any of the four models. This does not, of course, mean that the definitional effect is nonexistent. The reported regression coefficients indicate the total effect of incarceration on employment conditions, only a part of which is composed of the definitional effect. When the total effect is opposite the hypothesized direction for the definitional effect, or when the effects are not significant, there must be countervailing effects of incarceration that have not been considered in the literature where unemployment rates are recalculated. For example, it is plausible that a strong and active criminal justice system, as embodied in the incarceration rate, contributes to a secure environment, which promotes economic investment and thus job growth. Perhaps enough jobs are created to counteract the definitional effect.

The long-run, or causal, impact of incarceration would appear as a statistically significant positive coefficient for the third and fourth lags of the change in the prison population for models with the logit of the unemployment rate, and a negative coefficient for the third and fourth lags of the change in the prison population for models with the logit of the employment ratio. Yet, none of these coefficients

TABLE 6.3. *Maximum Likelihood Regressions of Unemployment Rate and the Employment-Population Ratio on State Prison Population (SPP)*

	Model 1	Model 2	Model 3	Model 4
	Logit (UR)	Logit (Emp-pop)	Logit (UR)	Logit (Emp-pop)
Intercept	−1.377*	−2.721	−0.257	−4.281*
	(2.024)	(2.156)	(1.735)	(1.840)
Lag(ln SPP)*	−0.119	0.135	−0.029	0.037
	(0.082)	(0.086)	(0.059)	(0.062)
Lag(%changeSPP)	0.109	−0.112	0.018	−0.009
	(0.092)	(0.098)	(0.082)	(0.088)
Lag2(%changeSPP)	0.153	−0.185	0.082	−0.105
	(0.093)	(0.100)	(0.091)	(0.098)
Lag3(%changeSPP)	0.128	−0.038	0.082	0.014
	(0.089)	(0.095)	(0.088)	(0.095)
Lag4(%changeSPP)	0.049	−0.094	0.024	−0.065
	(0.075)	(0.082)	(0.076)	(0.082)
Lag(GSP per capita)*	−0.370*	0.351*	−0.542*	0.533*
	(0.164)	(0.175)	(0.135)	(0.143)
Lag(% 16–19)	−9.705*	10.112*	−12.149*	12.738*
	(3.410)	(3.607)	(3.476)	(3.668)
Lag(% 20–24)	28	−3.297	4.631*	−4.817*
	(2.434)	(2.582)	(2.361)	(2.454)
Lag(% 55 and up)	−8.736*	8.774*	−5.472*	5.442*
	(1.741)	(1.842)	(1.245)	(1.305)
Lag(% black)	0.323	0.470	0.338	−0.338
	(5.167)	(5.447)	(0.001)	(0.889)
Lag(% metro)	−0.001	−0.002	0.003	−0.001
	(0.002)	(0.003)	(0.003)	(0.002)
Lag(%GSP mining & manufacturing)	−0.004	−0.004	−0.001	−0.004
	(0.004)	(0.004)	(0.004)	(0.003)
−2*Log-likelihood	−1171.3	−1018.0	−930.6	−777.1
F-test (%change variables)	0.80	1.22	0.31	0.73
	($p = 0.523$)	($p = 0.302$)	($p = 0.874$)	($p = 0.573$)

* State prison population (SPP); ** gross state product (GSP).

Note: Models 1 and 2 include fixed state and year effects (not reported); models 3 and 4 include random state and year effects (not reported). $N = 1{,}050$ for all models. Standard errors are in parentheses.

is statistically significant in the four models.[60] There does not seem to be a discernible long-term effect of incarceration on employment conditions.[61]

In summary, there is no discernible short-term effect of prison population size on either the unemployment rate or the employment population ratio. We conclude that, in the state-level panel data, there is no evidence that incarceration actually has the effects on unemployment proposed by Western and Beckett. We find no support for a definitional impact of incarceration on unemployment and, perhaps more surprisingly, little support for a causal effect of incarceration. It is difficult to "prove" a noneffect. Still, we have consistently found no evidence of relationships of the form hypothesized by Western and Beckett, even as we changed aspects of the model and estimation process.[62] It is possible that the long-term effects are right around the corner, but this seems increasingly unlikely.

CONCLUSION

Some scholars argue that America's reliance on mass imprisonment has caused, and will to continue to cause, great damage to American society, above and beyond the grinding deprivations of prison life for so many. High rates of imprisonment are "shattering communities in order to save them."[63] Along these lines, a number of studies claim to have found that mass imprisonment masks high rates of unemployment in the short run and generates high rates of unemployment in the long run.

The unemployment statistic was designed to measure one thing – slack in the economy. From the demand side, if new job opportunities become available, will people come running to them? From the supply side, how many people are currently excluded from the economy and have to face the pains of unemployment? Prisoners do not fit into this accounting; they are neither employed nor unemployed. Forcibly detained, prisoners cannot run to employment opportunities as they open up, and the distress caused by market exclusion becomes one of the many pains of imprisonment. Although prisoners contribute little to the GDP, their detainment may or may not have social purpose, as is discussed elsewhere in this book.

We have found that the recent recalculations of the unemployment rate to incorporate prisoners have given an undeserved impression of great effect. However, the larger point is that if unemployment is too narrow a concept to encompass prisoners, so, too, is productivity. Perhaps a new, broader measure should be developed to measure the sum total of "contributions" to society. However, in the absence of such a measure, we cannot expect the unemployment rate to proxy for concerns it was not intended to measure.

A main finding of this chapter is that, with regard to unemployment, the implications from the literature on recalculations of the unemployment rate and from the literature on the consequences of incarceration on individual-level employment outcomes do not translate into observable aggregate relationships. Mass imprisonment does not seem to have generated unemployment, at least as far as can be identified with variation across states in the extent of the buildup. There are many possible links from incarceration to the economy. The most obvious is that law enforcement activity is often necessary to re-create conditions conducive to economic activity. Such aggregate-level, general equilibrium consequences mean that the social calculation of the proper scope for incarceration is complicated.

Is it plausible that there is a zero aggregate effect of incarceration on employment in either the short or long run? Yes. Although the U.S. prison population is large relative to historical levels and to that in other countries, the overall numbers are small relative to the aggregate economy, especially once one takes into consideration that the potential labor market productivity of prisoners is relatively low (even if employment rates are higher than one might think). Thought experiments are useful for raising issues for further inquiry. However, no thought experiment can substitute for rigorously conducted empirical studies. Critics of the prison buildup have a number of solid grounds on which to challenge that high-cost policy. As far as we can tell, increased unemployment is not one of them.

Even if one were to grant that the prison buildup benefits society as a whole, this does not diminish the point that certain demographic groups, more than others, suffer the consequences of high rates of imprisonment on postprison employment. The idleness of incarceration represents a challenge for society to address, regardless of whether incarceration causes increased idleness. The most severe impact is on African American males, especially those with low levels of education. However, again, the policy implications of these "raw" findings do not suggest immediate policy implications.

More broadly, the painful reality of American society is that the issues of race and crime are not easily decoupled. The excellent work on employer discrimination, as reviewed previously, finds that employers

(1) discriminate against African American job seekers, (2) discriminate against job seekers with a criminal record, and (3) are especially harsh toward African American applicants with prison records, but (4) discriminate less against African American job seekers when they can be reassured that the applicants do not have a criminal record. The vast majority of African Americans have not violated the law; the problem is that they are stereotyped as otherwise. This form of statistical discrimination is difficult to break. Reducing the rate of imprisonment by a modest amount is unlikely to be very helpful in the near term.

CHAPTER SEVEN

Conclusion: Right-Sizing Prison

> Sanctions, penalties, and the fear of punishment are merely braces and not foundations.[1]

> The dominant competitive weapon of the twenty-first century will be the education and skills of the workforce.[2]

The prison buildup movement, we have argued, was a pragmatic effort to deal with an escalating crime rate rather than, as the critics claimed, an irrational expression of a disturbed population or an effort to achieve an otherwise extraneous political agenda. The critics include David Garland and Loïc Wacquant, in a tradition that springs from the work of Michel Foucault.[3] These attributions of irrationality, we found, do not fit the available facts. Yet, more generally, although social movements are pragmatic efforts to create new social forms, they are not deliberative bodies or research seminars. They do not collect evidence on the structures that they are seeking to bring, or have brought, into being. Data analysis (with all its complications) is not part of their "repertoire" for contention. Social movements are rational, but they are not hyperrational. If successful in achieving their immediate goals, they may not know how, or even when, to stop. More prisons, even if effective up to a point, may have exceeded that point during the buildup, as well as damaged society in other ways. The prison buildup movement may have unknowingly gone too far. Although social movements are strong in their mechanisms of mobilization, they have weak brakes.

To expand on these points, our analysis suggests that the prison buildup movement took the lead in a reasonable effort at social experimentation and change. Crime rates began to increase rapidly during the late 1960s. The initial response to this was to lower the level of imprisonment, both in absolute numbers of prisoners and more so relative to the escalating crime rate. The antiprison forces prevailed. This was the first break in the historic trend of nearly steady rates of imprisonment. When the crime rate turned even more serious, however, a crisis set in. A social movement from below came to demand greater punishment. There followed a switch in time.

The evidence bears out this part of the story. The American public came to demand tougher punishment, including more prisons. Our work suggests that this occurred for instrumental reasons. The upshot was that increasing numbers of people began to serve time behind bars, and the increase was substantial. Something new and different was being created: a society of captives writ large. This society was concentrated among the poorly educated and racial minorities.

So what has been the outcome? We have considered several dimensions: order behind bars, labor market impacts, reentry problems, and crime reduction. Also, in assessing these particular outcomes, what of a more general nature has been learned about prisons and how they perform?

COLLAPSE BEHIND BARS

Critics of the buildup expressed a reasonable concern that the buildup would result in an organizational collapse, a failed state–like situation. Some authors warned that the strains of an ever-increasing prison population would produce mass violence. This did not occur; in fact, quite the opposite. During the buildup period, prisons became much safer for inmates and correctional staff, and less prone to riots and disturbances. Prisons became more, not less, stable.

In Chapter 4, we argue that prisons are systems of cooperation, although hierarchical and authoritarian in nature. Correctional authorities (line staff through the chain of command to agency heads) issue orders, evaluate the inmates' response to those orders, and sanction them for noncompliance. Inmates may choose to comply with or resist these orders. Prison riots are the ultimate breakdown in cooperation; inmates seize territory and hold it for a time. This argument was rooted in the classic study of prisons by Gresham Sykes.[4]

However, in contrast to Sykes, as well as the buildup critics, we argued that effective institutional leadership might arise to meet severe challenges, including those associated with the buildup. As an example, the New York City Department of Correction experienced high rates of inmate-on-inmate and inmate-on-staff assault in the first half of the 1990s. This showed that management was not in control of the correctional facilities on Rikers Island, which housed nearly 20,000 inmates. The management response to this problem, known as TEAMS (the Total Efficiency Accountability Management System), began to hold every level of the agency accountable for its contribution to the chaotic culture and environment. The resulting reduction in disturbances in those facilities is astounding. As another example, the high-profile killing of a priest in a Massachusetts prison led to reforms to improve not only safety, but also daily life and efficiency throughout the prison system.[5] By addressing the institutional problems revealed by prison violence, corrections professionals, line staff, and politicians have been able to manage the consequences of the prison buildup fairly effectively.

These case studies, however, have not yet yielded a general understanding of the core features of effective correctional leadership and management. Nor do they indicate that all prisons are as safe, orderly, and supportive of reentry as they could be, as demonstrated recently in the findings of the Commission on Safety and Abuse in America's Prisons.[6]

Of related importance is the role of courts in creating, or destroying, order. Although this book did not conduct a detailed analysis of the judicial role in effecting prison reform, we would like to comment briefly on this role in so far as it bears on the issue of order. The courts may be seen as externally constraining of correctional operation, but real people (judges and their appointees) do the constraining. They can work more or less effectively. On the ineffectiveness side, judges are not trained as administrators, nor are they experts on the details of how prisons work. Heavy caseloads limit the time a judge can spend on any one case.[7] Moreover, judges cannot "order" effective institutional reform, any more than school principals can order learning in the classroom or chief executive officers can order their firms to avoid bankruptcy. Schools, business firms, and prisons may all fail, despite the "command" to succeed.

However, the judiciary may work effectively with corrections. We know this primarily though case studies, such as Leo Carroll's study of the transformation of Rhode Island's maximum security prison. An alliance was struck between the judiciary and prison officials, permitting the restoration of order. Likewise, Feeley and Rubin observed that judicial involvement in the Arkansas prison system showed signs of progressive administration.[8] The judge divided complex problems into manageable component parts, used both incentives and punishment to motivate slow-moving corrections officials, required detailed reports to enforce accountability, and fostered a moral commitment to the mission of the agency.

Another point is that too much weight can be given to the role of the courts in effecting positive reform. As a recent example of an excessively courtcentric approach, law professor James Q. Whitman compared U.S. prisons with those in continental Europe.[9] Although Whitman is highly critical of the greater harshness of U.S. prisons, he qualifies this by noting that U.S. prisons have improved, but only because "courts have actively engaged in improving American prison conditions."[10] In recent years, this intervention has waned and, in that measure, U.S. prisons will become correspondingly worse. Whitman links bad conditions with prison violence; thus, it would follow that rates of prison violence should have increased in the last quarter-century. Yet, we know, from Chapter 4, that rates of violence seem to be going downward, and we argue that internal leadership and management deserve some of the credit. Moreover, Whitman ignores the problem of institutional competence and capacity. For him, the good intentions of the judiciary and the alleged bad intentions of correctional administrators are the only relevant considerations. Our core point is that effective reform requires both good intentions and strong capacity among various actors.

In summary, prison order is best understood in dynamic terms, as a balance between institutional leadership from above and resistance and rebellion from below. In the period *prior* to the buildup, the forces of inmate resistance held the advantage. The rates of prison disturbances and assaults against staff were high. Buildup critics warned of a multiplying effect: the additional stress would cause the rates of violence and disorder to rise even higher. This was far too deterministic a prediction. Perhaps seeing the potentially explosive situation, institutional leadership undertook the measures needed to reduce stress and achieve stability.

LABOR MARKET CONSEQUENCES

Another consequence of mass incarceration that we considered is its effect on labor markets. Although there are reasons to believe that incarceration damages the employment prospects of inmates, the best studies fail to find evidence of large effects of the buildup. At the same time, these studies point out how poor the labor market prospects of inmates are, both before and after incarceration.

Yet, growing bodies of evidence show that employers strongly prefer to hire those without criminal records, and they discriminate against those who they believe have criminal records. This spills over into discrimination against African American males, in particular, without criminal records. We suspect that any efforts to convince employers not to discriminate against ex-prisoners will meet great resistance. One can too easily argue that such discrimination is reasonable, at least in those circumstances in which employee trust is crucial to firm performance, that is, most employment. The findings of discrimination against African Americans, such as in the work by Devah Pager, reveal the prevalence of intolerable racism.[11]

In this regard, prison buildup cuts both ways. To the extent that more prison reduces the crime rate, then the scope of discrimination will be attenuated. Employers will have more breathing room to hire the most qualified applicants. Yet, more prison also leaves more people vulnerable to discrimination for having served time. Clearly, though, emptying the prisons will not solve the discrimination problem. If only it were so easy.

Finally, when thinking about economic impacts of the buildup, it is important to remember that there is a substantial loss to the economy of having such a large prison sector because the human and financial resources used could be put to alternative uses. Again, there are tradeoffs. High crime rates also drag down the economy and, in various ways, make life a lot less pleasant. However, if the crime reduction benefits are small, the labor market and other costs appear unbearable.

MORE PRISON, LESS CRIME?

The consequence of mass incarceration that has generated the most interest is the crime rate. We found that the prison buildup has reduced the crime rate, but the qualifications on this finding may be as important as the initial finding itself. First, the effect is not large. Our preferred estimates find that, at the median rate of imprisonment over the period, a 10% increase in the state prison population would lower crime rates by 0.58%. Second, there are diminishing returns to the prison buildup. That is, as prison populations are larger (relative to population), the crime reductions associated with further expansions are smaller. This conclusion is consistent with both the case study inmate surveys and the statistical analysis conducted using national data. Furthermore, the regression results showed not just declining marginal returns but *acceleration* in the declining marginal return to scale.

One must assign values to the victimizations averted and to the losses associated with incarceration before determining whether the U.S. prison sector is "right sized" or not using these numbers. But it should be central to any discussion of the scale of imprisonment in the United States that the size of the victimization reduction is strongly related to the size of the prison population.

More generally, the right size of the prison population depends on how the impact is distributed. More prison brings about some reduction in the crime rates, and, to that measure, society is under a moral obligation to protect innocent victims. However, the elasticities linking prison to crime are much lower than 1, and falling lower. The case for tempering justice with mercy becomes all the more compelling the lower the elasticity.

PRISONER REENTRY

We also consider the fact that as prison populations increase, so do the numbers of inmates released back to civil society. Here, criminology meets head on with the full complexity of social life. There is currently a tremendous amount of energy, within corrections and outside, devoted to rationalizing institutional procedures and aligning the provision of social services behind bars and on the outside. At a minimum, practitioners and advocates in this field aim to remove unintended barriers to reintegration into community life. At the other extreme, prisoner reentry can be used as a window into the buildup itself. By seeing just how difficult the life circumstances are for some of those soon to be released from prison, one immediately notices how disproportionate the impact of mass incarceration is on poor and minority communities, the extreme disadvantages many inmates face, and how the buildup has led to a set of overlapping punishments (e.g., restrictions on access to public housing and employment checks on criminal records), which compound the challenges of reentry.

This documentation and analysis of how the buildup came about and some of its most important consequences brings us to the present. Now we look to the future, so naturally we must be more speculative

RIGHT-SIZING PRISON AND STATE BUDGETS

The recession that began in 2001 hit state budgets hard, resulting in major budget shortfalls in some states. Inevitably, some would argue that states, facing hard choices among competing priorities, should choose other priorities over prisons.[12] The economic recovery that has followed has eased the pressure on state budgets, as revenue growth became strong enough to support existing levels of spending, at least in most states.[13] Nevertheless, the demands on state spending continue to grow, revenue streams are uncertain,[14] raising the question of whether criminal justice policy should be strongly shaped by budgetary strains. (Of course, cost savings are always welcome.) For example, should we have fewer prisoners to allow for more college attendance as the Justice Policy Institute urges?[15]

To provide a perspective on state spending on corrections, consider total spending by states on the other major state functions. In 2005, states spent $283 billion on medicaid, $131 billion on higher education, and $43 billion on corrections.[16] Medicaid does appear to be exerting pressure on state budgets. Medicaid surpassed higher education as the second largest state program in 1990, and then in 2003, surpassed elementary and secondary education to become the largest budget item.[17] State higher education spending remains strong, at almost 11% of total state spending. In contrast, although corrections has grown dramatically in the past two decades, it takes up less than 4% of the state expenditures.

In summary, at $43 billion per annum, corrections has become an expensive program for states to administer. Because states cannot forever spend more revenue than they can raise through taxation, like all state spending programs, corrections spending competes for limited funds. Yet, when compared to other state spending programs, such as Medicaid, correctional spending does not appear to be the driving fiscal concern in most states. This, in turn, suggests that decisions on correctional programming should be best made on substantive, rather than purely fiscal, grounds.[18]

Despite this argument, it is more likely to be the case that the political agenda will be in large part driven by the need to manage budgets. As the prison population becomes increasingly populated by those who are middle aged or older, and as corrections departments and state budgets continue to be confronted with increasingly expensive physical and mental health costs, fiscal concerns will continue to demand attention. In many states, fiscal pressures will provide the impetus for pragmatic reforms that did not have any political traction during the most rapid years of the prison buildup.

Our own view is that we are past the point, at an aggregate basis, where prison expansion generates sufficient social benefits to justify the financial and social costs. This, of course, varies across states, with some now far beyond that point. Our prescription is that the next decade be a period of pruning, whereby the good that came from the buildup period, including increased concern with victims, improved management in corrections, and support for the larger law enforcement aim of relative safety on the streets, is sustained, while the problematic consequences of the buildup, including the underprovision of correctional programs, lack of systematic aid for rebuilding a life after incarceration, and the loss of crucial features of the social safety net, are rectified.

A NEW COUNTERMOVEMENT?

If the prison buildup movement has reached its limit, reversal may be the new challenge at hand. This suggests the need for a new social movement, one that would push for prison reduction and change. At this writing, the prisoner reentry effort appears to be a nascent social movement. It is providing some push back to some of the policies and practices adopted during the prison buildup, without taking on the sensitive issue of sentence lengths. Thus far, the reformers have found some success, mostly with regard to rhetoric. It remains to be seen whether these reformers will be able to implement and institutionalize practices that appreciably change prison life or the transition out of prison for a substantial fraction of the inmate population.

Strongly working in favor of the nascent movement is the fall in the violent crime rate since the mid-1990s. With security brought by lower crime rates, we are now freer to experiment and change. The threat of historically high crime rates has faded. Yet, the falling crime rate is *also* strongly working against this countermovement. If the prison buildup movement was born in crisis, then the absence of crisis may dampen the possibility of mobilization for something new and different. One task of political leadership is to replace complacency with a sense of urgency for change.

To take stock, prisons can be managed safely and state governments can afford the existing levels of correctional spending. Do we want to continue our commitment to imprison at these historic high levels? Although the prison buildup was not as catastrophic as some feared, we have demanded a lot of our prison system. Thankfully, institutional leadership has delivered to make most prisons relatively safe and secure. This is not a trivial achievement.

Yet, for new energy to be put in to the "prison" problem, given the absence of a sense of crisis in the "crime" problem, a link to broader issues may be required. New energy is needed. One such possible link (here, we are quite speculative) is to a potential social movement that would revitalize U.S. human capital formation.

EPILOGUE: THE ROLE OF HUMAN CAPITAL

Economist Claudia Goldin has called the twentieth century the "human capital century."[19] By this, she means that differences in investing in people, or human capital, explain how the United States surpassed other nations to become an economic superpower. At the turn of the century, the United States and Great Britain were the world's two leading economies, about even in their aggregate and per-capita

GDP. Early in the century, the United States embarked, for the first time in world history, in an effort to bring secondary and postsecondary education to the masses. By 1910, the United States began to pull away from all other nations in its rates of student enrollment in post primary schooling. There were, as well, significant changes in the content and organization of schools. The high school curriculum became more pragmatic and less classical, although still academic rather than vocational. Public education, at all levels, became more open, forgiving, secular, and gender neutral. The scope and virtues of American mass education, according to Golden, produced U.S. economic ascendancy. Other factors of development, such as technology and physical capital, were of secondary importance.

More recently, Isaac Ehrlich has come to much the same conclusion as Goldin; that is, that investment in human capital through education was the major instrument through which the United States achieved its rapid economic growth.[20] Ehrlich, however, adds an important caveat to the current situation – the United States is losing some of its advantage. A recent report by the Educational Testing Service paints a worrisome picture. For example, high school graduation rates peaked at 77% in 1969, fell to 70% in 1995, and have not changed since then. The United States now ranks sixteenth out of twenty-one OECD countries in graduation rates.[21] We agree with Ehrlich that cross-national convergence is of secondary importance to improvement of all nations' human capital. This would be a tide raising all boats.

In an impressive series of papers with several coauthors, Nobel laureate James Heckman has made the case for investment in children, particularly disadvantaged children, to reap rewards of economic growth, narrowing income inequality, and improved social outcomes, including crime.[22]

The case in favor of strengthening human capital formation calls for a broad social movement to achieve a revitalization of that sector. The challenges facing such a movement would be great because more funding alone would not be sufficient. The United States continues to outspend most other OECD countries on a per-student basis.[23] The problems are deeper than money alone can solve. As the analysis in this book revealed, the prison buildup was not the outcome of a single piece of legislation or blue ribbon panel. Just as with the buildup, any success at making reasonable reductions in the extent to which the Untied States uses incarceration will come from actions of many participants.

Under current levels of imprisonment, one in thirty-seven U.S. adults will spend a portion of their lives in either a federal or a state prison.[24] Among the incarcerated population, 65% do not have a high school diploma, a rate that is 3.5 times higher than the general population.[25] If the most pressing problem is a skyrocketing crime rate, then optimizing deterrence and incapacitation must be our most pressing goal. However, we are beyond this pure security issue. We are freer to think about what more prison can do to contribute to the social welfare. A human capital revolution for the population behind bars, and those at risk of being put behind bars, would contribute to the wider welfare.

The question we face now with regard to the scale of punishment is one of the optimal scope of government. We cherish liberty, which implies less government, but that is not our only value. American society faced a severe crisis of public safety. The prison buildup was a pragmatic effort to get a handle on this crisis, and it worked – our streets became safer. However, the size of the prison population is not necessarily a one-way ratchet. It can be lowered as the crisis begins to dissipate in intensity and fade in memory. No challenge is greater than developing the human capital of those at risk of incarceration or reincarceration.

Notes

Chapter 1. The Buildup to Mass Incarceration

1. Bill Clinton, *CNN Transcript of President Bill Clinton's Radio Address*, January 27, 1996.
2. Peter Gay, *Cultivation of Hatred: The Bourgeois Experience, Victoria to Freud* (New York: W. W. Norton, 1994), 35.
3. Chinese Premier Zhou En-lai, responding to a question about the significance of the French Revolution of 1789. Quoted in Simon Schama, *Citizens: A Chronicle of the French Revolution* (New York: Knopf, 1989), xiii.
4. Kathleen Maguire and Ann L. Pastore, *Sourcebook of Criminal Justice Statistics, 1998* (Washington, DC: Bureau of Justice Statistics, 1999).
5. Alfred Blumstein and Jacqueline Cohen, "A Theory of Stability of Punishment," *Journal of Criminal Law & Criminology* 64 (1973): 198–206.
6. Allen J. Beck, *Prisoners in 1999* (Washington, DC: Bureau of Justice Statistics, 2000).
7. Paige M. Harrison and Allen J. Beck, *Prisoners in 2005* (Washington, DC: Bureau of Justice Statistics, 2006).
8. Ibid., 8.
9. Thomas P. Bonczar, *Prevalence of Imprisonment in the U.S. Population, 1974–2001* (Washington, DC: Bureau of Justice Statistics, 2003), 1.
10. Historian Peter Gay observes that aggression implies attack, which in ordinary language discloses both negative and positive implications. In the negative, *attack* connotes a hostile setting upon, often with high-sounding rationalizations as justification. In its positive implications, *attack* connotes an adaptive mastery, perhaps of counteraggression in response to a real phenomenon. Gay, *Cultivation of Hatred*; Peter Gay, *Schnitzler's Century: The Making of the Middle-Class Culture, 1815–1914* (New York: W.W. Norton, 2002).

11. James Q. Whitman, *Harsh Justice: Criminal Punishment and the Widening Divide between America and Europe* (New York: Oxford University Press, 2003).
12. For evidence of the positive role of an independent judiciary on economic growth, see Kenneth W. Dam, "The Judiciary and Economic Development," John M. Olin Law & Economics Working Paper No. 287, The Law School, University of Chicago (March 2006), 1, www.law.uchicago.edu/Lawecon/WkngPprs_251-300/287.pdf. This theme is also developed by Richard A. Posner, "The Sociology of the Sociology of Law: A View from Economics," *European Journal of Law and Economics* 2 (1995): 268.
13. Margaret Werner Cahalan, *Historical Corrections Statistics in the United States, 1850–1984* (Washington, DC: Bureau of Justice Statistics, 1987), 69; James J. Stephan and Jennifer C. Karberg, *Census of State and Federal Correctional Facilities, 2000* (Washington, DC: Bureau of Justice Statistics, 2003), iv.
14. In 2001, federal, state, and local governments spent $60 billion for all aspects of corrections, including prison, jail, parole, and probation. *Direct Expenditures by Criminal Justice Function, 1982–2003* (Washington, DC: Bureau of Justice Statistics), www.ojp.usdoj.gov/bjs/glance/tables/exptyptab.htm.
15. For a full discussion, see Donald C. Light, *The True Size of Government* (Washington, DC: Brookings Institution, 1999).
16. Peter Zimmerman, "The Workforce: Not So Big," *Government Executive* 31 (1999): 41.
17. For a discussion of the position that prison privatization is a means to the end of less government, see Sean Nicholson-Crotty, "The Politics of Administration of Privatization: Contracting Out for Corrections Management in the United States," *Policy Studies Journal* 32 (2004): 59–75.
18. James Austin and John Irwin, *It's About Time: America's Imprisonment Binge, Third Edition* (Belmont, CA: 2001), 65.
19. An exception is in the custody of those detained for immigration violations. Here, private firms are playing an increasingly large role, currently housing about a fifth of the immigrants in detention. Meredith Kolodner, "Private Prisons Expect a Boom: Immigrant Enforcement to Benefit Detention Companies," *New York Times*, July 19, 2006.
20. Allen J. Beck and Jennifer C. Karberg, *Prison and Jail Inmates at Midyear 2000* (Washington, DC: Bureau of Justice Statistics, 2001); Paige M. Harrison and Allen J. Beck, *Prison and Jail Inmates at Midyear 2005* (Washington, DC: Bureau of Justice Statistics, 2006).
21. Geoffrey F. Segal and Adrian T. Moore, *Weighing the Watchman: Evaluating the Costs and Benefits of Outsourcing Correctional Services* (Los Angeles: Reason Public Policy Institute, 2002), 4.

22. James F. Blumstein and Mark A. Cohen, "Do Government Agencies Respond to Market Pressures? Evidence from Private Prisons," Law and Economics Working Paper No. 03–16, Vanderbilt University Law School, http://ssrn.com/abstract=441007.
23. A growing literature compares private and public prisons in term of their cost, quality, and safety. There is also a literature discussing whether prisons, as a matter of public philosophy, should be privatized. For summaries of recent research and discussions, see Travis C. Pratt and Jeff Maahs, "Are Private Prisons More Cost-Effective than Public Prisons? A Meta-Analysis of Evaluation Research Studies," *Crime and Delinquency* 45 (1999): 358–371; *Harvard Law Review*, "Developments in the Law – The Law of Prisons," *Harvard Law Review* 115 (2002): 1868–1891; Scott D. Camp and Gerald G. Gaes, "Growth and Quality of U.S. Private Prisons: Evidence from a National Survey," *Criminology & Public Policy* 3 (2002): 427–450; Anna Lukemeyer and Richard C. McCorkle, "Privatization of Prisons: Impact on Prison Conditions," *American Review of Public Administration* 36 (2006): 189–206.
24. Francis Fukuyama, *State-Building: Governance and World Order in the 21st Century* (Ithaca, NY: Cornell University Press, 2004); Peter B. Evans, "The Eclipse of the State? Reflections on Stateness in an Era of Globalization," *World Politics* 50 (1997): 62–87.
25. Fukuyama, *State Building*, 19. To illustrate the shift toward greater concern with the strength of the state, as against its scope, Fukuyama quotes Milton Friedman, a standard bearer of free market economics. In a 2001 interview, Friedman commented that a decade earlier he had three words of advice for societies seeking to transform their socialist economies: "privatize, privatize, privatize." Friedman goes on to say, "But I was wrong. It turns out that the rule of law is probably more basic than privatization" (quoted in Fukuyama, *State Building*, 19).
26. States vary in how they apply these sanctions. This section describes the "usual" ways that probation, parole, jail, and prison are defined.
27. Joan Petersilia, "Community Corrections," in James Q. Wilson and Joan Petersilia, eds., *Crime: Public Polices for Crime Control* (Oakland, CA: Institute for Contemporary Studies, 2002); Lauren Glaze and Seri Palla, *Probation and Parole in the United States, 2004* (Washington, DC: Bureau of Justice Statistics, 2005).
28. Federal Bureau of Investigation, *Crime in the United States, 2004*, www.fbi.gov/ucr/cius_04/persons_arrested/table_29.html.
29. Ibid., table 5.57. These data on adjudication outcomes are somewhat imprecise for the purposes here. The data are for felony defendants in the seventy-five largest counties in 2002. These counties accounted for 37% of the U.S. population, 50% of all reported serious violent

crimes, and 42% of all reported serious property crimes. Thomas H. Cohen and Brian A. Reaves, *Felony Defendants in Large Urban Counties, 2002* (Washington, DC: Bureau of Justice Statistics), 1.

30. *Sourcebook of Criminal Justice Statistics*, table 5.59. These data are, as those in note 29, from seventy-five largest counties and were collected in 2002. Data from state courts, in 2002, differ somewhat – of those convicted of a felony: prison, 41%; jail, 28%; and probation, 31%. For this data set, sentences other than prison, jail, and probation are included under probation. Taking this into account, the differences between the two data sets in the number assigned to probation are minor (28% vs. 31%). *Sourcebook*, table 5.47. Data on adjudication outcomes for misdemeanor charges are not available but are unlikely to show significant contributions to the prison population. The seventy-five largest-county data set (2002) reported on the sentencing of defendants with a felony arrest charge who were convicted of a misdemeanor: prison, 2%; jail, 58%; probation, 26%; and other, 14%. *Sourcebook*, table 5.59.
31. Thomas P. Bonczar, *Prevalence of Imprisonment in the U.S. Population, 1974–2001* (Washington, DC: Bureau of Justice Statistics, 2003).
32. As noted in the original study, the critical assumption is that the current age-specific rates of first incarceration continue in the future. Both policy changes and behavior of offenders and law enforcement will determine whether this occurs.

Chapter 2. Causes of the Prison Buildup

1. Henry Ruth and Kevin R. Reitz, *The Challenge of Crime: Rethinking Our Response* (Cambridge, MA: Harvard University Press, 2003).
2. Frank Weed, *Certainty of Justice: Reform in the Crime Victim Movement* (New York: Aldine de Gruyter, 1995); Lucy N. Friedman, "The Crime Victim Movement at Its First Decade," *Public Administration Review*, 45 (1985): 790–794; Valiant R. W. Poliny, *A Public Policy Analysis of the Emerging Victims' Rights Movement* (San Francisco: Austin and Winfield, 1994). The right of crime victims to be "heard" in court proceedings has been discussed extensively. See, for example, Walker A. Matthews, III, "Proposed Victims' Rights Amendment: Ethical Considerations for the Prudent Prosecutor," *Georgetown Journal of Legal Ethics* 11 (1998): 738–739, and Catherine Guastello, "Victim Impact Statements: Institutionalized Revenge," *Arizona State Law Journal* 37 (2005): 1321–1344.
3. David Garland, *The Culture of Control: Crime and Social Order in Contemporary Society* (Chicago: The University of Chicago Press, 2000), 194, emphasis added.

4. Thomas G. Blomberg and Karol Lucken, *American Penology: A History of Control* (New York: Aldine de Gruyter, 2000), 187.
5. William Lyons and Stuart Scheingold, "The Politics of Crime and Punishment," in Gary LaFree, ed., *The Nature of Crime: Continuity and Change* (Washington, DC: National Institute of Justice, 2000), 127.
6. Katherine Beckett, *Making Crime Pay: Law and Order in Contemporary American Politics* (New York: Oxford University Press, 1997), 108.
7. Michael Tonry, "Rethinking Unthinkable Punishment Policies in America," *UCLA Law Review* 46 (1999): 1781.
8. Ibid., 1786.
9. Ibid., 1788.
10. Jonathan Simon, "Megan's Law: Crime and Democracy in Late Modern America," *Law and Social Inquiry* 25 (2000): 1111–1150.
11. Theodore Caplow and Jonathan Simon, "Understanding Prison Policy and Population Trends," in Michael Tonry and Joan Petersilia, eds., *Prisons* (Chicago: The University of Chicago Press, 1999), 87.
12. Ibid., 79.
13. Anthony Bottoms, "The Philosophy and Politics of Punishment and Sentencing," in C. M. V. Clarkson and Rodney Morgan, eds., *The Politics of Sentencing Reform* (Oxford, UK: Clarendon Press).
14. Ibid., 47.
15. Jack A. Goldstone, "A New Look at Gamson's *The Strategy of Social Protest*," *American Journal of Sociology* 85 (1980): 1017–1043; Arthur L. Stinchcombe, "Tilly on the Past as a Sequence of Futures," in Charles Tilly, ed., *Roads from Past to Future* (Lanham, MD: Rowman & Littlefield, 1997).
16. Bruce Ackerman, "Revolution on a Human Scale," *Yale Law Journal* 108 (1999): 2279.
17. Walter Dean Burnham, "Constitutional Moments and Punctuated Equilibria: A Political Scientist Confronts Bruce Ackerman's *We The People*," *Yale Law Journal* 108 (1999): 2237–2278.
18. John P. Kotter, *Leading Change* (Cambridge: Harvard University Press), 45–46.
19. John P Kotter, "Leading Change: Why Transformation Efforts Fail." *Harvard Business Review*, 73 (March/April,1995): 62.
20. Neil J. Smelser, *Theory of Collective Behavior* (New York: Free Press, 1959).
21. John D. McCarthy and Mayer N. Zald, "Resource Mobilization and Social Movements: A Partial Theory," *American Journal of Sociology* 82 (1977): 1217–1218.
22. The violent crimes are murder and nonnegligent manslaughter, forcible rape, robbery, and aggravated assault. The property crimes are burglary, larceny theft, and motor vehicle theft.

23. The Federal Bureau of Investigation (FBI) began publishing crime statistics in 1932. However, the reporting procedures changed dramatically in 1960. The FBI recommends against using its crime data prior to 1960 in time-series comparisons, a recommendation that the *Sourcebook* respects.

24. Figure 2.2 shows the results of dividing the total number of offenders in state and federal prisons by the number of property and violent crimes for the period 1960 to 2004. The calculations are less than ideal because (1) prisoners (the numerator) include offenders incarcerated not only for property and violent crimes, but also for drug and public order crimes; (2) the numerator includes federal prisoners, a significant source of growth; and (3) the large number of larceny thefts could overwhelm the other crimes in the denominator. There are several ways to get around these problems, which, although not perfect, show essentially the same trends. One approach is to divide the number of prisoners in state prison for a specific crime, such as murder, by the incidence of that crime in that year. We do this, but only for the period from 1980 to 2003 because data on the crimes committed by prisoners prior to 1980 are unavailable. The following table shows that these calculations yield essentially the same story as the figures reported in Figure 2.2. For example, between 1980 and 2003, the ratio of prisoners (state and federal) to violent crime increased 4.2 times. During the same period, the ratio of murderers in state prison to murders increased by 6.1. Likewise, between 1980 and 2003, the ratio of prisoners (state and federal) to property crime increased 5.0 times. During the same period, ratio of state inmates convicted of burglary/burglaries increased by 5.3. Although these ratios are not identical, they are of the same order of magnitude and do not change the basic interpretation – prison growth relative to the crime rate.

	Increase in ratios, 2003/1980
Data used for Figure 2.2	
State and federal inmates/violent crime	4.2
State and federal inmates/property crime	5.0
*Additional data**	
State inmates convicted of murder/murders	6.1
State inmates convicted of robbery/robberies	3.2
State inmates convicted of auto theft/auto thefts	4.8
State inmates convicted of burglary/burglaries	5.3

* *Source:* Bureau of Justice Statistics, *Prisoners in 1994*, http://www.ojp.usdoj.gov/bjs/pub/pdf/pi94.pdf; Bureau of Justice Statistics, *Prisoners in 2005*, www.ojp.usdoj.gov/bjs/pub/pdf/p05.pdf.

25. Tom R. Tyler and Robert J. Boeckmann, "Three Strikes and You Are Out, But Why? The Psychology of Public Support for Punishing," *Law and Society Review* 31 (1997): 237–265.
26. Stuart A. Scheingold, "Constructing the New Political Criminology: Power, Authority, and the Post-liberal State," *Law and Social Inquiry* 23 (1998): 779.
27. James Q. Wilson, *Thinking about Crime* (New York: Basic Books, 1975); John J. DiIulio, Jr., "Arresting Ideas: Tougher Law Enforcement Is Driving Down Urban Crime," *Policy Review* 74 (1995): 12–17.
28. In this chapter, we do not take a stand on the empirical validity of this argument.
29. For recent efforts along these lines, see Theda Skocpol, *Diminished Democracy: from Membership to Management in American Civil Life* (Norman: University of Oklahoma Press, 2003); Robert D. Putnam, "*E Pluribus Unum*: Diversity and Community in the Twenty-first Century. The 2006 Johan Skytte Prize Lecture," *Scandinavian Political Studies* 30 (2007): 137–174.
30. Carl I. Hovland and Robert R. Sears, "Minor Studies of Aggression: VI. Correlation of Lynchings with Economic Indices," *Journal of Psychology* 9 (1940): 301–310.
31. Donald P. Green, Jack Glaser, and Andrew Rich, "From Lynching to Gay Bashing: The Elusive Connection Between Economic Conditions and Hate Crime," *Journal of Personality and Social Psychology* 75 (1998): 82–92.
32. Alan B Krueger and Jorn-Steffen Pischke, "A Statistical Analysis of Crime Against Foreigners in Unified German," *Journal of Human Resources* 32 (1997): 182–209.
33. Donald P. Green, Dara Z. Strolovitch, and Janelle S. Wong, "Defended Neighborhoods, Integration, and Racially Motivated Crime," *American Journal of Sociology* 104 (1998): 372–403.
34. Beckett, *Making Crime Pay.*
35. Ibid., 15–16.
36. Ibid., 16.
37. Ibid., 22.
38. Moreover, as Philip Cook points out, high levels of concern about crime can lead people to take protective measures. If those measures are effective, then increased concern will produce lower crime rates. "The Demand and Supply of Criminal Opportunities," in Michael Tonry and Norval Morris, eds., *Crime and Justice: An Annual Review of Research, Vol.* 7 (Chicago: The University of Chicago Press, 1986).
39. For additional discussion of Beckett's analysis, see Bert Useem, Raymond V. Liedka, and Anne Morrison Piehl, "Popular Support for the Prison Buildup," *Punishment and Society*, 5 (2003): 5 – 33.

40. Kathlyn T. Gaubatz, *Crime in the Public Mind* (Ann Arbor: University of Michigan Press, 1995).
41. Ibid., 12, 162–163.
42. Ibid., 161.
43. Ibid., 140.
44. Ironically, Gaubatz criticizes the respondent for being too instrumental, or at least instrumental on behalf of the "wrong" values. The respondent favors the rehabilitation of offenders, but "just for society's sake. Not *even* for society's sake and the offender's sake – but *just* for society's sake." Lacking are a "sense of compassion for offenders" and a "critique of criminogenic social conditions for which we bear some collective responsibility." Gaubatz, *Crime in the Public Mind*, 62, 63, emphasis in original.
45. Ibid., 153.
46. Franklin E. Zimring, Gordon Hawkins, and Sam Kamin, *Punishment and Democracy: Three Strikes and You're Out in California* (New York: Oxford University Press, 2001).
47. For the complete wording of the questions, the response categories, and the years in which the questions were asked, see Useem, Liedka, and Piehl, "Popular Support."
48. Year was coded as a set of dummy variables.
49. In Richard Posner's list of the 100 most prominent academic public intellectuals, Foucault received more than twice as many citations in the scholarly literature as the second most cited public intellectual. Richard A. Posner, *Public Intellectuals: A Study of Decline* (Cambridge, MA: Harvard University Press, 2001), 213. Sociologist Dan Clawson ranked *Discipline and Punish* as one of sociology's "most influential books," even though Foucault was not a sociologist. Dan Clawson, ed., *Required Reading: Sociology's Most Influential Books* (Amherst: University of Massachusetts Press, 1998). Although Foucault's prominence cannot be doubted, some commentators have gone overboard. Jonathan Simon, in a retrospective review of *Discipline and Punish*, states that "virtually nothing written in the field since has been able to ignore Foucault's startling way of recounting the place of prison in the self-interpretation of modernity." Nothing? Jonathan Simon, "Review of *Discipline and Punish*," *Contemporary Sociology* 25 (1996): 316.
50. Michel Foucault, *Discipline and Punish: The Birth of the Prison*. Trans. Alan Sheridan (New York: Vintage, 1977).
51. Ibid., 16.
52. Ibid., 228.
53. Loïc Wacquant, "Deadly Symbiosis: When Ghetto and Prison Meet and Mesh," *Punishment and Society* 3 (2001): 97.

54. Frances Fox Piven and Richard A. Cloward, *Regulating the Poor: The Functions of Public Welfare* (New York: Pantheon Books, 1971).
55. Loïc Wacquant, "The New 'Peculiar Institution': On the Prison as Surrogate Ghetto," *Theoretical Criminology* 4 (2000): 378.
56. Wacquant, "Deadly Symbiosis," 105.
57. In another context, theorists of revolution have shown that peasants rebel against landlords only when they develop partly autonomous communal organizations. Theda Skocpol, *States and Social Revolutions* (New York: Cambridge University Press, 1979); Eric R. Wolff, *Peasant Wars of the Twentieth Century* (New York: Harper & Row, 1970).
58. Wacquant, "Deadly Symbiosis," 103, 118.
59. Ibid., 114.
60. Ibid., 116. Some observers contend that hip-hop music, in its hostile and sexist lyrics, combined with fantasies of youth revolution achieved through confrontations on the street, genuinely holds back black youth and seriously harms the black community. John H. McWhorter, "How Hip-Hop Holds Blacks Back," *City Journal* 13 (2003): 66–75. Wacquant would probably disagree, although he is not explicit on this point. Andreana Clay has written a more sympathetic account of hip-hop music, arguing that this musical form is a means to "authenticate a Black identity." "Keepin It Real: Black Youth, Hip-Hop Culture, and Black Identity," *American Behavioral Scientist* 46 (2003): 1346–1358.
61. Wacquant, "Deadly Symbiosis," 116. The quote within the quote is from Jerome G. Miller, *Search and Destroy: African American Males in the Criminal Justice System* (Cambridge, UK: Cambridge University Press, 1997), 101.
62. Wacquant, "Deadly Symbiosis," 108.
63. Ibid., 119, 121.
64. Peter Gay criticizes Foucault's approach to the study of the history of sexuality along much the same lines. Foucault's procedure, Gay asserts, "is anecdotal and almost wholly unencumbered by facts." *The Bourgeois Experience: Victoria to Freud. Volume I, Education of the Senses* (New York: Oxford University Press), 468. In fairness, Gay and Foucault are poles apart in their substantive conclusions. For a similarly negative assessment of Foucault's approach to literary criticism, see Francis-Noël Thomas and Mark Turner, *Clear and Simple as the Truth* (Princeton, NJ: Princeton University Press, 1994), 55–56. A more positive treatment of Foucault can be found in John S. Ransom, *Foucault's Discipline: The Politics of Subjectivity* (Durham, NC: Duke University Press, 1997).
65. Foucault claims modern prisons are exemplars of extreme order and detailed surveillance. Wacquant claims that the distinctive feature of modern prison is disorder, racial conflict, gang rule, and unpredictability. Both claims – prisons are highly chaotic and prisons are

highly orderly – cannot be true. Neither author presents evidence along these lines.

66. Christopher Uggen and Jeff Manza, "Democratic Contraction? The Political Consequences of Felon Disenfranchisement in the United States," *American Sociological Review*, 67 (2002): 696.
67. Sentencing Project, "Felony Disenfranchisement Laws in the United States," www.sentencingproject.org/Admin/Documents/publications/fd_bs_fdlawsinus.pdf.
68. Ibid., 1.
69. Uggen and Manza provide additional evidence to support their assumption that the political behavior of felons matches the political behavior of demographically similar nonfelons. They use arrest data from a longitudinal survey of Minnesota youth, tracking them from ninth grade through ages 23 to 25. They estimated a regression model to determine whether having been arrested had any impact on voter turnout and party preference. The impact was minor to nonexistent once control variables were introduced for race, gender, education, income, employment, and marital status. Although these finding support their case, they are far from decisive. A small number of respondents had been in jail, but none had been in prison. Uggen and Manza, Democratic Contraction, 790–791.
70. Christopher Jencks, *Rethinking Social Policy: Race, Poverty, and the Underclass* (Cambridge, MA: Harvard University Press, 1992), 92. The association between party and crime rate may have broken down in more recent years because Democrats have increasingly taken a "get-tough" approach to crime. This only complicates the modeling problem we identify. As a brief historical note, Uggen and Manza observe that Nixon may have defeated Kennedy in 1960 if the correctional population had been at its current level. Yet, it is also the case that Nixon defeated Hubert Humphrey in 1968 in part based on a "law and order" theme. Philip Converse and colleagues argue about this election, "In the broad American public, then, there was a widespread sense of breakdown in authority and discipline that fed as readily on militant political dissent as on race riots and more conventional crime.... Thus, the 'law and order' phrase, ambiguous though it might be, had considerable resonance among the voters, and deserves to be catalogued along with Vietnam and racial crisis among major issue influence on the election." Philip E. Converse, Warren E. Miller, Jerrold G. Rusk, and Arthur C. Wolfe, "Continuity and Change in American Politics: Parties and Issues in the 1968 Election," *American Political Science Review* 63 (1969): 1083–1105.
71. Richard A. Posner, *Law, Pragmatism, and Democracy* (Cambridge, MA: Harvard University Press, 2003), 235.

72. Chambliss, *Power, Politics, and Crime*, 130–131.
73. John J. DiIulio, Jr. "Two Million Prisoners Are Enough," *The Wall Street Journal*, March 12, 1999.

Chapter 3. More Prison, Less Crime?

1. Barrington Moore, Jr., *Reflections on the Causes of Human Misery and Upon Certain Proposals to Eliminate Them* (Boston: Beacon Press, 1970), 25.
2. William Chambliss, *Power, Politics, and Crime* (Boulder, CO: Westview Press, 1999), 5, emphasis added.
3. Loïc Wacquant, "The Great Leap Backward: Incarceration in America from Nixon to Clinton," in John Pratt, David Brown, Mark Brown, Simon Hallsworth, and Wayne Morrison, eds., *The New Punitiveness: Trends, Theories, Perspectives* (Portland, OR: Willan, 2005), 15.
4. Ibid., 22.
5. Dina R. Rose and Todd R. Clear, "Incarceration, Social Capital, and Crime: Examining the Unintended Consequences of Incarceration," *Criminology* 36 (1998): 441–479.
6. James P. Lynch and William Sabol "Assessing the Effects of Mass Incarceration on Informal Social Control in Communities," *Criminology and Public Policy* 3 (2004): 267–294.
7. In one study, researchers compared state court records of offenders being sent to prison and state correctional records of offenders entering the prison. There was a close correspondence, suggesting confidence in both data sets. Patrick A. Langan and David Levin, *Assessing the Accuracy of State Prisoner Statistics* (Washington, DC: Bureau of Justice Statistics, 1999).
8. The percent of crimes reported to the police is based on the National Crime Victimization Survey, which collects data from a representative sample of the American public. The crimes include both violent and property crimes, but do not include murder. Details on the survey can be found at www.ojp.usdoj.gov/bjs/cvict.htm. The clearance rates are based on the FBI's Uniform Crime Report, calculated on the eight index crimes, which includes murder. Kathleen Maguire and Ann L. Pastore, eds. *Sourcebook of Criminal Justice Statistics 2000* (Washington, DC: Bureau of Justice Statistics, 2001), tables 3.38 and 4.21.
9. In a survey of a representative sample of state and federal inmates, 64% of those responding said "yes" to the question, "Before your trial for the [the offender's offense], did you reach an agreement with a prosecutor to plead guilty to a lesser charge or to fewer counts." *Survey of Inmates in State and Federal Correctional Facilities, 1997*, National Archive of Criminal Justice Data, www.icpsr.umich.edu/NACJD/.

10. Violent offenses include murder, negligent and nonnegligent manslaughter, rape, sexual assault, robbery, assault, extortion, intimidation, and criminal endangerment. Property offenses include burglary, larceny, motor vehicle theft, fraud, possession and selling of stolen property, destruction of property, trespassing, vandalism, and criminal tampering. Drug offenses include possession, manufacturing, and trafficking. Public order offenses include weapons, drunk driving, escape/flight to avoid prosecution, court offenses, obstruction, commercialized vice, morals and decency charges, and liquor law violations.
11. Federal Bureau of Prisons, "Code Tables, IIS Offense Codes," October 7, 2001.
12. These figures include prisoners whose offenses could not be classified into one of the four main categories. Federal jurisdiction includes all sentenced inmates without regard to sentence length.
13. This is based on 2002 data, the last year for which state data broken down by inmate crime are available.
14. These criteria are suggested by Matthew R. Durose and Christopher J. Mumola, *Profile of Nonviolent Offenders Exiting State Prisons* (Washington, DC: Bureau of Justice Statistics, 2004). They used the four criteria to examine a somewhat different population than the one we are looking at.
15. Eric L. Sevigny and Jonathan P. Caulkins, "Kingpins or Mules: An Analysis of Drug Offenders Incarcerated in Federal and State Prisons," *Criminology and Public Policy* 3 (2004): 401–434.
16. Ibid., 421.
17. Ibid., 425.
18. See Mark Moore, "Policies to Achieve Discrimination on the Effective Price of Heroin," *American Economic Review* 63 (1973): 270, and Matthew D. Adler and Eric A. Posner, eds., *Cost–Benefit Analysis: Legal, Economic, and Philosophical Perspectives* (Chicago: University of Chicago Press, 2001).
19. Edwin W. Zedlewski, *Making Confinement Decisions* (Washington, DC: Bureau of Justice Statistics, 1987).
20. Zedlewski determined the cost of a single crime by dividing the total annual costs of the criminal justice system by the number of crimes committed in that year. We note here that measuring the costs of crime should take into account the full set of effects of crime on society, such as the pain and suffering of crime victims, deceased quality of life associated with fear of crime, public security expenditures, and private self-protective measures. Zedlewski captured some, but not all, of these costs. For example, he calculated the costs of private security dogs, but did not take into account victims' pain and suffering. Economists

have debated one "cost" of crime. Some economists argue that stolen property is not destroyed, it is "transferred" to others. Therefore, the value of the stolen property should not count as a social cost. Taken seriously, this should argue for subtracting the entire value of property taken from social loss estimates. This seems extreme because we know that the "resale" price of stolen property is much lower than the replacement value. Subsequent work has improved on these measures, as discussed later.

21. Edwin W. Zedlewski, "New Mathematics of Imprisonment: A Reply to Zimring and Hawkins," *Crime & Delinquency* 35 (1989): 171.
22. This work was undertaken with John J. DiIulio: John J. DiIulio, Jr., and Anne Morrison Piehl, "Does Prison Pay? The Stormy National Debate over the Cost Effectiveness of Imprisonment," *The Brookings Review* 9 (Fall 1991): 28–36; Anne Morrison Piehl and John J. DiIulio, Jr., "Does Prison Pay? Revisited." *The Brookings Review* (Winter 1995): 21–25; Anne Morrison Piehl, Bert Useem, and John J. DiIulio, Jr. *Right-Sizing Justice: A Cost–Benefit Analysis of Imprisonment in Three States. A Report of the Manhattan Institute for Policy Research Center for Civic Innovation* (New York: Manhattan Institute, 1999).
23. Although the Manhattan Institute used improved estimates of the social costs of crime compared to those used in Brookings, the consequences were slight. For New York, Arizona, and New Mexico, the correlation between using the social cost estimates calculated using the old estimates and the new estimates was 0.993.
24. Although the samples of women inmates in the three states were small, it appears that the incapacitation benefits are lower for women than they are for men. An important dimension of this finding is that the proportion of "drug-only" offenders is as high or higher for women than men. This is especially the case if "drug possessors" are included in the category of drug-only offenders. Given the small sample size, the numbers of dimensions that can be analyzed, as well as the reliability of the estimates, are limited. Here we must rely primarily on the Arizona data, which include seventy-one women inmates with crimes associated with social costs. Relative to the men in Arizona, at each point in the distribution, the social costs associated with the women were lower than for the men, although these differences were not always statistically significant.
25. Jan M. Chaiken and Marcia R. Chaiken, *Varieties of Criminal Behavior* (Santa Monica, CA: Rand Corp., 1982) 215, table A15.
26. "As the war [on drugs] heated up in the late 1980s, the street price of cocaine should have increased. . . . Instead, the street price of cocaine *fell.*" Steven R. Donziger, ed., *The Real War on Crime: The Report of the*

National Criminal Justice Commission (New York: HarperCollins, 1996), 116, emphasis in original.

27. Thomas B. Marvell and Carlisle E. Moody, "Prison Population and Crime Reduction," *Journal of Quantitative Criminology* 10 (1994): 109–139; Steven D. Levitt, "The Effect of Prison Population Size on Crime Rates: Evidence from Prison Overcrowding Litigation," *Quarterly Journal of Economics* 111 (1996): 319–352; Robert Witt and Anne Witte, "Crime, Prison, and Female Labor Supply," *Journal of Quantitative Criminology* 16 (2000): 69–85. For a discussion of these studies that highlights their methodological strengths and weaknesses, see Bert Useem, Anne Morrison Piehl, and Raymond V. Liedka, "Crime Control Effect of Incarceration: Reconsidering the Evidence, Final Report," National Institute of Justice, U.S. Department of Justice, NCJRS Document No: 188265, www.ncjrs.gov/pdffiles1/nij/grants/188265.pdf.
28. William Spelman, "The Limited Importance of Prison Expansion," in Alfred Blumstein and Joel Wallman, eds., *The Crime Drop in America* (New York: Cambridge University Press, 2000).
29. The results are reported in much greater detail in Raymond V. Liedka, Anne Morrison Piehl, and Bert Useem, "The Crime-Control Effect of Incarceration: Does Scale Matter?" *Criminology and Public Policy* 5 (2006): 249–251.
30. For many more estimates, see Ibid.
31. For example, Levitt used prison overcrowding litigation as an instrument to break the simultaneity. Levitt, "The Effect of Prison Population." Yet, there are problems with this approach: (1) it is difficult to see how, if rising crime rates cause increases in prison populations, they do not also play a role in determining overcrowding litigation because the rising crime rate leads to the overcrowding; (2) only twelve states experienced systemwide litigation during the period Levitt studied, all of them either Southern or small; and (3) the instrument is available only for one point in time, not allowing for estimation using current data. For a more complete technical discussion, see Liedka, Piehl, and Useem, "The Crime-Control Effect of Incarceration."

Chapter 4. Prison Buildup and Disorder

1. William Butler Yeats, "The Second Coming," in Richard J. Finneran, ed., *The Collected Poems of W.B. Yeats*, rev. 2d ed., (New York: Simon and Schuster, 1996), 187.
2. D.W. Brogan, *The Price of Revolution* (New York: Grosset & Dunlap, 1951), 7.
3. John Hagan, "The Imprisoned Society: Time Turns a Classic on Its Head," *Sociological Forum* 10 (1995): 524.

4. Ibid., 520,
5. Thomas G. Blomberg and Karol Lucken, *American Penology: A History of Control* (New York: Aldine de Gruyter, 2000), 132.
6. Jack A. Goldstone, Ted Robert Gurr, Barbara Harff, Marc A. Levy, Monty G. Marshall, Robert H. Bates, David L. Epstein, Colin H. Kahl, Pamela T. Surko, John C. Ulfelder, Jr., and Alan N. Unger, *State Failure Task Force Report: Phase III Findings* (McLean, VA: Science Applications International Corporation, September 30, 2000), http://globalpolicy.gmu.edu/pitf/SFTF%20Phase%20III%20Report%20Final.pdf; Gary King and Langche Zeng, "Improving Forecasts of State Failure," *World Politics* 53 (2001): 623–658; Frances Fukuyama, *State-Building, Governance, and World Order in the 21st Century* (Ithaca, NY: Cornell University Press, 2004); Robert I. Rotberg, "The Failure and Collapse of Nation-Sates: Breakdown, Prevention, and Repair," in Robert I. Rotberg, ed., *When States Fail: Causes and Consequences* (Princeton, NJ: Princeton University Press, 2004); Stephen D. Krasner, "Sharing Sovereignty: New Institutions for Collapsed and Failing States," *International Security* 29 (2004): 85–120.
7. Arthur L. Stinchcombe, "Ending Revolutions and Building New Governments," in Nelson Polsby, ed., *Annual Review of Political Science* (Palo Alto, CA: Annual Reviews, 1999), 49–73.
8. David F. Greenberg and Fay Stender, "The Prison as a Lawless Agency," *Buffalo Law Review* 21 (1972): 799–833; Dan M. Kahan, "What Do Alternative Sanctions Mean?" *University of Chicago Law Review* 63 (1996): 591–653; Richard H. McAdams, "An Attitudinal Theory of Expressive Law," *Oregon Law Review* 79 (2000): 339–389; Cass Sunstein, *Why Societies Need Dissent* (Cambridge, MA: Harvard University Press, 2003).
9. Gresham M. Sykes, *The Society of Captives: A Study of a Maximum Security Prison* (Princeton, NJ: Princeton University Press, 1958); Gresham M. Sykes, "The Structural-Functional Perspective on Punishment," in Thomas G. Blomberg and Stanley Cohen, eds., *Punishment and Social Control* (New York: Aldine de Gruyter, 2003); Erving Goffman, *Asylums: Essays on the Social Situation of Mental Patients and Other Inmates* (New York: Anchor Books, 1961); Richard A. Cloward, "Social Control in the Prison," in Richard A. Cloward, Donald R. Cressey, George H. Grosser, Richard H. McCleery, Lloyd E. Ohlin, Gresham M. Sykes, and Sheldon L. Messinger, eds., *Theoretical Studies in Social Organization of the Prison* (New York: Social Science Research Council, 1960).
10. We draw on E.V. Walter's insightful discussion of authoritarian regimes as systems of cooperation, *Terror and Resistance: A Study of Political Violence* (New York: Oxford University Press, 1969).
11. Sykes, *Society of Captives.*

12. John J. DiIulio, Jr., *Governing Prisons: A Comparative Study of Correctional Management* (New York: Free Press, 1987).
13. For additional discussion along the same lines, see William D. Hagedorn and John J. DiIulio, Jr., "The People's Court? Federal Judges and Criminal Justice," in Martha Derthick, ed., *Dilemmas of Scale in America's Federal Democracy* (Washington, DC, and Cambridge, UK: Woodrow Wilson Center Press and Cambridge University Press, 1999).
14. Leo Carroll, *Lawful Order: A Case Study of Correctional Crisis and Reform* (New York: Garland, 1998).
15. Ibid., 73–96.
16. Ibid., 316.
17. Ibid., 94.
18. Ibid., 314.
19. Jack A. Goldstone and Bert Useem, "Prison Riots as Microrevolutions: An Extension of State-Centered Theories of Revolution," *American Journal of Sociology* 67 (1999): 985–1029; Bert Useem and Jack A. Goldstone, "Forging Social Order and Its Breakdown: Riot and Reform in U.S. Prisons," *American Sociological Review* 67 (2002): 499–525.
20. Goldstone and Useem, "Prison Riots as Microrevolutions."
21. Useem and Goldstone, "Forging Social Order."
22. Two public employee unions brought the suit. They claimed that sending inmates out of state violated California's civil service laws. *New York Times*, "Transfer of Prisoners Is Ruled Illegal," February 21, 2007; Associated Press, "Judge Rules California Inmate Transfers Are Illegal," February 27, 2007.
23. *The Arizona Republic*, "Arizona Saw Problems Just before Prison Riot," April 25, 2007; Arizona Department of Corrections, "Short of Prison Beds, Arizona Plans Expansion Program," May 7, 2007, www.azcorrections.gov/adc/news/2007/050707_short_prison_beds_expansion_prog.html.
24. Ronald Anderson and Craig Hanks, "Memo: Post Event Analysis of the New Castle Correctional Facility Disturbances on April 24, 2007," Indianapolis, Indiana, Department of Corrections, May 23, 2007.
25. Author interview with New Castle Correctional Facility staff, August 2, 2007.
26. Ibid.
27. Inmates were notified at midnight that they were being transferred to another state and boarded a plane at 5:00 A.M. the next morning. Even on the plane, they were unaware of their destination. Author interview with New Castle Correctional Facility staff, August 2, 2007.
28. *Indiana Star*, "Abrupt Transfer to Indiana Stoked Anger in Arizona Inmates, Loved Ones," May 1, 2007.

29. California Department of Corrections and Rehabilitation Expert Panel on Adult Offender Reentry and Recidivism, *Report to the California State Legislature: A Roadmap for Effective Offender Programming in California.* (Sacramento: California Department of Corrections and Rehabilitation, June 29, 2007) http://ucicorrections.seweb.uci.edu/pdf/Expert_Panel_Report.pdf
30. Charles Tilly, *From Mobilization to Revolution* (Reading, MA: Addison-Wesley, 1978); Arthur L. Stinchcombe, *Theoretical Methods in Social History* (New York: Academic Press, 1978).
31. Electronic retrieval services, such as Westlaw and LexisNexis, permit a more comprehensive listing of riots using regional papers. However, these services began indexing regional newspapers in the mid-1980s. Thus, to use that information for the later years, but not to have it available for the earlier years, would introduce the sort of bias we most want to avoid. We are more interested in trends over time than the absolute number of riots. Newspaper coverage of prison riots may have improved over time, but that would work against our general argument.
32. Rare here does not imply nonexistent, or a permanent feature.
33. If there has been a large change in the composition of the inmate population, especially toward the imprisonment of increasingly large proportions of nonviolent offenders, then the use of total prison population would be an inappropriate denominator. Data in Chapter 3 show some, but not dramatic, changes in "who" goes to prison over time.
34. Our argument parallels the one developed by Matthew Silberman, *A World of Violence: Corrections in America* (Belmont, CA: Wadsworth, 1995), 121.
35. Loïc Wacquant, "Deadly Symbiosis: When Ghetto and Prison Meet and Merge," *Punishment and Society* 3 (2001): 111.
36. See Franklin E. Zimring and Gordon Hawkins, *Crime Is Not the Problem: Lethal Violence in America* (New York: Oxford University Press, 1997), 40–44. Best measured does not imply perfectly measured. For example, homicides may be mistaken for suicides, and vice versa. James Q. Wilson and Richard J. Herrnstein, *Crime and Human Nature* (New York: Simon & Schuster, 1985), 34–35.
37. The prison population differs greatly from the U.S. resident population in terms of their demographic characteristics. Christopher Mumola of the Bureau of Justice Statistics calculates the homicide rate among the general population if they were matched to the prison population by gender, age, and race. Using 2002 data, he calculates that the resident population would have had a homicide rate of 35 per 100,000, which is almost nine times greater than the rate of homicide

in state prisons. Christopher Mumola, *Suicide and Homicide in State Prisons and Local Jails* (Washington, DC: Bureau of Justice Statistics, 2005), 11.

38. These data should be treated with caution. In varying degrees, states mix in with their counts of escapes, attempted escapes, and walkways from low-security facilities. However, as long as this mix does not change over time, these reporting problems will not affect the overall trends.
39. Protective custody units segregate inmates from the rest of the population to protect, rather than to punish, them. They are typically single cells, and are labor intensive for staff and expensive to operate. Although systematic data are unavailable, veteran corrections administrators assert that protective custody was used little before the 1960s. Ron Angelone, "Protective Custody Inmates," in Peter M. Carlson and Judith Simon Garrett, eds., *Prison and Jail Administration: Theory and Practice* (Gaithersburg, MD: Aspen, 1999).
40. In the 2000 Census, BJS adopted the term "major disturbance" rather than "riot" for classifying incidents involving five or more inmates. This change does not affect the results we report.
41. John J. Gibbons and Nicholas de B. Katzenbach, *Confronting Confinement: A Report of the Commission on Safety and Abuse in America's Prison* (New York: Vera Institute of Justice, 2006).
42. Ibid., 11–12, 110.
43. Ibid., 110.
44. Only seven of the ninety-eight witnesses were either prisoners or family members of prisoners.
45. Ibid., 22.
46. These questions ask inmates about assaults that may have occurred any time since the start of their most recent incarceration. The longer an inmate is in prison, the more likely he or she will have experienced at least one such incident. In 1991, the average amount of time served was 32.4 months; in 2004, this average increased to 54.5 months. This upward trend strengthens the finding of a modest decline in the number of assaults behind bars from 1991 to 2004.
47. *Corrections Yearbook* (South Salem, NY, and Middletown, CT: Criminal Justice Institute, annually, 1987–2002).
48. For example, for 1986, the *Corrections Yearbook* reports the number of "total assaults" by inmates against staff and inmates. The next year, the yearbook reports only the number of "serious assaults" by inmates against staff and inmates. Along the same lines, for the years 1989 through 1993, an assault against an inmate was counted only if the assaulted inmate required medical attention.

49. The Bureau of Justice Statistics defines a confinement institution as one in which less than one-half of the prisoners are permitted to leave the prison unaccompanied by staff.
50. These trends should be treated cautiously. Facilities do not always distinguish the various forms of restrictive housing (e.g., disciplinary segregation, administrative segregation, protective custody). Although there is no reason to believe this reporting problem has changed over time, it may have.
51. David A. Ward, "Supermaximum Facilities," in Peter M. Carlson and Judith Simon Garrett, eds., *Prison and Jail Administration: Theory and Practice* (Gaithersburg, MD: Aspen, 1999); Chase Riveland, *Supermax Prisons: Overview and General Considerations* (Washington, DC: National Institute of Corrections, 1999).
52. Roy D. King, "The Rise and Rise of Supermax: An American Solution in Search of a Problem?" *Punishment and Society* 1 (1999): 163–186.
53. Leena Kurki and Norval Morris, "The Purposes, Practices, and Problems of Supermaximum Prisons," in Michael Tonry and Joan Petersilia, eds., *Crime and Justice: A Review of Research* (Chicago: University of Chicago Press, 2001), 385–424.
54. King, "The Rise and Rise of Supermax."
55. Hans Toch, "Trends in Correctional Leadership," *Corrections Compendium* 27 (2002): 24–25.
56. Jesenia Pizarro and Vanja Stenius, "Supermax Prisons: Their Rise, Current Practices, and Effects on Inmates," *The Prison Journal* 84 (2004): 248–264.
57. Jonathan Simon, "The 'Society of Captives' in the Era of Hyper-Incarceration," *Theoretical Criminology* 4 (2000): 301.
58. We are addressing here the narrow issue of the effect of supermaxes on prison order. One can both believe that supermaxes fail to meet ethical and legal standards of just punishment, and that they do not contribute to order. For example, Craig Haney offers a highly negative assessment of the harmful psychological consequences of supermax prisons. Without contradiction, Haney can also approvingly cite Brigg's study (noted in note 57), indicating that supermax confinement does not reduce systemwide violence. Craig Haney, "Mental Health Issues in Long Term Solitary and 'Supermax' Confinement," *Crime and Delinquency* 49 (2004): 130; Craig Haney, *Reforming Punishment: Psychological Limits to the Pains of Imprisonment* (Washington, DC: American Psychological Association, 2006), 217.
59. Chad S. Briggs, Jody L. Sundt, and Thomas C. Castellano, "The Effect of Supermaximum Security Prisons on Aggregate Levels of Institutional Violence," *Criminology* 43 (2003): 1341–1376.

60. For a broader discussion of the effects of supermax facilities on prison order, drawing a similar conclusion, see Daniel P. Mears and Michael D. Reisig, "The Theory and Practice of Supermax Prisons," *Punishment and Society* 8 (2006): 33–57.
61. Malcolm M. Feeley and Edward L. Rubin, *Judicial Policy Making and the Modern State: How the Courts Reformed America's Prisons* (Cambridge, UK: Cambridge University Press, 1998); Margo Schlanger, "Inmate Litigation," *Harvard Law Review* 116 (2003): 1557–1706.
62. Feeley and Rubin, *Judicial Policy Making*, 617.
63. Ibid., 657.
64. Margo Schlanger, "Inmate Litigation."
65. Ibid., 1694.
66. Ibid., 1672.
67. Ibid., 1690.
68. Feeley and Rubin, *Judicial Policy Making*, 655.
69. Richard Posner points out that judges develop an "institutional competence" in matters that routinely come before them, such as accidents, contracts, and ordinary crime. On other issues, such as national security, they may have little background knowledge and have neither the time nor the staff to overcome this deficiency. Richard A. Posner, *Not a Suicide Pact: The Constitution in a Time of National Emergency* (New York: Oxford University Press, 2006), 35–36. Likewise, there is no reason to believe that judges are experts in correctional administration. Clair Cripe, former general counsel of the Federal Bureau of Prisons, observes, "What federal judge has *any* knowledge of about how a prison should be run? Not a single one that I know of." Clair A. Cripe, "Courts, Corrections, and the Constitution: A Practitioner's View," in John J. DiIulio, Jr., ed., *Courts, Corrections, and the Constitution: The Impact of Judicial Intervention on Prisons and Jails* (New York: Oxford University Press, 1990), 279, emphasis in original.
70. John J. DiIulio, Jr., *Governing Prisons*, 294, fn. 23.
71. Ibid., 86.
72. DiIulio, however, points out weaknesses in the Huron Valley's architecture. For example, the gun towers were poorly positioned and the control centers were open, allowing inmates to move around the desks at which the officers sat.
73. DiIulio, *Governing Prisons*, 86.
74. Howard Bidna, "Effects of Increased Security on Prison Violence," *Journal of Criminal Justice* 3 (1975): 33–46.
75. New York State Commission of Correction (NYSCC), *Investigation of Disturbances at Otis Bantum Correctional Center, August 14, 1990* (Albany: NYSCC, 1991); NYSCC, *Inquiry into Disturbances on Rikers Island, October 1986* (Albany: NYSCC, 1987).

76. Rotberg, "The Failure and Collapse of Nation-States," 4.
77. Ann Chih Lin, *Reform in the Making: The Implementation of Social Policy in Prison* (Princeton, NJ: Princeton University Press, 2000).
78. Joan Petersilia, "From Cell to Society: Who Is Returning Home?" in Jeremy Travis and Christy Visher, eds., *Prisoner Reentry and Crime in America* (New York: Cambridge University Press, 2005), 41.
79. Ibid.

Chapter 5. The Buildup and Inmate Release

1. Former Attorney General Janet Reno asking Jeremy Travis, director of the National Institute of Justice under Reno. Quoted in Ellis Cose, "The Dawn of a New Movement," *Newsweek*, April 24, 2006.
2. Many of the ideas in this chapter were developed during a long collaboration between the author (Piehl) with Stefan LoBuglio, now Chief of the Montgomery County (Maryland) Pre-release and Reentry Services Division. We are indebted to him for the work underlying this chapter.
3. Joan Petersilia, *When Prisoners Come Home* (New York: Oxford University Press, 2003); Jeremy Travis, *But They All Come Back: Facing the Challenges of Prisoner Reentry* (Washington, DC: Urban Institute Press, 2005).
4. Allen J. Beck and Bernard E. Shipley, *Recidivism of Prisoners Released in 1983* (Washington, DC: Bureau of Justice Statistics, 1989); Patrick A. Langan and David J. Levin, *Recidivism of Prisoners Released in 1994* (Washington, DC: Bureau of Justice Statistics, 2002).
5. John Hagan and Ronit Dinovitzer, "Collateral Consequences of Imprisonment for Children, Communities, and Prisoners," in Michael Tonry and Joan Petersilia, eds., *Prisons* (Chicago: University of Chicago Press, 1999); Joan Petersilia, *When Prisoners Return to the Community: Political, Economic, and Social Consequences* (Washington, DC: National Institute of Justice, 2000).
6. Douglas C. McDonald, "Medical Care in Prisons," in Michael Tonry and Joan Petersilia, eds., *Prisons* (Chicago: University of Chicago Press, 1999), 121–163; Laura M. Maruschak and Allen J. Beck, *Medical Problems of Inmates, 1997* (Washington, DC: Bureau of Justice Statistics, 2001); Gerald G. Gaes and Newton Kendig, *The Skill Sets and Health Care Needs of Released Offenders,* (Washington DC: Urban Institute, 2002).
7. James Austin, John Irwin, and Patricia Hardyman, *Exploring the Needs and Risks of the Returning Prisoner Population* (Washington, DC: Urban Institute, 2001); Creasie Finney Hairston, *Prisoners and Families: Parenting Issues During Incarceration* (Washington, DC: Urban Institute, 2001); Dina R. Rose and Todd R. Clear, *Incarceration, Reentry and Social*

Capital: Social Networks in the Balance (Washington, DC: Urban Institute, 2001).

8. Results of this effort can be found at www.svori.org.
9. See the Urban Institute web site for descriptions of released inmates in several states, www.urban.org/center/jpc/index.cfm.
10. Harry J. Holzer, *Employer Attitudes towards Hiring Ex-Offenders* (Washington, DC: Urban Institute, 2000); Marc Mauer and Meda Chesney-Lind, eds., *Invisible Punishment: The Collateral Consequences of Mass Imprisonment* (Washington, DC: New Press, 2002); Nancy Fishman, *Briefing Paper: Legal Barriers to Prisoner Reentry in New Jersey* (Newark: New Jersey Institute for Social Justice, 2003).
11. For proposals on reentry, see Faye S. Taxman, Douglas Young, James M. Byrne, Alexander Holsinger, and Donald Anspach, *From Prison Safety to Public Safety: Innovation in Offender Reentry* (Washington, DC: Bureau of Governmental Research, University of Maryland, 2001); The Re-Entry Policy Council, *Charting the Safe and Successful Return of Prisoners to the Community* (New York: The Counsel of State Governments, 2006).
12. Descriptions and analyses of reentry issues faced by the 12 million releasees from local jails each year were produced for a joint effort of the Urban Institute; John Jay College of Criminal Justice at the City University of New York; and Montgomery County, Maryland. They can be found at www.urban.org/projects/reentry-roundtable/roundtable9.cfm.
13. Characteristics of inmate populations can be found in the prisoner self-report surveys discussed previously or in administrative data available from the Bureau of Justice Statistics or compiled in Petersilia, *When Prisoners Come Home.*
14. James P. Lynch and William J. Sabol, *Prisoner Reentry in Perspective* (Washington, DC: Urban Institute Justice Policy Center, 2001).
15. Ibid; Joan Petersilia "Understanding California Corrections: Summary," University of California Irvine, Center for Evidence-Based Corrections. May 2006. http://ucicorrections.seweb.uci.edu/pdf/cprcsummary.pdf.
16. Alfred Blumstein and Allen J. Beck, "Reentry as a Transient State between Liberty and Recommitment," in Jeremy Travis and Christy Visher, eds., *Prisoner Reentry and Crime in America* (Cambridge, UK: Cambridge University Press, 2005), 67.
17. Joan Petersilia, "Parole and Prisoner Reentry in the United States," in Michael Tonry and Joan Petersilia, eds., *Prisons* (Chicago: University of Chicago Press, 1999), 554; Michael Tonry, *The Fragmentation of Sentencing and Corrections in America* (Washington, DC: National Institute of Justice, 1999).
18. Daniel Glaser, *The Effectiveness of a Prison and Parole System* (Indianapolis, IN: Bobbs-Merrill, 1964).

19. Timothy Hughes, Doris James Wilson, and Allen J. Beck, *Trends in State Parole, 1990–2000* (Washington, DC: Bureau of Justice Statistics, 2001).
20. Lauren E. Glaze, *Probation and Parole in the United States, 2001* (Washington, DC: Bureau of Justice Statistics, 2002).
21. The Violent Crime and Law Enforcement Act of 1994 (P.L. 103–322).
22. Paula M. Ditton and Doris James Wilson, *Truth in Sentencing in State Prisons* (Washington, DC: Bureau of Justice Statistics, 1999).
23. Lauren E. Glaze and Seri Palla, *Probation and Parole in the United States, 2004* (Washington, DC: Bureau of Justice Statistics, 2005).
24. Glaze, *Probation and Parole in the United States, 2001*. It is hard to reconcile these figures with others on the use of probation for postincarceration supervision. For more details, see Anne Morrison Piehl and Stefan F. LoBuglio, "Does Supervision Matter?" in Jeremy Travis and Christy Visher, eds., *Prisoner Reentry and Crime in America* (Cambridge, UK: Cambridge University Press, 2005), 105–138.
25. In some cases, offenders may receive postrelease supervision from more than one agency. Anne M. Piehl, *From Cell to Street: A Plan to Supervise Inmates after Release* (Boston: Massachusetts Institute for a New Commonwealth, 2002).
26. There is, of course, a federal jurisdiction for sentencing, incarcerating, and providing postincarceration supervision. In this chapter, we emphasize the fifty state jurisdictions that cover approximately 90% of both those on parole and those incarcerated in prisons. We exclude the District of Columbia from direct analysis because of its peculiar and changing relationship to the federal system.
27. Federal legislation (Violent Crime Control and Law Enforcement Act of 1994 and its 1996 amendments) provided grant incentives for states to increase the use of incarceration for those convicted of violent offenses. One standard in the grant program was that offenders should serve 85% of the imposed sentence. A comprehensive analysis of sentencing reforms in the mid- and late 1990s argues that the impact of the federal grant program on the states was modest and that it reflected reform in the states more than it influenced it. William J. Sabol, Katherine Rosich, Kamala Mallik Kane, David P. Kirk, and Glenn Dubin, *The Influence of Truth-in-Sentencing Reforms on Changes in States' Sentencing Practices and Prison Populations* (Washington, DC: Urban Institute, Justice Policy Center, 2002).
28. Paula M. Ditton and Doris James Wilson, *Truth in Sentencing in State Prisons* (Washington, DC: Bureau of Justice Statistics, 1999).
29. Ilyana Kuziemko, "Going off Parole: How the Elimination of Discretionary Prison Release Affects the Social Cost of Crime" (Cambridge, MA: Harvard University Economics Department, 2006).

30. Massachusetts Sentencing Commission, *Survey of Sentencing Practices, FY 1999*, January, 2000, table 23.
31. These numbers come from Jamie Watson, *Community Corrections Programs at the Suffolk County House of Correction: Strategies for Optimizing Use while Minimizing Risk* (Cambridge, MA: Kennedy School of Government, Harvard University, 2002).
32. Subsequent to the study, the halfway house placement rates increased noticeably, which were the result of better procedures to track inmates who were eligible for prerelease from the moment of their admission to the Suffolk County House of Correction. For more on implementation of reentry programming, see Anne M. Piehl, Stefan LoBuglio, and Richard B. Freeman, *Prospects for Prisoner Reentry*, Economic Policy Institute Working Paper No. 125 (Washington, DC: Economic Policy Institute, 2003).
33. Lynch and Sabol, *Prisoner Reentry in Perspective*; Petersilia, *When Prisoners Come.*
34. Glaser, *The Effectiveness of a Prison and Parole System.*
35. Piehl and LoBuglio, "Does Supervision Matter?"
36. One of the more compelling aspects of the Boston strategy against youth violence in the 1990s was the blurring of support and surveillance functions, both within and across agencies. See Anne Morrison Piehl, David M. Kennedy, and Anthony A. Braga, "Problem Solving and Youth Violence: An Evaluation of the Boston Gun Project," *American Law and Economics Review* 2 (2000): 58–106. Other examples abound. For exemplary programs in reentry, see www.reentrypolicy.org/reentry/Program_Examples.aspx.
37. Amy L. Solomon, Vera Kachnowski, and Avi Bhati, *Does Parole Work? Analyzing the Impact of Postprison Supervision on Rearrest Outcomes* (Washington, DC: Urban Institute, 2005). A synopsis of the study and reaction pieces are in *Perspectives: The Journal of the American Parole and Probation Association* 30 (2006): 26–61.
38. Hughes, Wilson, and Beck, *Trends in State Parole, 1990–2000*; Jeremy Travis and Sarah Lawrence, *Beyond the Prison Gates: The State of Parole in America* (Washington, DC: Urban Institute, 2002).
39. Glaze and Palla, *Probation and Parole in the United States, 2004.*
40. Hughes, Wilson, and Beck, *Trends in State Parole, 1990–2000.*
41. Because California is so large and is an outlier, the nationwide figures are very sensitive to the experience of this state. In fact, the Bureau of Justice Statistics reports that "when California data are excluded, the 'success' rate for all parole discharges rises to 53% (from 42%), and the rate for mandatory parolees increases to 64% (from 33%) in 1999." Glaze, *Probation and Parole in the United States, 2001.*
42. Hughes, Wilson, and Beck, *Trends in State Parole, 1990–2000.*

43. Kevin Reitz, "Questioning the Conventional Wisdom of Parole Release Authority," in Michael Tonry, ed., *The Future of Imprisonment in the 21st Century* (New York: Oxford University Press, 2004), 215.
44. Piehl, *From Cell to Street.*
45. Kuziemko, *Going Off Parole.*
46. Reitz, "Questioning the Conventional Wisdom of Parole Release Authority."
47. Piehl and LoBuglio, "Does Supervision Matter?"
48. Glaser, *The Effectiveness of a Prison and Parole System.*
49. Joan Petersilia and Susan Turner, "Intensive Probation and Parole," in Michael H. Tonry, ed., *Crime and Justice: A Review of Research* (Chicago: University of Chicago Press, 1993).
50. Ibid.
51. Ibid.
52. Anne Morrison Piehl, "Debating the Effectiveness of Parole," *Perspectives: The Journal of the American Probation and Parole Association* 30(2): 54–61.

Chapter 6. Impact of the Buildup on the Labor Market

1. Richard B. Freeman, "Why Do So Many Young American Men Commit Crimes and What Might We Do About It," *Journal of Economic Perspectives* 10 (1996): 27.
2. U.S. Department of Labor, Bureau of Labor Statistics, "Unemployment Level," 2006, http://data.bls.gov/cgi-bin/surveymost?ln.
3. Lawrence E. Katz and Alan B. Krueger, "The High Pressure U.S. Labor Market of the 1990s," *Brookings Papers on Economic Activity* 1999 (1991): 1–65; Bruce Western and Katherine Beckett, "How Unregulated Is the U.S. Labor Market? The Penal System as a Labor Market Institution," *American Journal of Sociology* 104 (1999): 1030–1060; Bruce Western and Becky Pettit, "Incarceration and Racial Inequality in Men's Employment," *Industrial and Labor Relations Review* 54 (2000): 3–16; Bruce Western, *Punishment and Inequality in America* (New York: Russell Sage Foundation, 2006).
4. Bruce Western and Becky Pettit, "Black–White Wage Inequality, Employment Rates, and Incarceration," *American Journal of Sociology* 111(2005): 553–578; Western, *Punishment and Inequality.*
5. Western and Pettit, "Incarceration and Racial Inequality"; Amitabh Chandra, "Is the Convergence in the Racial Wage Gap Illusory?" Working Paper 9476, National Bureau of Economic Research, Cambridge, MA, 2003.
6. Western and Beckett, "The U.S. Penal System."

7. Starting in July 2001, the sample size was increased to 60,000 households. *Current Population Survey: Design and Methodology. Technical Paper 63RV* (Washington, DC: Bureau of Labor Statistics and U.S. Census Bureau, 2002), www.census.gov/prod/2002pubs/tp63rv.pdf. For a brief discussion of the conceptual and practical difficulties in calculating the population of potential workers, see U.S. Department of Labor, Bureau of Labor Statistics, "Labor Supply in a Tight Labor Market," *Issues in Labor Statistics,* Summary 00–13, June 2000.
8. Many inmates work while incarcerated, in prison jobs, in prison industries (run by public or private companies), or in the private sector through work release programs. None of these categories of work are captured in labor market statistics.
9. In the long run, even those who have withdrawn from the labor market may respond to incentives to return. So, the unemployment rate captures a short- to medium-run phenomenon.
10. Western and Beckett, "The U.S. Penal System."
11. We note that many prison systems have contracts with private companies to provide inmate labor. Although these agreements tend to cover a small number of those incarcerated at any given time, it is possible that they would continue to expand if demand for labor grows.
12. Economist Bernard Salanié, for example, develops some evidence that the riots that swept across France in 2005 were the by-product of high rates of unemployment, especially for young workers. Bernard Salanié, "The Riots in France: An Economist's View," Social Science Research Council, http://riotsfrance.ssrc.org/Salanie/. Several studies have examined whether unemployment contributed to the wave of U.S. urban riots from 1964 to 1971. For a finding of "no effect," see Seymour Spilerman, "Structural Characteristics of Cities and Severity of Racial Disorders," *American Sociological Review* 36 (1976): 771–793. More recent work has found a link between unemployment and rioting in this period. See, e.g., Daniel Myers, "Racial Rioting in the 1960s: An Event History Analysis of Local Conditions," *American Sociological Review* 62 (1997): 94–112, and Susan Olzak and Suzanne Shanahan, "Deprivation and Race Riots: An Extension of Spilerman's Analysis," *Social Forces* 77 (1996): 941–961.
13. Western and Beckett, "The U.S. Penal System."
14. Ibid., 1038.
15. Ibid., 1039. Western and Beckett define the influence of incarceration on "the unemployment rate by keeping those with high unemployment risk out of the labor market" as the "causal" effect of incarceration. The extent to which unemployment is "hidden" because of removal of jobless inmates from the statistics is referred to as the "accounting" effect. Ibid., 1038.
16. Ibid., 1040.

17. Ibid., 1042, figure 2.
18. Some of these concerns raised by Clogg are arguably less relevant during periods when economic activity is high. Clifford C. Clogg, *Measuring Underemployment: Demographic Indicators for the United States* (New York: Academic Press, 1979).
19. Jeffrey R. Kling and Alan B. Krueger, "Costs, Benefits, and Distributional Consequences of Inmate Labor," *Proceedings of the 53rd Annual Meeting of the Industrial Relations Research Association*, 349–358.
20. Ibid.
21. Bruce Western and Becky Pettit, "Incarceration and Racial Inequality in Men's Employment," *Industrial and Labor Relations Review* 54 (2000): 3–16.
22. Katz and Krueger, "The High Pressure U.S. Labor Market."
23. Western and Beckett, "The U.S. Penal System as a Labor Market."
24. Western and Pettit, "Incarceration and Racial Inequality," 4.
25. Ibid., figure 1.
26. In his more recent publication, Bruce Western takes a similar approach. He calculates the "true rate" of joblessness by adding to the unemployed prison and jail inmates. The effects of this addition are highlighted by focusing on the demographic group most likely to be incarcerated, men aged 22 to 30 years. Using data for 2000, adding prisoners and jail inmates, increases unemployment by 35% for black young men, 14% for Hispanic young men, and 12% for white young men. *Punishment and Inequality*, 89–90.
27. Katz and Krueger, "The High Pressure U.S. Labor Market"; Western and Beckett, "The U.S Penal System."
28. Ibid.
29. Jeffrey R. Kling, "Incarceration Length, Employment, and Earnings," *American Economic Review* 96 (2006): 863–876.
30. Ibid.
31. To be sure, there are differences in the way the questions are worded. The Current Population Survey asks about activity "last week," whereas the inmate survey asks whether the respondent had a job "during the month before your arrest." Furthermore, the Current Population Survey questions are more detailed than the inmate survey about the reasons a respondent may not have been at work. However, the inmate survey does ask a question that allows one to define who might be in the labor force but not working. See U.S. Department of Labor, Bureau of Labor Statistics, 2001, *How the Government Measures Unemployment*, www.bls.gov/cps/cps_htgm.htm and U.S. Department of Justice, Bureau of Justice Statistics and Federal Bureau of Prisons, *Survey of Inmates in State and Federal Correctional Facilities, 1997*, National Archive of Criminal Justice Data, www.icpsrumich.edu/cocoon/NACJD/STUDY/02598.xml.

32. Western and Beckett, "The U.S. Penal System."
33. The 1997 numbers appear to be quite similar. The authors' calculations from U.S. Department of Justice, *Survey of Inmates*, reveal that 68% of state inmates were employed in the month prior to the current arrest.
34. David Greenberg develops a similar critique that the counterfactual unemployment rates used by Western and Beckett are too high. His paper also provides citations to additional data sources to support this position. David F. Greenberg, "*Novus Ordo Saeclorum?* A Commentary on Downes, and on Beckett and Western," *Punishment & Society* 3 (2001): 81–94.
35. Lisa Barrow, "Is the Official Unemployment Rate Misleading? A Look at the Labor Market Statistics over the Business Cycle," *Federal Reserve Bank of Chicago Economic Perspectives* 28 (2004): 21–35.
36. For a negative assessment, see Austan Goolsbee, "The Unemployment Myth," Op-ed, *New York Times*, November 30, 2003. He states about the expansion of Social Security Disability Insurance, "Almost all of the increase came from hard-to-verify disabilities like back pain and mental disorders. As the rolls swelled, the meaning of the official unemployment rate changed as millions of Americans were left out."
37. Western and Beckett, "The U.S. Penal System," 1037.
38. Katz and Krueger, "The High Pressure U.S. Labor Market"; Western and Beckett, "The U.S Penal System"; Western, *Punishment and Inequality*.
39. Western and Beckett, "The U.S. Penal System," 1051.
40. In terms of raw counts, the number of juveniles detained for law violations grew from 62,248 in 1983 to 96,655 in 2003, an increase of 55% (authors' calculations from Office of Juvenile Justice and Delinquency Prevention [OJJDP], *OJJDP Statistical Briefing Book*, 1999 and ojjdp.ncjrs.gov/ojstatbb/corrections/qa08201.asp?qaDate=2003). For the same period, the number of adults in the custody of state and federal prisons rose from 487,593 to 1,390,279, an increase of 185%. U.S. Department of Justice, Bureau of Justice Statistics, *Key Facts at a Glance*, http://www.ojp.usdoj.gov/bjs/glance/tables/corr2tab.htm. Levitt reported evidence that the rate of incarceration per offense grew substantially for adults relative to juveniles through 1993. Steven D. Levitt, "The Effect of Prison Population Size on Crime Rates: Evidence from Prison Overcrowding Litigation," *Quarterly Journal of Economics* 111 (1996): 319–352.
41. Western, "Punishment and Inequality," 115–116.
42. Kling, "Incarceration Length, Employment, and Earnings."
43. Ibid., 864.

44. Karen Needels, "Go Directly to Jail and Do Not Collect? A Long-Term Study of Recidivism, Employment, and Earnings Patterns among Prison Releasees," *Journal of Research in Crime & Delinquency* 33 (1996): 471–496, and John H. Tyler and Jeffrey R. Kling, "Prison-Based Education and Reentry into the Mainstream Labor Market," unpublished paper, Brookings Institution. See also reviews by Anne Morrison Piehl, "Economic Conditions, Work, and Crime," in Michael Tonry, ed., *Handbook on Crime and Punishment* (New York: Oxford University Press, 1988), and Bruce Western, Jeffrey R. Kling, and David F. Weiman, "The Labor Market Consequences of Incarceration," *Crime and Delinquency* 47 (2001): 410–427. A forthcoming volume, edited by Shawn Bushway and colleagues, contains essays from these and other researchers analyzing institutions driving labor markets for those with prison experience and criminal records. As with our reading of the literature, the evidence assembled in the new volume is not generally optimistic about the prospects for improving labor market outcomes for those recently released from prison. Shawn D. Bushway, Michael Stoll, and David Weiman, eds., *Barriers to Reentry? The Labor Market for Released Prisoners in Post-Industrial America* (New York: Russell Sage Foundation, 2007).
45. Joan Petersilia, *When Prisoners Come Home* (New York: Oxford University Press, 2003), 119.
46. Amy L. Solomon, Kelly Dedel Johnson, Jeremy Travis, and Elizabeth C. McBride, "From Prison to Work: The Employment Dimensions of Prisoner Reentry," Urban Institute, Justice Policy, 2004, www.urban.org/UploadedPDF/411097_From_Prison_to_Work.pdf.
47. Matthew R. Durose and Christopher J. Mumola, *Profile of Nonviolent Offenders Exiting State Prisons* (Washington, DC: Bureau of Justice Statistics, 2004).
48. Harry J. Holzer, Steven Raphael, and Michael A. Stoll, *Employer Demand for Ex-Offenders: Recent Evidence from Los Angeles* (Washington, DC: Urban Institute).Harry J. Holzer, Steven Raphael, and Michael A. Stoll, "The Labor Market for Ex-Offenders in Los Angeles: Problems, Challenges, and Public Policy" (Washington, DC: Urban Institute), http://urbaninstitute.org/UploadedPDF/410779_ExOffenders.pdf.
49. Holzer, Raphael, and Stoll, "Employer Demand," 8.
50. Holzer, Raphael, and Stoll, "The Labor Market for Ex-Offenders," 8.
51. Ibid, 11.
52. Devah Pager, "The Mark of a Criminal Career," *American Journal of Sociology* 108 (2003): 937–975.
53. A problem with "audit" studies is that the auditors may be aware of the purposes of the experiment, and either consciously or unconsciously act in ways to generate data consistent with hypothesis of the

experiment – here to find evidence of racial and offender discrimination. To get around this problem, Bertrand and Mullainathan sent fictitious resumes to help wanted ads in Boston and Chicago, with each resume randomly assigned either a very "white" or very "black" first name. Consistent with Pager findings, resumes with "white" names resulted in 50% more callbacks than resumes with "black" names. Marianne Bertrand and Sendhil Mullainathan, "Are Emily and Greg More Employable Than Lakisha and Jamal? A Field Experiment on Labor Market Discrimination," *American Economic Review* 94 (2004): 991–1013. Pager addresses the issue of "experimenter effect," but almost exclusively in terms of auditors acting differently when they were assigned a "criminal record" ("Mark of a Criminal Record," 969–970). Bertrand and Mullainathan findings are important in this regard because employers are reacting to nonvarying resumes rather than potentially varying people. There can be no experimenter effect.

54. Devah Pager, "Double Jeopardy: Race, Crime, and Getting a Job," *Wisconsin Law Review* 617 (2005): 617.
55. Western and Beckett, "The U.S. Penal System."
56. Richard B. Freeman and William M. Rodgers III, "Area Economic Conditions and the Labor Market Outcomes of Young Men in the 1990s Expansion," in Robert Cherry and William Rodgers III, eds., *Prosperity for All? The Economic Boom and African Americans* (New York: Russell Sage Foundation, 2000).
57. More details about the data and results reported here are available from the authors.
58. If "P" is the unemployment rate or the employment ratio, then the dependent variable is log(P/1–P).
59. Because of the various lags of the percent change in SPP, the first 3 years of data (1982–1984) are lost to missing data on male incarceration prior to 1981. The total sample size for all the models is 1050 (21 years × 50 states).
60. In an effort to test liberally for any effects of the lags of the change in SPP, an omnibus F-test for the inclusion of the lags as a group was conducted. However, this test is not significant in any model.
61. We conducted a large number of robustness checks to be sure that small changes in model specification did not yield dissimilar findings. We performed four types of checks. First, we reestimated the equations using untransformed values of the unemployment rate and employment ratios, as well as an additional transformation as an alternative to the logit, the arcsin transform. Second, the models were reestimated for only 1990s data in case the relationships in the data had changed over time. Third, the models were again reestimated, but weighting

for each state's population relative to the national total. Finally, we estimated partial and full error correction models to provide more structure to the estimation strategy.

62. Western and Beckett, "The U.S. Penal System."
63. William Lyons and Stuart Scheingold, "The Politics of Crime and Punishment," in Gary LaFree, ed., *The Nature of Crime: Continuity and Change* (Washington, DC: National Institute of Justice, 2002), 104.

Chapter 7. Conclusion: Right-Sizing Prison

1. E. V. Walter, "Power, Civilization, and the Psychology of Conscience," *American Political Science Review* 53 (1959): 642.
2. Lester C. Thurow, "Changing the Nature of Capitalism," in Rowan Gibson, ed., *Rethinking the Future: Rethinking Business, Principles, Competition, Control and Complexity, Leadership, Markets and the World* (London: Nicholas Brealey, 1997), 233.
3. We are using the term "tradition" loosely here. The connection between Wacquant and Foucault is much more direct than between Garland and Foucault, and Garland has criticized Foucault quite extensively.
4. Gresham Sykes, *Society of Captives: A Study of a Maximum Security Prison* (Princeton, NJ: Princeton University Press, 1958). We also drew on the work of E. V. Walter, especially *Terror and Resistance: A Study of Political Violence* (New York: Oxford University Press, 1969).
5. The Commonwealth of Massachusetts, Department of Correction Advisory Council, "Preliminary Report," June 17, 2005, www.mass.gov/Eeops/docs/eops/DCAC_prelim_report_061705.pdf.
6. John J. Gibbons and Nicholas de B. Katzenbach, *Confronting Confinement: A Report of the Commission on Safety and Abuse in America's Prison* (New York: Vera Institute of Justice, 2006).
7. For a discussion of the growth of the workload in federal courts, with supportive data, see Richard A. Posner, *The Federal Courts: Challenge and Reform* (Cambridge, MA: Harvard University Press, 1996), ch. 3.
8. Feeley and Rubin, *Judicial Policy Making*, 65–79.
9. James Q. Whitman, *Harsh Justice: Criminal Punishment and the Widening Divide between American and Europe* (New York: Oxford University Press, 2003).
10. Ibid., 60.
11. Devah Pager, "The Mark of a Criminal Career," *American Journal of Sociology* 108 (2003): 937–975.
12. Robin Campbell, *Dollars and Sentences: Legislators' Views on Prison, Punishment, and the Budget Crisis* (New York: Vera Institute of Justice, 2003).

13. *The Fiscal Survey of States* (Washington, DC: National Governors Association and National Association of State Budget Officers, 2006), 1.
14. Robert D. Behn and Elizabeth K. Keating, *Facing the Fiscal Crisis in State Governments: National Problem; National Responsibility* (Cambridge, MA: The Taubman Center for State and Local Government, John F. Kennedy School of Government, Harvard University, 2004).
15. Justice Policy Institute, "Cellblocks or Classrooms?: The Funding of Higher Education and Corrections and Its Impact on African American Men," Washington, DC, 2002, www.soros.org/initiatives/justice/articles_publications/publications/cellblocks_20020918.
16. The category "corrections" includes both the cost to build and operate prisons and, for some states, probation, parole, and juvenile justice functions. Spending on prisons alone cannot be broken out with this data set. Excluded is spending on federal and local corrections.
17. *Fiscal Survey of the States*, 8.
18. Donald Boyd also makes this recommendation in *State and Local Governments Face Continued Fiscal Pressure* (Albany, NY: The Rockefeller Institute of Government Fiscal Studies Program, January 2005).
19. Claudia Goldin, "The Human-Capital Century and American Leadership: Virtues of the Past," *Journal of Economic History* 61 (2001): 263–292.
20. Isaac Ehrlich, "The Mystery of Human Capital as an Engine of Growth, or Why the US Became the Economic Superpower in the 20th Century," NBER Working Paper, No. 12868, National Bureau of Economic Research, Cambridge, MA, 2007.
21. Irwin Kirsch, Henry Braun, Kentaro Yamamoto, and Andrew Sum, *Policy Information Report: America's Perfect Storm: Three Forces Changing Our Nation's Future* (Princeton, NJ: Educational Testing Service, 2007).
22. See, among others, James J. Heckman and Dimitriy V. Masterov, "The Productivity Argument for Investing in Young Children," NBER Working Paper 13016, National Bureau of Economic Research, Cambridge, MA, 2007; F. J. Cunha, J. J. Heckman, L. J. Lochner, and D. V. Masterov, "Interpreting the Evidence on Life Cycle Skill Formation," in E. A. Hanushek and F. Welch, eds., *Handbook of the Economics of Education* (Amsterdam: North-Holland, 2006); James J. Heckman, J. Stixrud, and S. Urzua, "The Effects of Cognitive and Noncognitive Abilities on Labor Market Outcomes and Social Behavior," *Journal of Labor Economics* 24 (2006): 411–482; and James J. Heckman, "Skill Formation and the Economics of Investing in Disadvantaged Children," *Science* 312 (2006): 1900–1902.
23. U.S. schools ranked third among twenty-two OECD countries in per student spending in both primary and secondary education. United

States spends $5,300 per pupil for primary schools, 75% more than the international average of $3,033. For secondary schools, the United States spends $6,680 per pupil, 54% more than the $4,335 international average. Herbert J. Walberg, *Spending More While Learning Less: U.S. School Productivity in International Perspective* (Washington, DC: The Thomas B. Fordham Foundation, 1988).

24. Thomas P. Bonczar, *Prevalence of Imprisonment in the U.S. Population, 1974–2001* (Washington, DC: Bureau of Justice Statistics, 2003), 1.
25. Caroline Wolf Harlow, *Education and Correctional Populations* (Washington, DC: Bureau of Justice Statistics, 2003). Literacy comparisons also show the relative deficits of those in prison. See Elizabeth Greenberg, Eric Dunleavy, and Mark Kutner, *Literacy Behind Bars: Results from the 2003 National Assessment of Adult Literacy Prison Survey* (Washington, DC: National Center for Education Statistics, U.S. Department of Education, 2007).

Index

Other books in the series (*continued from page iii*)

The Criminal Career: The Danish Longitudinal Study, by Britta Kyvsgaard

Gangs and Delinquency in Developmental Perspective, by Terence P. Thornberry, Marvin D. Krohn, Alan J. Lizotte, Carolyn A. Smith, and Kimberly Tobin

Early Prevention of Adult Antisocial Behaviour, by David P. Farrington and Jeremy W. Coid

Errors of Justice, by Brian Forst

Violent Crime, by Darnell F. Hawkins

Rethinking Homicide: Exploring the Structure and Process Underlying Deadly Situations, by Terance D. Miethe and Wendy C. Regoeczi

Situational Prison Control: Crime Prevention in Correctional Institutions, by Richard Wortley

Prisoner Reentry and Crime in America, edited by Jeremy Travis and Christy Visher

Choosing White Collar Crime, by Neal Shover and Andrew Hochstetler

Marking Time in the Golden State: Women's Imprisonment in California, by Candace Kruttschnitt and Rosemary Gartner

The Crime Drop in America (revised edition), edited by Alfred Blumstein and Joel Wallman

Policing Gangs in America, by Charles M. Katz and Vincent J. Webb

Street Justice: Retaliation in the Criminal Underworld, by Bruce Jacobs and Richard Wright

Race and Policing in America: Conflict and Reform, by Ronald Weitzer and Steven Tuch

What Works in Corrections: Reducing Recidivism, by Doris Layton MacKenzie

Police Innovation: Contrasting Perspectives, edited by David Weisburd and Anthony A. Braga

The Prison and the Gallows: The Politics of Mass Incarceration in America, by Marie Gottschalk

Understanding Crime Statistics: Revisiting the Divergence of the NCVS and the UCR, edited by James P. Lynch and Lynn Addington

Key Issues in Criminal Career Research: New Analyses of the Cambridge Study of Delinquent Development, by Alex R. Piquero, David P. Farrington, and Alfred Blumstein

Drug-Crime Connections, by Trevor Bennett and Katy Holloway

CPSIA information can be obtained at www.ICGtesting.com
Printed in the USA
BVOW011606220911

271840BV00001B/43/P

9 780521 713399